Wilhelm Sasnal
Untitled (Reader)

Verlag der Buchhandlung
Walther und Franz König, Köln
2022

Wilhelm Sasnal
Untitled (Reader)

Edited by
Adam Szymczyk

'Do you have the rest of your payment?'

'Yes, of course.'

'Here.'

'Wh-where is your partner going?'

'He's phoning ahead to the men who will meet you at the border. He'll join us on the train - don't worry!'

But, of course, we *did* worry...

So, all of us together started on our journey...

We traveled less than an hour 'til we came to Bielsko-Biala [*sic*]. Here I used to have my factory. And here the smugglers disappeared.

It was a big commotion... Gestapo came on every side

'Here they are!'

'Juden raus!'

In Katowice, it was only to them the smuggler phoned.

They marched us through the city of Bielsko. We passed by the factory what once I owned...

We passed the market where always we bought to eat, and passed even the street where we used to live, and we came 'til the prison, and there they put us.

Text transcribed from Art Spiegelman, *Maus: A Survivor's Tale*, New York: Pantheon Books, 1986, p. 155.

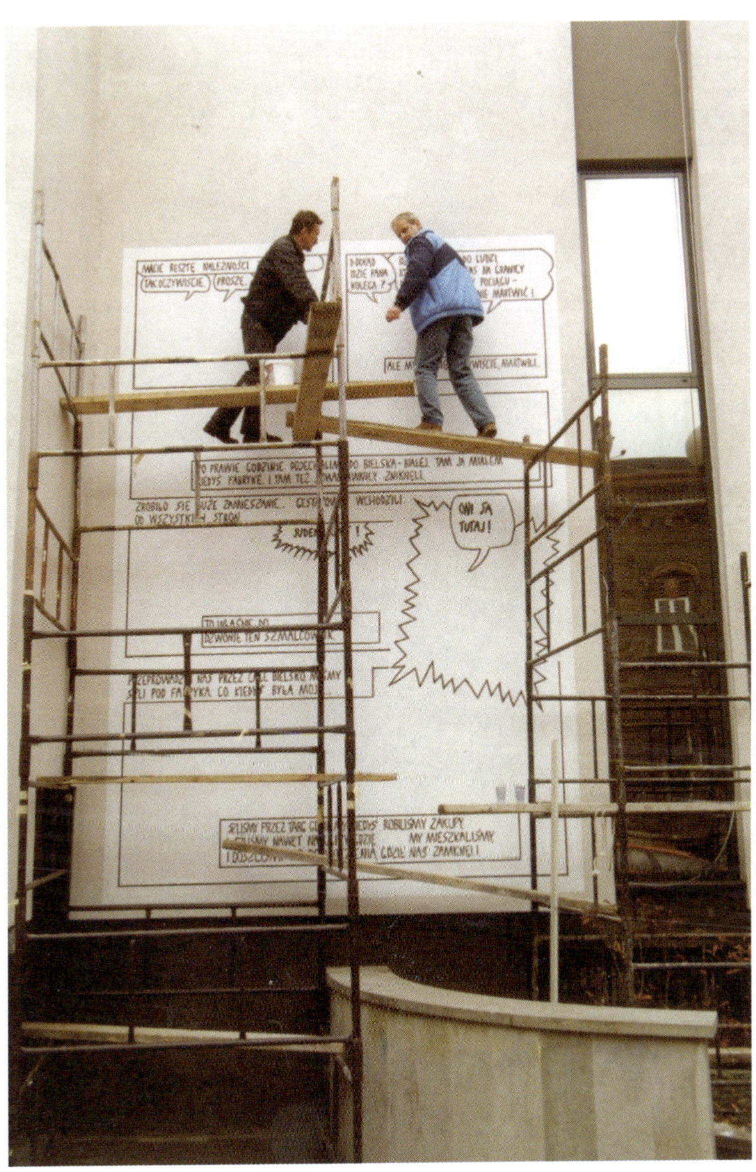

Workers dismantle the scaffolding after the mural
on the wall of Galeria Bielska BWA in Bielsko-Biała was completed

Untitled, 2007

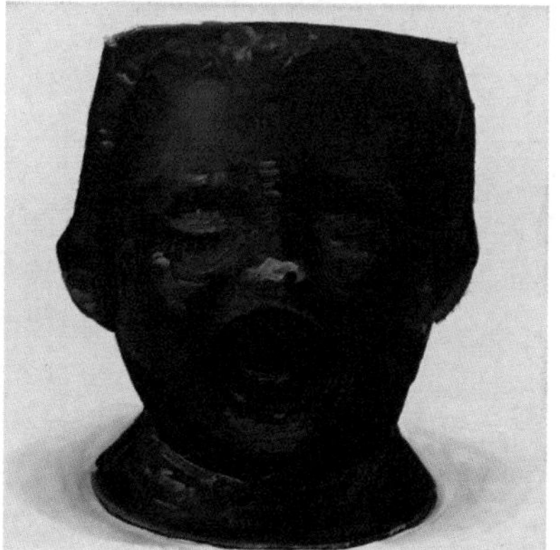

Untitled (Hitler), 2010

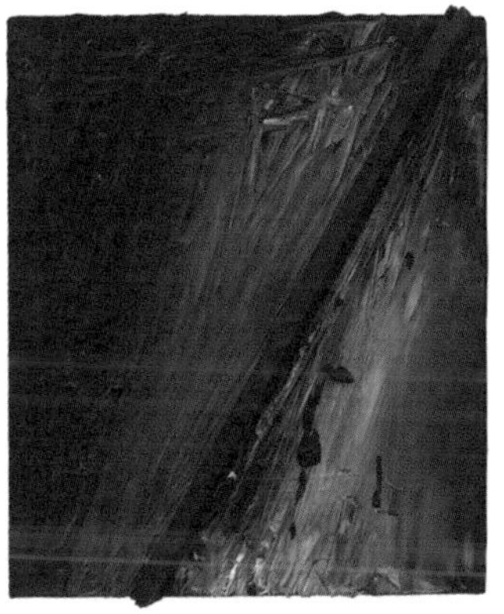

Invitation to Read, Call to See
By Adam Szymczyk

Translated from the Polish by Eliza Rose

For eight months, from May 2021 to January 2022, the exhibition *Such a Landscape*, which I curated, was on view at the POLIN Museum of the History of Polish Jews in Warsaw. Consisting of some seventy paintings by Wilhelm Sasnal, the show was seen by seventy-six thousand visitors. Although there is no obvious explanation for this impressive figure, the perennial question 'why make exhibitions?' seemed answered, at least for the time being. It was not in vain that Sasnal, born in 1972, had worked on these paintings over the last twenty years. The work evidently touched a vital nerve – something unstated but intuitively felt and shared in his home country. It is likely for this reason that the show exceeded the salon scale of the modest crowds typically drawn to contemporary art in Poland, without being reduced to mere blockbuster or spectacle.

The show's title is taken from the 1966 poem 'Taki pejzaż' (Such a Landscape) by Andrzej Szmidt, sung by Ewa Demarczyk in 1967, which includes the following stanzas that I've translated here from the Polish:

trees to flowers
flowers to prickles
onto our dreams
corpses flow in trickles
[...]

winds are blowing
pine trees are askew
inadequate
but oh-so true

such a landscape
such a landscape

In 2001, Sasnal created a large black and white mural on an external wall of a municipal gallery in Bielsko-Biała in southern Poland, recreating, and enlarging to the full height and width of the wall, a page from Art Spiegelman's comic book *Maus*, which was published in Polish for the first time in the same year. The artist kept the page's original layout, but he removed all drawings while keeping the empty frames and dialogues between Spiegelman's characters - Pigs, Cats and Mice, who stand for Poles, Germans and Jews. The gallery was built in the 1960s on the site of a synagogue that had been destroyed by the Nazis on 13 September 1939. The page Sasnal used referred to an episode in which the Spiegelman family is passing through Bielsko - where they had had properties and lived before the German occupation of Poland - after they were traded to the Nazis by local Polish *szmalcowniks* (blackmailers) and led through the city together with other Jews caught in a roundup.[1] Two years later, he painted a portrait cycle of Jewish musicians whose faces are erased (*Gonzalez*, *Beck* and *John Zorn*, all 2002). He made portraits and landscapes based on stills from Claude Lanzmann's 1985 film *Shoah* (*Translator* and *Forest*, both 2003) as well as abstract works with ropes affixed to the canvases (*Untitled (Broken Tree)*, 2017) or using blinding, acidic colours (*Untitled (Afterimage)*, 2019). The above works are all tied (some explicitly, others less so) to entanglements and afterimages of Polish-Jewish history. Yet the actual operation they perform upon history is to turn a sharp eye towards a barely visible past, narrating that which resists being visualised or named, which is shameful and often left unsaid. Narrating - through some mediating term or object that serves as a decoy, such as a black bicycle with panniers left standing unmanned in the foreground of a painting that represents a part of former

1 For more on *szmalcowniks*, see p. 133, n. 22 in this book.

concentration camp, watchtowers and barbed wire fences under the blue sky, some clouds. The formlessness or narrative suspension that the paintings evoke edges in the direction of some dim, elusive, abandoned place that asserts its presence even as it resists disclosure in the form of an image. The paintings speak volumes about the current state of Polish-Jewish relations, embedded as they are in a far-reaching history of defence mechanisms and politicised rewritings of the catastrophes in which we, as humans, are mired. Following the publication of Jan Tomasz Gross's *Sąsiedzi. Historia zagłady żydowskiego miasteczka* (2000; *Neighbors: The Destruction of the Jewish Community in Jedwabne, Poland*, 2001 [2000]), it seemed that we - mine and Sasnal's generation born in 1970s Poland - had taken a decisive step forward. But today we all face a renewed need to venture into the muted realms of the unsaid - into shadows thickened with indifference. We again probe half-truths and 'new truths' that blot out historical reality together with its potential advantages for life.

Wilhelm Sasnal's exhibition at the POLIN Museum was, then, an effort to touch the outer limits of this formless region and to fathom its depths. The actual environment made visible in the gallery, completely redesigned for the occasion according to a display concept by architect Johanna Meyer-Grohbrügge, was a landscape of disintegration: installed on walls fully clad in reflective tin curving around their edges, Sasnal's paintings depicted abandoned houses, empty temples, mould-streaked walls, silt-slick trenches, public bus stops in rural sprawl, train tracks leading who knows where, pigsties and stables, rust-corroded fences, obsolete monuments, muddy roads and menacingly tedious fields, swampy backwaters with no special role to play in history, landscapes empty of symbolism, objects cast aside. This Polish tableau lies searingly close to the heart and summons the melancholic, sentimental voids of the post-romantic landscape - of the crossroads and fields of lost battles canonised in nineteenth-century Polish painting, and later, in films. In Sasnal's hands, however, this all-too-familiar setting takes on an altogether new form. His is a landscape of insidious suspicions, of still unanswered questions, of endless doubts that will never be put to rest - a landscape we roam, light in hand, seeking out an honest face, a landscape we peer into as into a mirror.

This book appears after the exhibition's run as an expanded introduction to the issues it took up, or rather, as its discursive, reflexive and critical elaboration. The texts making up this publication comprise a constellation of thoughts on art and history writing, their failures and the advantage of hindsight they offer. A discontinuous polyphony of voices I gathered together while planning the show, the texts appear alongside reproductions of paintings, which were selected, for the most part, from those included in the exhibition. The majority of texts are previously unpublished, including two new, expansive essays by art historians: Noit Banai sketches the possibility of collectively building a 'post-national culture of remembering' on the ruins of national, politically fuelled obsessions with the exclusivity of traumas, while Luiza Nader summons us to do the active work of 'seeing in spite of all' (to paraphrase Georges Didi-Huberman). Also in print for the first time is Joanna Tokarska-Bakir's essay 'Monologue for Claude Lanzmann' – a montage of recorded and accurately transcribed oral accounts of 'eight residents of the hamlet of Rechta, Strzyżewice commune, Lublin Voivodeship, Poland, concerning the 1 November 1943 murder of thirteen Jews – while hiding in an underground "bunker" on a farmstead owned by Adam Kułaga – at the hands of National Armed Forces (Narodowe Siły Zbrojne, NSZ) partisans. Kułaga was subsequently apprehended by the Germans and died at the Majdanek concentration camp.'

'Manuscripts do not burn', replies Woland to the Master who has just said that he has burned his own book in a stove. Voices, too, have a way of persisting over time. *There's no escaping our own history* – thus the title of Jan Tomasz Gross's new introduction accompanying the publication of his own article 'Eastern Europe's Crisis of Shame', first published on the English-language website *Project Syndicate* and later, in Polish, in an online edition of *Krytyka Polityczna* magazine. Written in the context of the 'refugee crisis' of 2015, the essay ties Eastern European countries' response to an anticipated and feared arrival of people of different creed and skin colour to a long narrative of recent and chronic antisemitic – a fundamental human crisis rearing its head yet again, this time in the form of post-communist nations' refusal to take in refugees.

Several more essays were commissioned for this book: Dariusz Stola, historian and former director of the POLIN Museum, provides an overview of public debates on Polish-Jewish relations in Poland; political scientist Piotr Forecki exposes classist overtones in artists' narratives that relegate responsibility for Polish complicity in crimes against Jews to peasants; Berlin-based Cameroonian curator Bonaventure Soh Bejeng Ndikung explores contemporary mutations of xenophobia in Germany, prompted by questions posed by the author's ten-year old son. Opening the book are historical texts: Milena Jesenská's 'Judge Lynch in Europe' (1938), W. E. B. Du Bois's 'The Negro and the Warsaw Ghetto' (1952), and Adolf Muschg's 'Distancing from Participation: If Auschwitz Were in Switzerland' (1997). These interventionist essays, all originally published as press articles, capture their authors' immediate reactions to the respective moments in European history, which is also a history of antisemitism and xenophobia in their veiled and overt forms. Together, these texts afford a broadened picture that nevertheless remains incomplete. Rather than fixating on individual nations, the texts operate in response to any complex of national superiority and, ultimately, all forms of the innately racist 'coloniality of knowledge' (Aníbal Quijano) constitutive of modernity. In an article first delivered as a speech during an event that honoured heroes of the Warsaw Ghetto Uprising organised by *Jewish Life* (now *Jewish Currents*) in New York on 15 April 1952, and later published in that same magazine, Du Bois thus reflected upon his visit of the ghetto in ruins: '[T]he race problem in which I was interested cut across lines of colour and physique and belief and status and was a matter of cultural patterns, perverted teaching and human hate and prejudice, which reached all sorts of people and caused endless evil to all men.'

This book's intention is to show that, circumscribed within the rectangular frame of a painting, images offer one means to describe an endless evil that again threatens to 'reach all sorts of people'.

Untitled, 2017

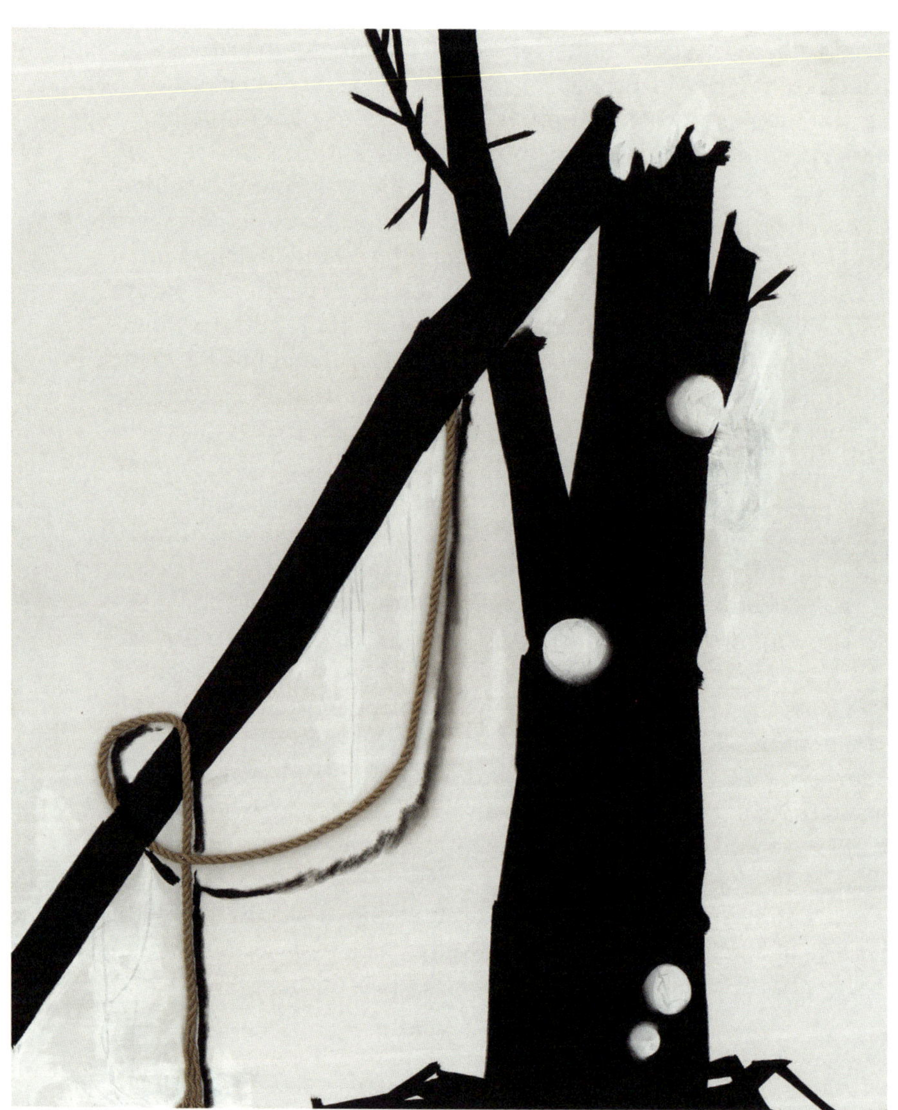

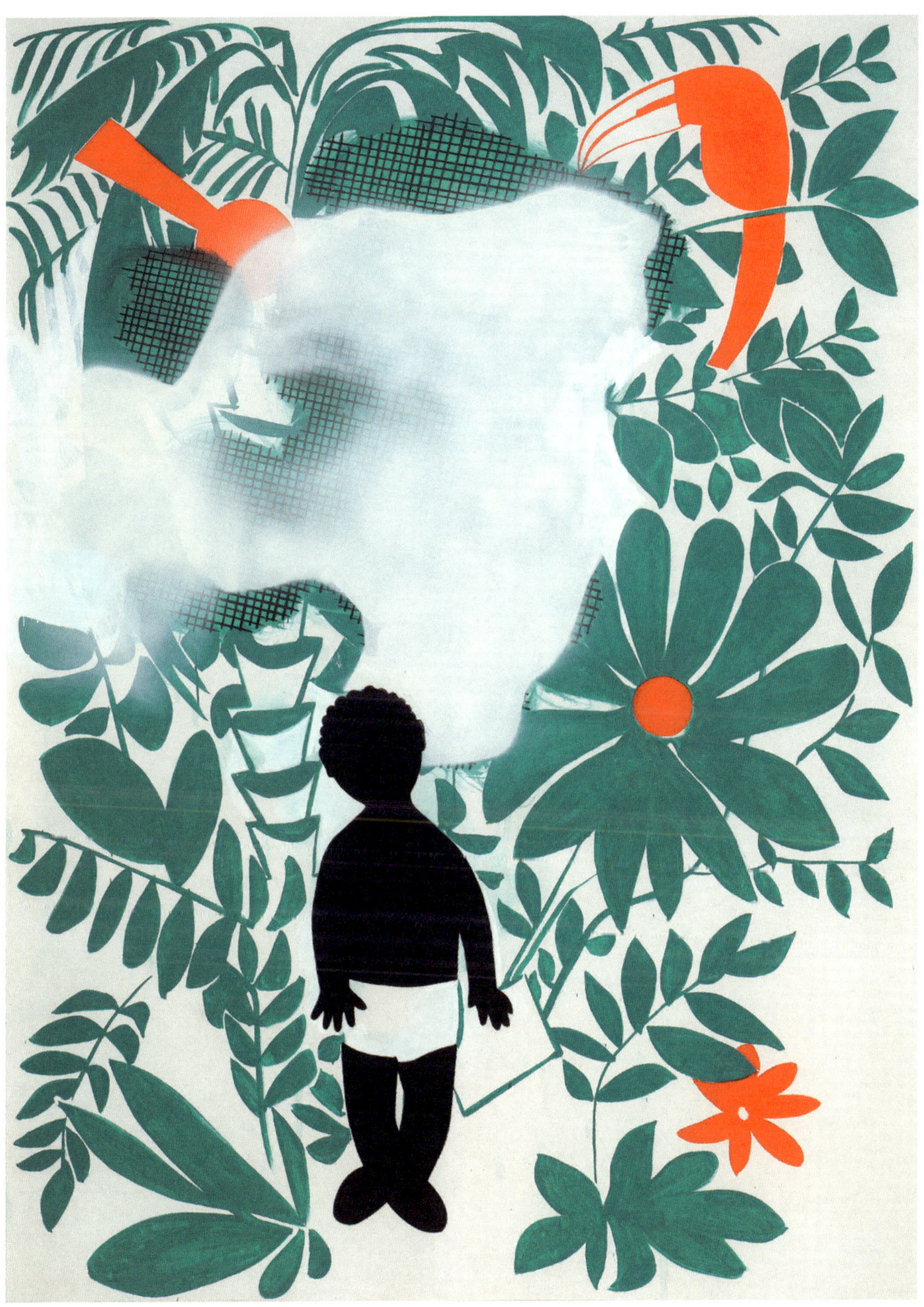

Murzynek is a diminutive of the Polish N-word 'Murzyn'. In the 1930s, when the poem 'Murzynek Bambo' was written and included in a schoolbook for children, the word was common and completely naturalised, without any questioning about the racist undertone of its use. This discussion only came about recently in Poland, following the ongoing debates in the US and Europe.

Judge Lynch in Europe
By Milena Jesenská

First published in 1938 in Czech newspaper *Přítomnost*, Prague
and translated by Kathleen Hayes

Perhaps a foreigner, driving through an unfamiliar city and looking out over the sea of houses, might think he had a great metropolis in front of him. But a person who lives in a city so large that not once in his life does he see how it empties into the fields knows that really there are no big cities in the world. There are only streets running into one another and houses pressed close together with no gardens or fields; there are square stone cages in five storeys on top of one another. In a big city, the individual lives as he would in a village. Among neighbours, with the tobacconist's shop across the road and the grocer on the corner. The concierge, the mailman, the tax collector, the telephone, work, a few friends and that is all. In the morning, the shop assistant leaves milk and a bag of rolls in front of the door; the man who lives next door goes off to work; the girl who lives across the way and has a night shift at some bar comes home from work. The day begins with an indifferent greeting of good morning. All fates are noted in the tobacconist's across the road. The walls have ears; women and children are talkative. So the whole building knows what debts and worries you have, what clothes you wear and what political convictions you hold. The man from the first floor greets you a little carelessly on account of those political convictions and the man from the second floor is particularly polite on account of them. If you belong to the same camp as the landlord, you can get away with paying the rent a little late. If your membership card is different from that of the concierge, your son has to wipe his shoes with particular care so as not to dirty the stairs. If the woman from the third floor passes by, the building grimaces quietly, today a little maliciously: that woman is a Jew. And if the student in the white knee-socks from the fourth floor makes a ruckus on the stairs, he walks through an icy calm on the scowling streets of today.

That is how the political life of the ordinary man looks in private. His political life is so blatantly private and so intertwined with his personal situation that it is closer to his skin than his own sense of honour. The radius of his political activities usually does not extend beyond the radius of his daily movements: across the square and three streets down, the way to work, the way home, the pub on the corner, the tobacconist's across the road and the eight square metres that are called home. From this reality there arises what is known as a pogrom. A pogrom is, among other things, the ordinary man taking revenge on the ordinary man, a battle across a gallery railing, from one storey to another. Long suppressed anger - whipped up and exploited by some propaganda - concentrates on a certain concept, crystallises and explodes.

Blacks in Europe

In more peaceful - and peaceful - eras all different kinds of people probably lived next to one another and did not bother much about politics. It did not trouble them; it did not seem to touch them but was played out in some distant place. Today politics has entered the dwellings of ordinary people, the two-room flats with kitchen, bathroom and lavatory; it has sat down at the table with crocheted covers and it jangles from the radios, which used to play nothing but songs. Today Mr Novotný is above all a Czech and a good neighbour, Mr Kohn is a Jew and the son of the tenant Keller is a very square-shouldered, very athletic youth in white Bavarian knee-socks - in the middle of tranquil Smíchov,[1] where there are no mountains far and wide - and Mr Svoboda, the tailor in the basement, is a social democrat. There are also two émigrés living in the basement, German socialists; they

1 Smíchov is a district in Prague. [All notes by Kathleen Hayes unless otherwise indicated.]

survive on a registration card, without work or documents and all the tenants in the building - Czech, German, Jewish - are a little uncomfortably offended by their presence.[2] Because an émigré is a black man and what's more, a black man among whites, living where he does not belong, damn nigger![3] In four years, Europe has changed so that it is full of blacks. Black men, as is well known, are not allowed to touch white women: they must live in quarters that are assigned to them and they are second-class citizens. Blacks in Vienna today - those are the Jews, the socialists, the former Austrian nationalists, the monarchists, Czechs here and there and often Catholics as well. In America it sometimes happens that a crowd, maddened by racial pride, hangs a black youth from the nearest tree - because he is black. Some time ago, the whole world stirred with a justified compassion for three black youths from Scottsborough [*sic*], who were sentenced to death on the basis of the false testimony of a white prostitute.[4] Europe welcomed their mother with open arms; Europe, through the voices of its best people, asked for freedom for the three innocent, sentenced youths. Europe spoke

2 The socialists would have been refugees from Germany. The registration cards were issued by the charitable organisations that supported the German refugees. The cards functioned as a form of identification for people who did not have valid passports. Černý lists seven organisations of this sort. Bohumil Černý, *Most k novému životu: německá emigrace v ČSR v letech 1933-1939* (Bridge to a New Life: The German Emigrés in Czechoslovakia 1933-1939), Prague: Lidová demokracie, 1967, p. 24.

3 The phrase 'damn nigger' is used in English in the original Czech article.

4 She refers to the Scottsboro Case, in the city of Scottsboro, Alabama, USA. In this case, nine black youths were charged with the rape of two white women. They were brought to trial in April 1931. The doctors who examined the women testified that no rape had occurred. Nonethless, the all-white jury convicted the nine and all but the youngest (12 years old) were sentenced to death. The cause of the 'Scottsboro Boys' was taken up by liberal and radical groups - in particular the Communist Part of the USA - in the north. In 1932, the US Supreme Court overturned the convictions. There followed further retrials of the accused by the state of Alabama, more re-convictions and successful appeals. The state finally freed the four youngest and paroled all but one. *The New Encyclopaedia Britannica*, vol. 10, 15th edn, Chicago: Encyclopaedia Britannica Inc, 1992, p. 568. [Editor's note: as of 1938, charges against four had been dropped, in addition to those dropped for the youngest, with additional charges brought to another of the youths related to an assault on return from trial in 1937. The last of the nine was paroled in 1946. See 'People and Events: Ozie Powell, 1917- ?', *Scottsboro: An American Tragedy*, web page for film, PBS, 2000, http://www.shoppbs.pbs.org/wgbh/amex/scottsboro/peopleevents/p_powell.html.]

with the centuries-old traditions of its culture to the rather young and rather noisy America. In Vienna they do not hang anyone from trees. In Vienna today there are a good half-million blacks. For the moment, no one has done them any great harm. They have 'only' been forbidden to work. Doctors are not allowed to treat patients; lawyers are not allowed to conduct their practice; no one is allowed to listen to writers or musicians. In addition, 'only' their property has been confiscated and they have been given to understand that they should leave - needlessly, because those who could leave have already gone. *Otherwise*, however, they can live. Strange, terrible, *lawful* Judge Lynch!

For four years those people lived in Vienna hardly daring to breathe. Over four years they learned all sorts of ways to deny themselves and to keep quiet. They took pains to be inconspicuous and to avoid giving cause for offence - because they wanted to live. In his last attempt to maintain Austrian independence, however, the former Chancellor Schuschnigg made an appeal to these very people.[5] To the very people who had defended Austrian independence in February 1934. These people came out of hiding, out of the silence that was so difficult to learn

5 Kurt von Schuschnigg (1897-1977), a Catholic lawyer and Christian social from Tyrol, was named Federal Chancellor of Austria after Engelbert Dollfuss's (1892-1934) assassination by Austrian Nazis in July 1934. Dolfuss was killed shortly after suppressing the outbreak of civil war. Fighting broke out in Vienna in February 1934 between the private army supporting the Social Democratic Party, the Republican *Schutzbund* and the government forces. In addition to the police and the army, the government had the support of a para-military, anti-Marxist, anti-parliamentarian, pro-fascist organisation, the *Heimwehr* (Home Defence Unity). The fighting in Vienna lasted for a week and was limited mainly to the outer proletarian districts. The aims of the *Schutzbund* members were mainly defensive: to resist seizure of their weapons and defend themselves against the army. The government forces lost 105 dead and 300 wounded; the *Schutzbund* lost 137 dead and 400 wounded. As a result of the fighting, the Social Democratic Party and its associated organisations were outlawed. Jesenská refers to the plebiscite that Schuschnigg intended to hold, in 1938, on the question of Austrian independence. He hoped that the plebiscite would put a stop to Nazi pressure on Austria. The former social democrats would have supported Schuschnigg in the plebiscite against Hitler. The latter, however, demanded on 11 March that Schuschnigg cancel the plebiscite, which he did. Schuschnigg was compelled to resign and the German army marched into Austria on 12 March 1938. See Elisabeth Barker, *Austria 1918-1972*, Basingstoke and London: Macmillan, 1973, pp. 84-112 and F. L. Carsten, *The Rise of Fascism*, London: Batsford ltd, 1967, pp. 223-29.

and they spoke: in the streets, at meetings, at home, on the stairway, on the gallery, in the pub, at the tobacconist's. They made themselves known once again. They cast off the four years of quiet denial like a mask and prepared to say 'yes' to Schuschnigg's question. When Schuschnigg resigned on 12 March 1938, these people stood revealed for a *second time* and defenceless before their enemies, this time with faces completely black.[6] Four years of silence and humility were in vain. A third of the white people in Austria lost their rights, work and civic existence among white people in Austria. In Europe today people do not have to have skin of colour in order to become blacks.

No one really knows exactly how many of these white blacks there are in Europe today. In the League of Nations they have statistics on post-war emigration, but these were outdated long ago and give only an approximate picture of the political migration of nations. Numbers also do not say *why* ordinary citizens have suddenly become blacks in some countries. Jews have almost always and everywhere been in a distinct position and in Eastern Europe they were essentially blacks even in the era considered to be the golden age of blossoming European culture and civilisation. How many Jewish blacks are there today? In the Third Reich about half a million. In Vienna and in Austria about 300,000. In Hungary there are Jewish mulattos, who are allowed to live and work and thus far also have civil rights, but all the same are bound by the laws of *numerus clausus*.[7] Only a certain percentage of Jews are permitted to study and it is almost impossible for Jews to become state employees or officials. Almost half a million Hungarian Jews are living this kind of lifelong quarantine, although they have been distinguished by their great patriotism. In Poland, where the number of Jews

6 After the German army occupied Austria, there was a wave of arrests of government leaders, Christian socials, social democrats, Jews and others. The number arrested has been estimated at 70,000. The Nazis had at their disposal the police records of the Schuschnigg regime. See Barker, *Austria 1918-1972*, pp. 114, 128.

7 The first *numerus clausus* law, limiting attendance at universities, was introduced in Hungary in 1920, but was not strictly applied. On 29 May 1938, the First Jewish Law was passed restricting the percentage of Jews to be employed in business, banks, the professions, journalism and the entertainment industry. Ezra Mendelsohn, *East Central Europe between the Wars*, Bloomington: Indiana University Press, 1987, pp. 105, 116. [Editor's note: mulatto is an outdated and racist term that was used to describe people of mixed African and European ancestry.]

is several times greater, the restrictions are even more severe and thus you meet in Prague, in Paris and in London poor and undernourished Polish Jewish students, who study medicine passionately and with amazing diligence, only to find, once they receive their doctorates, that they are not permitted to pursue their profession anywhere in the world. The situation is similar in Romania. There are about fifteen million Jews in the world, but a third of them live outside the law.

Nonetheless, there are far fewer Jewish blacks in the world than there are other, literally Aryan, blacks. For five years, many thousands of German émigrés have been wandering over all countries and continents; now the outcasts from former Austria have multiplied their ranks. How many of them are there? About 300,000, according to reliable estimates. Thousands and thousands are in prisons and concentration camps. Does that account for all of them? Not by a long shot. Today even a full-blooded Aryan can easily become a black in his own country if he is a socialist or a democrat, or if he considers the Gospel, for example, to be a higher law than various decrees. The number of such blacks, who have remained at home, who have not left and cannot leave, is boundless. Over their lives, thoughts and dreams, over their every day and every step, house patrols are watching, as well as neighbours, co-workers at the factory, the office, school or sports club. Social and political *activity* has always had certain consequences, but it is only today that a part of Europe is in such a state that millions of people are blacks only because they are, because they exist and have opinions and have the sort of parents they have. They do not have to do anything forbidden; indeed, they are not even permitted to conform (Jews in Vienna are not allowed to hang flags with the swastika); they suffer only because they are in the world.

Events Flare Up Over the Border

The press and radio bring news of events that are flaring up close at hand. There are people among us who have gained much self-confidence from these events abroad. Vigorous youthful calves in white knee-socks march over the Prague pavement with unusual energy. Then there are people among us who are under the impression that even here the development of events might produce blacks overnight. There are accounts of émigrés who go from one border to the next and are always turned away. Every country now harbours more of these people of colour than it can afford economically. The states have closed their borders; the flood of foreigners threatens their internal balance. But people come anyway, without documents, on foot, with empty hands. Wandering among us is the reflection of many hundreds of appalling human fates, hundreds and thousands of painful partings, suicides and injustices. Many people have grown nervous. The ceaseless flurry of classification of people has descended on us as well. In the Vinohrady, Smíchov, Karlín, Holešovice, Libeň and other suburban [areas], a quiet breeze of mutual tension is blowing from person to person. A dangerous breeze from a distant, German, alien country. In the small pubs, people sit debating. What will England do, how will France act, what will Hitler undertake? In truth, these are very urgent and important questions; for all of us, they stick to our skin like a shirt; it is impossible not to think of them. But above all we have to know something else: and that is, what we will do ourselves. Not on that great, international scale, but on our private scale, the radius of which is three and a half streets, the way home and a two-room apartment with a kitchen. We have to know what we will do on this very piece of earth where we are standing and in this very sphere of ordinary work that we are carrying out. Perhaps the outlines of this will become clear in our thoughts if we recall the dead engineer Weissl and the eleven living *Schutzbund* members.

Eleven *Schutzbund* Members

The last year truly was not stingy when it came to terrible news. We heard so many terrible tidings from the world that we almost grew numb to them. Bombarded cities and dead people were practically part of the daily routine. Before the feature film we used to see regularly photographs of women searching for their children and husbands in the wreckage, wringing their hands over the ruins of buildings, or something lying in the street - it looked like a grotesque rag, but it was a dead man. I do not know if the world can offer us even greater horrors. But three days ago, a little piece of news in tiny brevier type went through the papers and stopped the hearts of those who read it. An account of eleven Austrian *Schutzbund* members - firemen.[8]

These *Schutzbund* men fought with guns in February 1934 against Austrian fascism. They fought, they fell, they lost and - they were put on trial. Weissl had led those eleven arrested people. He was not a political leader or a political functionary; no one really knew him; he had never done anything political. He was a private individual like you or me, an individual who was, by conviction, an anti-fascist and a socialist. For many years his convictions were a purely private matter, falling in between his private life and work. But then there came a time when in Austria people took up guns on behalf of such convictions and Weissl stood at their head. Not because he had any rank, or because anyone commanded him to - only because of that inner human command that proclaims that there are things we love more than our lives. He was wounded, he was arrested, he was dragged from the hospital on a stretcher and, straight from the hospital stretcher, he was hanged. He died without saying much, very peaceful and matter-of-fact, with a salutation to freedom on his lips. The world had only just learned about Weissl - and the world soon forgot him. Beside him, however, there stood eleven fellow fighters, eleven *Schutzbund* members, who could not and should not forget. The Nazis put a question to these eleven people: do you want to swear the *same loyalty* to your new leader as you once showed for your ideals? *And those eleven people said: yes.*

The last month in the world perhaps did not provide a more oppressive or cautionary testimony. It would be good to consider these eleven people as a great warning for all of us who are not politicians, who do not have an impact on events except through the personal weight

8 According to the account in the newspaper *Lidové noviny*, the Nazis promised that those who had lost their jobs because of their participation in the civil war in February 1934 would be returned to their former positions. The account also mentioned that eleven former members of the Social Democratic Republican *Schutzbund*, who had fought in the Am Spitz fire station in the 21st district in Vienna on 12 February 1934, had recently been ceremoniously accepted back into the firemen's force. Their leader, the head officer of the firemen, Weisel [*sic*], had taken all the responsibility for the fighting upon himself and had been hanged. See nč, 'Nacisté získávají rakouské dělníky' (Nazis Win the Austrian Workers), *Lidové noviny*, 23 March 1936, p. 1.

of our fundamental beliefs. It is not true that we do not matter. Today all of us matter - but also each one of us matters. If some day someone requires of us a complete reversal of convictions and we are willing to answer 'yes', there is no salvation for us. Because first and foremost a person must save himself and only then can one help him. We do not know those eleven *Schutzbund* members by name. Nor does anyone know us by name. but the greatest illness of the European individual is the easy willingness to retreat, to offer no resistance, to surrender and to conform 'because one has to live, after all!' It is more urgent that we know *how* we want to live and that we consider this *how* to be as important as life itself. A difficult task faces each of us today - to find the precise boundary between prudence and cowardice, between daring and an outburst of passion. Today, not only the leading people of this state must find this boundary, but also every ordinary person, even the most ordinary. We can think with respect of the brave-hearted people in Barcelona and Madrid who work, sell, teach, go to the cinema and live right under the rain of bombs. And we must remember without sympathy the eleven *Schutzbund* members who raised their right arms to greet the new leader.

These two reminders delineate for us the course needed to create a quiet courage in the people of this country. If I were not ashamed of quotations and big words, I would dig out from the awestruck memories of my childhood the saying to the effect that people who are as hard as flint create a nation made of ashlars.[9]

9 She quotes from Canto XXVI of Jan Neruda's (1834–91) *Písně kosmické* (Cosmic Ballads): 'if each one of us is as hard as flint, / the whole nation will be made of ashlars.' Jan Neruda, *Písně kosmické*, Prague: 1878, p. 47.

Shoah (Translator), 2003

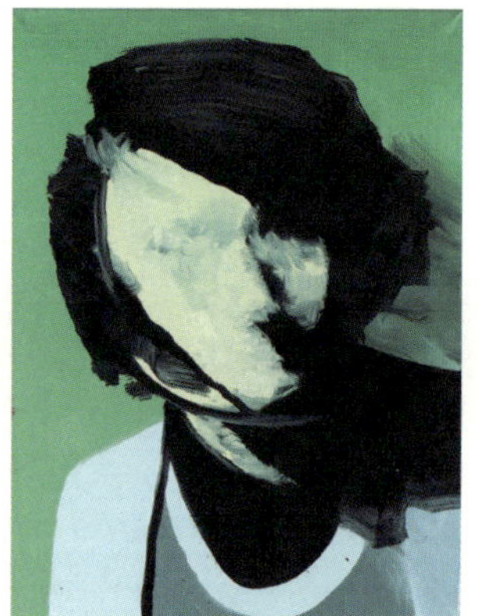

Shoah (Forest), 2003

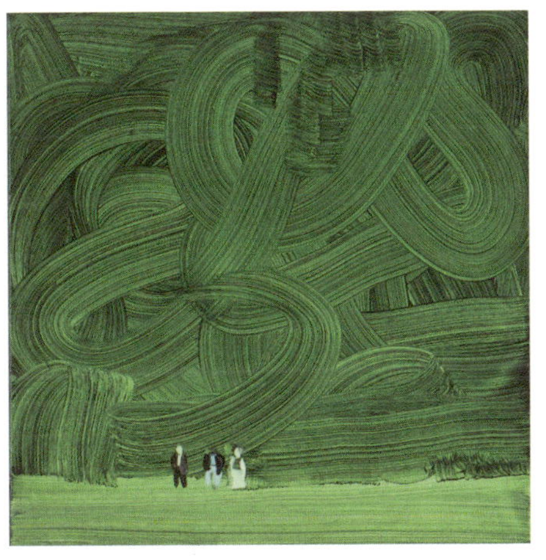

A Monologue for Claude Lanzmann[1]
By Joanna Tokarska-Bakir

1 This is a compilation of verbatim statements by eight residents of the hamlet of Rechta, Strzyżewice commune, Lublin Voivodeship, Poland, concerning the 1 November 1943 murder of thirteen Jews - while hiding in an underground 'bunker' on a farmstead owned by Adam Kułaga - at the hands of National Armed Forces (Narodowe Siły Zbrojne, NSZ) partisans. Kułaga was subsequently apprehended by the Germans and died at the Majdanek concentration camp. From 1949, the killers' cases were tried and retried at the District Court in Lublin. Their very punitive sentences (including two death penalties) were gradually commuted, and one died in prison. On the initiative of the Jewish community, the site of the crime was to be commemoratively marked in 2010. The project remains unrealised to this day. All we can read on the Strzyżewice commune website is a commemoration of the German crimes perpetrated 'in 1943 in Bystrzyca Stara, Dębszczyzna, Kiełczewice, and Pawłów', where German soldiers executed thirty Jews by shooting. Rechta hamlet was formerly Kolonia Dębszczyzna or Dębniak, subsequently Dębina. These interviews were recorded by Agata Fiedotow and Anna Górska in September 2010 as part of research conducted by the Ethnographic Archive of which I was head and which was founded in 2004 as part of the Institute of Applied Social Sciences, University of Warsaw and Institute of Slavic Studies of the Polish Academy of Sciences (see https://www.academia.edu/34435015/ Archiwum_Etnograficzne_EN_doc). See also Paweł P. Reszka and Dariusz Libionka, 'Święto Zmarłych w Rechcie' (All Souls' Day at Rechta), *Karta*, vol. 46, 2005, pp. 122–35; P. P. Reszka, 'Pomordowani z mojego podwórka' (The Murdered Ones from My Neighbourhood), Gazeta Wyborcza, 10 April 2011) and Gmina Strzyżewice: historia (Strzyżewice commune: history), https://archiwalna.strzyzewice.lubelskie.pl/his.html.

Translated from the Polish by Jerzy Juruś

No more farming for me. Not any more. All I have is the sick pension. 670 zloty. Next to nothing isn't it. You have to live lean. Can't even afford ham. You just plant a few potatoes there, some carrots there, some parsley. My hands are crooked now, and my joints.

Before the war, things were hard too. My mum and dad were working at the manor, Kozaryn's.
In the summer, at least you could go to the manor and make some money, but in the winter, in autumn, the work was over, the manor itself had nothing to give.
Life wasn't easy; poverty.
Lice bit us and poverty bit us. Where they had more kids, they lived real poor. One pair of shoes for all of 'em; when one went outside, another one had to wait for 'em to come back.
If you started at one end of Dymniak and reached the other end - and even the village of Kiełczewice - they had borscht and potatoes for breakfast and lunch in every home. That's the kind of food there was.

I had a brother. But he died. He was twenty-seven. The heart.

And when I married my husband, I had to cook, go work in the fields, and pick up mown crops. Then come back and cook again. Take care of the horses, too, the cows, the pigs. After lunch, back into the field.

Heat or no heat. And today? A combine harvester comes, does the thrashing, the pressing and..., and no need to go into the fields.

Over there, around Bychawka, there used to be a lot of Jews. A lot of Jews. It was almost like a Jewish town there. Nothing but Jews there. Hardly a Pole. The Jewish houses are still there, near the church. The old ones, where the Jews used to be. There was this man, Pakularz. We used to go to Bychawa, I was a girl of fourteen or so.

What'd they look like? Normal. There were some that were hardly different from a Pole.
Jews were pretty. Or those Jewish kids, such good-looking lads they were, well, well.
Krymkas, that's what they had. There were those *krymkas*, they put 'em on their heads. We used to call it *gimerka*. A kind of cap, their own kind, here. Oh, look, must be a Jew! Walking by in a *gimerka*.

The older ones mostly had beards and those..., such long ringlets they had. But the younger ones, whether male or female, some of 'em were hardly different. It was just their speech that was. Jewish. Such gibberish.

Swine meat they wouldn't eat, just hen meat. Except, they wouldn't kill it themselves, but had to go to a butcher, that's what they said, to a butcher in Bychawa. A Jewish fellow would take some hens in a bag and carry them to Bychawa, to a butcher; a butcher had to do the killing, and then he would bring 'em back, and they would dress it and such. There was this man Pinchas here, a poor old Jew. So the Jews would have a whip-round to give him some money for the road. So he would go to Bychawa, to the rabbi, to have those hens slaughtered.

When I was a small girl, I couldn't wait for Saturday. Because the thing with Jews is they won't strike a match on a Saturday. It was all loaded in the stove, the wood and the chips, soaked with kerosene. I would go, start the fire, and here come candies or grains into my pocket. They would give me some I mean.

Back then, they mostly ate those challahs. A kind of roll they were. And my, were they good! And back then in the village, our mothers would seldom bake like that. For a holiday, perhaps. So when I was over at their place, the Jewish woman would cut a piece of challah for me. They'd prepare so many every Saturday! All kinds of lovely pierogi. Or fried fish, all kinds of stuff, this or that. They'd prepare for it like we would for Easter Sunday or Christmas. The Jews would prepare that for every Saturday.

They used to buy orchards in our village. I remember (next to our place, there are large orchards) when I was a little girl, about ten I think, I used to go and help myself to apples.
They had those booths. Because, in autumn, if there was a big orchard, there'd be such a booth there, covered with straw. So they'd sit inside and guard the apples. They'd pick 'em neatly too, never broke a twig. If a wormy apple fell, they'd pick it up, cut it into strips and leave it to dry in the sun. And then bag it. Nothing would go to waste.

Over here, the Jews even had a shop too, there on the low land, near that house by the river. There was this man Berek, he kept it. And when I was a child, daddy would say: 'Baby, go..., go to Berek's and get me a corner of makhorka.' It was tobacco in such small packets; the man in the shop would cut it in four, so everyone could buy a quarter, a 'corner'.

I know that Srul lived in one of these homes, he had two children, over here, the second house, starting here. Then there was Lejba, and over there, in the third one, that was Mosiek, so called, Lejzor or Mendel. And Berek had a water mill and he built a little prayer house. Such an old hut it was. Later people took it apart for boards.
And there were Jews living across from the school, a Jewish woman.
And also further down there, by the fire hall.
Quite a few Jews there were, quite a few.

They were into trading, the Jews were. Jews used to be better at trading than Polish people! It was easier to come to an agreement with a Jew. People used to say: he sold a needle and a button, and he had gold. So they would go to a Jew's place because it was cheaper. And Jews would come to the village. They'd buy eggs, hens and such. And they had goods, shoes and everything, the Jews had, just like in a shop these days. They had jewellery, and everything, everything. And clothes, jumpers, tights, you could buy everything from 'em.

Well, they were people. Just like us.

And the doctor was Jewish. For the whole area here. If you went to him, he would see you. I had diphtheria twice and it was then that he saved me.

There were Jews going to school with us. We would rush out during the break, the Poles I mean. We screamed and ran around, and the Jews just stood in the corner in the corridor, talking about something in their own way. Those kids were more serious.

Esta Nissenbaum - I actually shared a desk with her. A pretty girl she was too. Her complexion was so white, and her hair black, curly. We didn't quarrel, didn't yank each other.
She survived the war; it must've been three days that she spent at our place. She was put up upstairs.
Once, she even came here after the war, with two military men. People said she'd gone to see the Stępieńs. Came back to pick up the things she'd left with 'em. But the old woman hid from her and the young ones said they didn't know anything.
She came in June, when the cherries were in season, and she had such a dress, the same colour.
I asked her: 'Is it you?' - 'It's me', she said.
That man, Szymon Nissenbaum, was her father. They had a shop with goods, so they would always trade with us. They'd buy a calf, eggs, and they'd bring thread, a needle, everything, or a piece of meat for the holidays.

And they were all such decent people. Well, what more can I tell you? It was better to trade with Jews than with Poles. 'Cause a Jew would keep reducing the price.

A man named Radomski used to have a shop in Sobieszczany. Before the war, I mean. And he and a Jew did some business. And that Jew cheated him. He started a quarrel. 'Let's go to the rabbi,' he said. 'So we're going to the rabbi.' A rabbi is like our priest. They both went to the rabbi. The Jew and that fellow. 'Tell me, Radomski, what's going on?' A true Jew with a curly sidelock! Those rabbis, I mean, they have such long sidelocks. He heard that one out, and then the Jew. And spoke his mind: 'You, Mosiek, need to pay him the difference, so and so.' And Mosiek took out the money, paid the difference, and said nothing. With our people, if a priest told him to do something like that, he would raise hell: 'What? Let him *** off from me.' But that one said nothing, damn. That was discipline.

Some time ago, in Poland, they didn't forbid the Jews from doing anything. It was only when the Germans invaded. But even earlier, I remember how, er ..., it got more and more hostile, those writings, 'Don't buy from a Jew.' This and that. Because, you know, a Jew had no state of his own and no home, so his home and his country were everywhere.

I heard that children would go missing in the city, for matzah people said. Even older people used to tell me that Jews captured kids for matzah. They were trying to scare me, saying that they captured kids, put 'em in a barrel and turned something, and they baked flatbreads on that blood, and had such a Shabbos. I heard that they'd put one in a barrel [*laughter*] and drew blood for matzah. Polish blood, Catholic. Well, when they take this barrel and halve it, then a lot of blood [*laughter*] will flow down, won't it? Martyred...

In '39, I remember, we used a horse engine for the thrashing machine, such an ordinary machine, and suddenly: aeroplanes. I remember the 17th of September. Over here, there was a meadow, some grass. A lot of Ruski cars came, they ran into our neighbour's place, killed his hog right away, a heifer at another's place; spent about twenty-four hours and drove on...

God, I was shaking like a leaf!
During the war, we used to pray outside the Kudels' place, there's a shrine here, so we would sing May devotion songs throughout May.

Why did those things happen like that during the war? I don't know myself. And I can't stop wondering. The Germans are such an educated people, with such culture. And they brought themselves to do such crimes: set up camps, burn people! Well I never!

The rich Jews, the Mendels, must've left for some other place, only the poor ones were decimated like that later on.

After all, it's the Germans who gave the order. They didn't like those Jews. '*Jude!*' they would shout, '*Jude!*' When they walked to work, spades on their backs, they walked in fours, a German told 'em to sing: 'Hitler, a man of gold, has taught us how to work, and Śmigły-Rydz didn't know the first thing about anything.' When those Germans saw them on the road, in the middle of the road, they started killing 'em off. The Germans would annihilate Jews like that. Not the Poles. Mostly Germans. As for Poles, the Jews have no reason to complain about them. The Germans were cruel. They took all of 'em. They drove 'em out to Belzec.

But once they were gone, then instantly, yeah, people took over the homes... Because that is also what Polish people are like.

Some Germans kept their horses at our place. Eighteen weeks. So the Germans would get so cosy with us, almost like family. I'd ask 'em: 'Why are the Germans murdering Poles?' And he'd say: 'That's not true that Germans are murdering Poles. It's Poles murdering Poles.' So I get back at him with: 'How d'you mean, Poles?' 'Well, how would I know what you are if your neighbour hadn't told on you?'

Because Poles denounced..., told on other Poles.

During the occupation, there were village guards, right? My father also stood watch like that once. Suddenly he sees a Jewish woman with a small child, near the woods over there. She was staying all the way at Bychawka, also over at Bajdówka. She had another support there. So she was coming with this child in her arms and she was carrying cooked groats. Such a little potful, for the kid, hot groats.

And the other guy says: 'Look, a Jew; gotta kill him.' And my father says: 'Would your conscience allow you to? Kill a child? It's a human being.' And he says: 'Run this way 'cause it's guards on a watch here and they'll hand you over to the Germans. If they don't kill you, they'll hand you over. Run, and I mean now! Straight along this dirt road to the woods and run through the woods!' He says the child understood. He just grabbed his mother's neck like that. And she ran. And she was gone. She used to come there for quite a long time. Because I was at Bychawka some time later and I asked about her; they'd say that Jewish woman keeps coming, she's over at this or that house. But later, they didn't know what was with her any more 'cause she no longer came. And a Jew is a human being too! Yes.

There was also a tailor, Szlama; he would come to my father. He made clothes, suits, that kind of stuff for him. So later he would come to my father, a few times, because he was in hiding. He was at some place but wouldn't say at whose place. Later he'd just say: 'Stach, Stach! Open up.' So I know that my father would go out and give him fatback and bread. He would say, 'Run' cause if they meet you here, they'll kill you. ... They'll kill you. And they'll burn me.'
So he came a couple of times. And daddy gave 'im a wreath of onions, too. He'd say, 'Run away or they might burn my place. Don't come here!' He'd say, 'At night, at night. Better yet, don't come any more.' But he did come a few times.
A lot of Jews used to come. People would give 'em whatever they could. Yeah.

At one farmer's place there was this couple from Lublin, living there. The Jewish woman was pretty, and he was a kind of Chassid. And he would say to his host: 'Pan Staszek, I wouldn't be residing in a wooden house but for the war. Because the tree grew, then it was cut down and hewn. It hurt.' And also: 'I wouldn't be here, but there's a war, so I have to.' It was all in his books. They had such a shallow chimney in there, so he would raise the stove grates: 'Pan Staś, the wood is weeping, I can't sleep.'[1]

Partisans? Well, yes, I don't really...
A Pole would kill a Pole, a father a son, a son a father.

They must've killed 'em, the partisans, those Jews in Rechta.

1 In the original Polish: 'Panie Staszku, ja bym w mieszkaniu drewnianym nie siedział, żeby nie wojna. Bo to drzewo rosło, jego potem zrzęli, obrąbili, jego bolało.' I jeszcze: 'Ja bym nie siedział, tylko, że wojna, to muszę.' On w tych księgach to miał. U nich komin był taki płytki, to jeszcze podnosił te ruszta: 'Panie Stasiu, drzewa mi płaczą, nie mogę spać.'

Why? Well, they must've been rich.

It's the partisans who did it.

Er..., here, at the village end, it was the NSZ, or something like that? The noblemen's party. I don't know much about this party. I just know from my husband there were two outposts in our village, the nationalists headed by Bolek Świątek and the Home Army headed by Roman Kawecki. They cooperated.
Thirty people in each.
Who belonged? You should rather ask who didn't! Only a coward or an old duffer. Some duffer afraid of everything.
Everyone belonged. The young ones, you couldn't keep 'em away from it. Almost every fellow belonged. Whoever had served in the army, a military man, you know, full of vigour, they were all partisans.
And there had to be outposts, because there were terrible thefts where there was no outpost.
They kept order! Made sure there were no thieves.

In Bychawa, there was a family named Rajs, three or four little Jews, two old ones, the rest were women.
First they hid at Franciszek Baran's place in Górne Kiełczewice, at Kolonia.
Then Stefan Mazur brought 'em over here.
Then they moved up there to Dymniak. Adam Kułaga kept 'em.
Obviously they were kept in hiding by those, well, the ones who benefited from them, from the Jews.

Why did they keep 'em? Because the Jews were rich. Those were Bychawa Jews, they had hard hides, but there were also those who used to have a coach service before the war, what they call PEKAES nowadays. The people there were hardly poor. When they kept 'em, the Jews must've given them a few zloty for that.
Well, you had to bake bread every other day, you know, to feed 'em.

Kułaga's son-in-law kept some, Adam Radomski. Right away he set up beehives, in his father-in-law's field.
There were about a hundred and fifty hives, with bees. And here they had

nice mushrooms and tomatoes, and sunflowers, and flowers and stuff. He built such a new fence, huge, blackthorn wood, a metre and a half high. Everyone said Radomski had a devil, that if you walked into his field of beehives, you'd never walk back out. Everyone was scared, every child.

Well, I was just a girl, but they were boys, so they'd walk in, wouldn't they?
And he was black-haired, his head was so curly, Radomski's was, and so much hair on his chest. And when the sun shone, it was hot, he'd stand among those hives without much clothing... kind of like... well, like a devil he looked.
So he carried food to them there, Mr Radomski did. He'd carry food to them, in buckets on a shoulder yoke, making like it was for the bees. That he was feeding bees. And people didn't even know that he was feeding people there and not the bees. Because everyone..., they'd tell everyone that he had bees there. So no one would go there.
Bees they say, so bees it is. No one looked in there; what business was it of anybody's, right?
You're carrying something, go ahead.
Later it came out who'd been eating that bread.

Someone denounced them, said they were over at Dymniak, in Kułaga's barn. There was a basement dug out. Somewhere in the barn, under the straw heap, they made 'em such a hiding place and they were staying in there. Access was through a sort of wardrobe. They were staying in the ground, covered over with boards, and straw put on top. It was sand, so the sides were laid with boards, like formwork, to make sure it wouldn't slide down. And a number of Jews inside, I don't know how many. Thirteen? Fourteen?

So, well, the partisans came at night and killed off the Jews. Well, there were two of 'em, the leaders, er..., of the partisans, who did time in prison under communism. One of 'em, Jan Gajowiak (his commander was Kawecki) came back but he's no longer alive, and the other one, Franciszek Mańko, well, he died in prison.

How far away he lived, that partisan leader? A hundred metres from the house with the hiding place. But then, to feed so many people, there

must've been something, some suspicion, when that Mańko fellow, almost a neighbour, must've noticed something.
And so, well, they sniffed 'em out somehow, and it was mostly those nationalist partisans who sniffed those Jews out in there.

Why did they kill 'em off? How can I know? There was one who was sent to spy at some point and he found out. Perhaps he wanted to rob 'em? Rob 'em, maybe? Maybe he thought they had gold. Because it was possible that, if it was a Jew, Jews, then they had gold. On account of the gold perhaps; damned if I know on account of what. For sure, there must've been a reason. Must've been on account of some possessions. They thought that the Jews, when leaving home, must've taken some with 'em, must've had some.

And at that time there was a fire at a Jewish place, a Jewish house. The last night of October, into the first of November 1943. They set the fire to that house, Szymon Nissenbaum's, where the shop was, where Esta...

The partisans arranged the fire to keep the people busy with the fire, while they...
The ones who were trying to put out the fire said: 'We were fighting the fire and in there - we listened in - knock, silence, knock.'
They went there to rape them.

We were guests at a wedding, and came back late at night.
I remember how I ran because there was a fire, and then, in the morning, I hear that Jews have been killed, a number of 'em.

It was later, we were on our way to church as it was All Souls' Day, so we went to have a look.
Because some fellow came and said: 'Ma'am, aren't you coming to look at the herrings?' And my mum asked him, 'What herrings? Where's herrings? Who threw them away and where?'
And everyone went, and our folks went too, and there were the herrings.
The Jews, all killed, laid out [*pause*] like herrings.
And they were massacred too.
I looked once, and off I went! Headed home.

I remember Antek Król from Strzyżewice was there too. He was an older man. Forty perhaps?
And he said: 'What have you done?' Because there were lots of people around. Perhaps some of 'em were actually the same that had been there at night.
'What have you done? This is a human being. You should all be hanged' - there was a forest nearby - 'on those spruce trees.' Yes.

People say they were all battered, pecked with an axe. They shot 'em and then pecked 'em with axes on the bullet holes, so the Germans wouldn't know they'd been killed with firearms.

And the Germans came right away to get Kułaga. For harbouring them, they were both taken to Majdanek, but the Kułaga woman came back soon, in December. And he was burned in a furnace at Majdanek in Lublin.

And then, after they locked up Kułaga, er..., the lads started walking among Radomski's beehives, to get tomatoes and sunflowers.
They said: 'The devil's gone!'

The Germans came so someone must've tipped 'em off, what else?
So the Germans told the neighbours who were there to bury them, right outside the window, to spite the Kułagas.
And one was buried outside the window, another one in the hall, and the third one here. And the village head had to obey the order and bury them where the Germans told 'im to.
There are such thick oaks growing there.

So when the Kułagas were at Majdanek, he, the Gajowiak fellow, was courting a girl. So he came over, and I used to go over there too, 'cause he was such a lad, we had fun, he may have been two years older than me. So I went there, and stayed too long, so my mum took a rod and came to fetch me. And he was just telling us how he'd pulled out those Jews, how they'd given 'em gold, and such. And my mum was just standing in the hall and listening outside the door; the door into the hall was open. And then she comes in and says: 'I was gonna flog my dear daughter but actually it's you that should get one in the mug to shut you up. Don't you brag!'

And so, the Jews were, er..., done. That's it.
So they killed 'em all.
They killed 'em, buried 'em, and there you have it.
Put 'em in the ground and goodbye.

There was supposedly one Jewish kid who survived. He was nine or so. There were those boards there, so he crawled in, as kids do, under that boarding, and they didn't notice him. And, well, supposedly he survived and when all quieted down he came out and went to the people who'd kept 'em. First, there was this one fellow that kept 'em, so he went to that one, not where they'd been killed but to the other one, because there were two, two kept 'em; one kept 'em, and later he installed them at the other place. So he went there and stayed in hiding all the way through, somewhere.

Going towards the fields from Kułaga's, there was a place where the Adamczyks lived. And this child came up, the Jewish lad did. And they took him in. And they lived in the fields. And kept him through. And he was here, people say, after the liberation. When the Ruskis came in, then whoa, he came here, the Jew, the Jewish lad. And said he'd hidden under some kind of board and survived and asked about those that had kept 'em, those Jews.

No one saw it at night. Everyone would be afraid to come up there. It all happened at night. It was only much later that everything became known. Not right away. But it was later that people felt the right moment and began to chip, and chip and chip. And so they chipped things out.

Well, there were young Jewish women in that basement.
All over and done! The partisans had killed 'em all, and that's it.
There were Jews; the Jews were killed off, so they plundered.
The money.
They took a bunch of hides, because the Rajses had leather for boots; shoemakers used to buy supplies from them.
They took whatever was there.
If a Jew had something in her bra, they'd take it. And they had bras, like women had back then... Nowadays they thread whalebones through, right? Well, they had pieces of sheet gold sewn into theirs. There were a few, some young people shared 'em apiece.

What could they have, really? Say they had some money, so the partisans would've taken that when they killed them. Or those clothes of theirs?! Bloody rags, who would've taken that?

Later, when the young ones went there, they took some, such rags, the pieces that seemed better. What was left of the Jewish things. Even Feluś Adamczyk's grandmother went there. And walked in on 'em. And there was this dead Jewish kid, just like their own son. They gave 'er a jacket and she came back and rinsed it 'cause it was bloodstained. Went down to the river to wash it, went towards the valley over there. Kept soaping it. There were golden coins sewn in it. Every Jew had some sewn in for the road, to support themselves. When they moved out, every one of 'em had some sort of supplies. But granny didn't know what kind of money it was. She came and said: 'Something, some kind of money. Some un-Polish money?'
She told people in the village, someone told someone else, and that one yet another. He came at night and said: 'Adamczykowa, give me that money that you have!'
He'd found out and came, the partisan who'd killed 'em, done the killing. In the evening he came and [threatened] the Adamczyk woman, just like this!
So granny gave it up right away.

Later, after the war, the UB [security police] summoned her. She said: 'It was something shiny so that you just couldn't look at.' Were those pearls or what? Or diamonds? He said to her: 'Lady, you could've bought the best house in Lublin for it.'

My mother-in-law, when she was still alive, found some trousers there, or a jacket, so she had some, some of that gold that was sewn in. She found it. But there was one fellow, he's no longer alive, Józiek Teter; he came and said she must give it up. Give him the jacket, there's nothing in it, and he took that jacket. And there was gold in those, those... And he took it from her.

And what did people say in the village? You know how things are in a village... They say: that one found gold; another, they say, didn't get any gold. They blamed everything on... on Mańko. Mańko was, so to speak, and so was Józiek Teter, harassed. And that man Gajowiak and Teter came back, and Mańko's punishments were the greatest, he didn't come back.

But he must've, must've gained something, seeing as they later quit farming. The wife and the children sold the farm, and moved to Lublin.

Did Teter build a house later? Well, he did, he built a home.

They took all kinds of Jewish gold. The ones who killed 'em; they did nothing with that gold later... Because no one got rich on this whole business. Nobody. None of 'em was shiny all over.

And later, in his old age, in his eyes, whenever he drank, he must've seen all those Jews that he'd killed. Because something like that will stand up before your eyes, won't it? When you do something bad, won't it stand up before your eyes?
He confessed to my mum. There were eight of 'em, the Gajowiaks. They'd grown up together with my mum. They lived next door, so she would ask him. 'Janek,' she'd say, 'don't they stand up before your eyes?' And he'd go: 'Hush, Lodzia, don't say nothing!'

His wife said he was unbearable when he drank, he talked in his sleep, when he was asleep, right? In his sleep, she said, he talked, er..., he shouted. So, there must've been something on his conscience.

So he died, but when he died, it was a sunny day. And here's the priest with the burial sermon at the cemetery, and then how it began to pour down, like from a bucket, as if someone poured out a bucket. So people say it was Lord God crying over his soul.

And the ones who had kept the Jews in hiding, they didn't sell their farmstead. Wasn't really much of a farm, just a little forest and a cottage, a hut standing there, such a small one. That family stayed on around here. They weren't harassed by anyone.

No one was granted any title for harbouring Jews.
And even if someone was granted one? Who would admit he was?
No one will.

You're saying it was an honourable thing to harbour them? I don't know... They won't admit they did; someone would find fault with 'em, blame 'em for getting rich on Jewish gold.

If someone had gold, they knew where to put it in, and they'd tell nobody.
One family *really* camouflaged themselves. And they were cross at everyone: what are they accusing us of, right? Because someone would tell 'em something sometimes, lay it all out. But actually they were quite immune to all that. They bought houses for their children, one in Gdańsk, one in Świdnik, one in Bychawa. In those days the countryside was poor, wasn't it?

Did anyone punish 'em for the killing? You know, ma'am, they bought their way out. So no one would say anything after that. And later, those that did confess... they didn't buy those out at all.
One would tell on another, and that's how things went.
Well, but there's this innocent blood, and that's all bound to come out into the open, too.

And they spent some time in prison, and one got death penalty, then it was turned into life, then twenty-five years, and then, when all the fuss started about the letters, when the Jews started leaving for Israel under Gomułka, Gajowiak was released.[2]
And I think one of 'em actually got damages for wrongful accusation. So there were different stories here. Later, those who had money could buy themselves out.

A local may know. But he may be afraid to tell.
There's this elderly fellow living there, keeps pigeons, lives alone.
In his childhood, he saw it all but he won't talk about it now.
He's alone; his parents passed away. It's his parents who harboured

2 Władyslaw Gomułka was first secretary of the United Polish Workers' Party and leader of Poland (1956–70). In 1967–68 in Poland the 'anti-Zionist' campaign followed the victory of Israel over Soviet-backed Arab states in the Six-Day War. Most of the remaining Polish Jews were coerced into leaving the country on one-way 'travel documents' that declared the holders had renounced Polish citizenship.

[Jews]. But he won't talk to this day, even though he's well over seventy now.
Everyone knows, more or less, who did what, but no one will spill the beans.
The older generation is gonna take this knowledge to their graves.

Politics is nothing but falsifying history.
Just like there's falsification of history to this day.
That's what it's like now: falsified.

When they taught us history, they said we wouldn't give up a single button! You understand? Meaning that Poland was so strong that no one, no other country would come and jump us. And then, how shall I tell you this to make sure it's the real truth? Three days later, after we found out that the Germans declared war on Poland, the whole thing was over. And the Russians, there's even no knowing when they declared it, the war against Poland. Whoever rode over there, he died in Russia.
And they said..., that's what they taught us at school: we won't give up a single button!

I disliked history more than anything 'cause I didn't like to study those kings. Because what business did I have with kings?
Where would any of 'em go? They had their feasts, balls and dresses-like they have in theatre or ballet.
All I was interested in was that people should have good lives.

If someone had it written at birth what he was going to go through, he would die right away.

And this is a human being, all of 'em are! Whether a Pole or a Ruthenian, or a Jew, or a German, or, or a Ukrainian; they're ordinary folk. It's just those in the government that pit one people against another, to stir up more evil.

People would drown one another in a spoonful of water.
I remember once, the light was on at home longer than usual in the evening, so the ground outside the window was trampled all over.
Anonymous denunciations were a major thing. I was accused eighteen

times during one year. Because of anonymous denunciations. And none of 'em was true.

But other than that, no one has claimed anything, no one has anything against it.
No one. There's a photographer in one house that used to be Jewish. Here, going towards the church. He takes photos for identity cards, as far as I know. That's in that one. Does anyone live in the one further down? I don't know. There are shops in there now. But those are Poles who live in there. But how did they get it? Did they buy it or did the government give it to them? Or did it become communal property, or what? I don't know. People have demolished the old houses by now, built new ones.
There's none here any more.
No trace of the Jews.

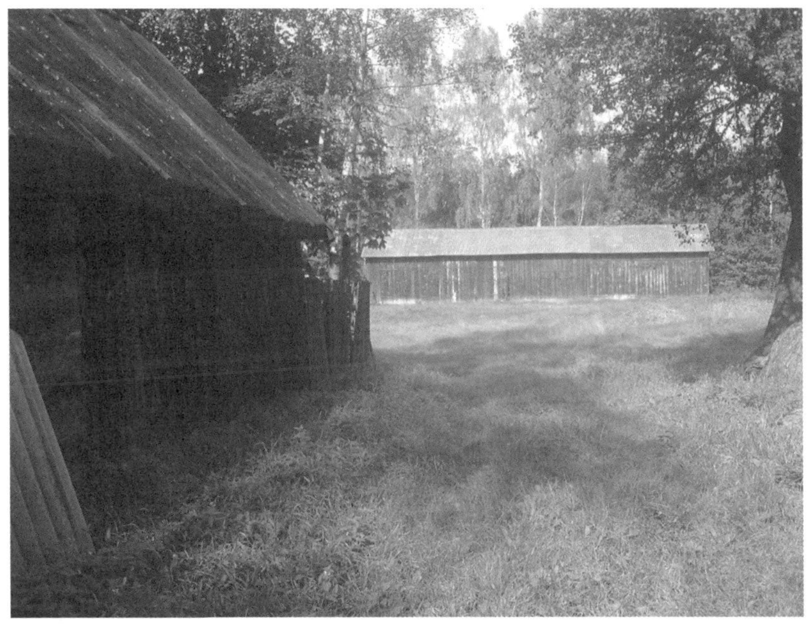

The site of the murder seen from the direction of Jan Adamczyk's house, Dębina. Photo: Agata Fiedotow and Anna Górska, 14 September 2010

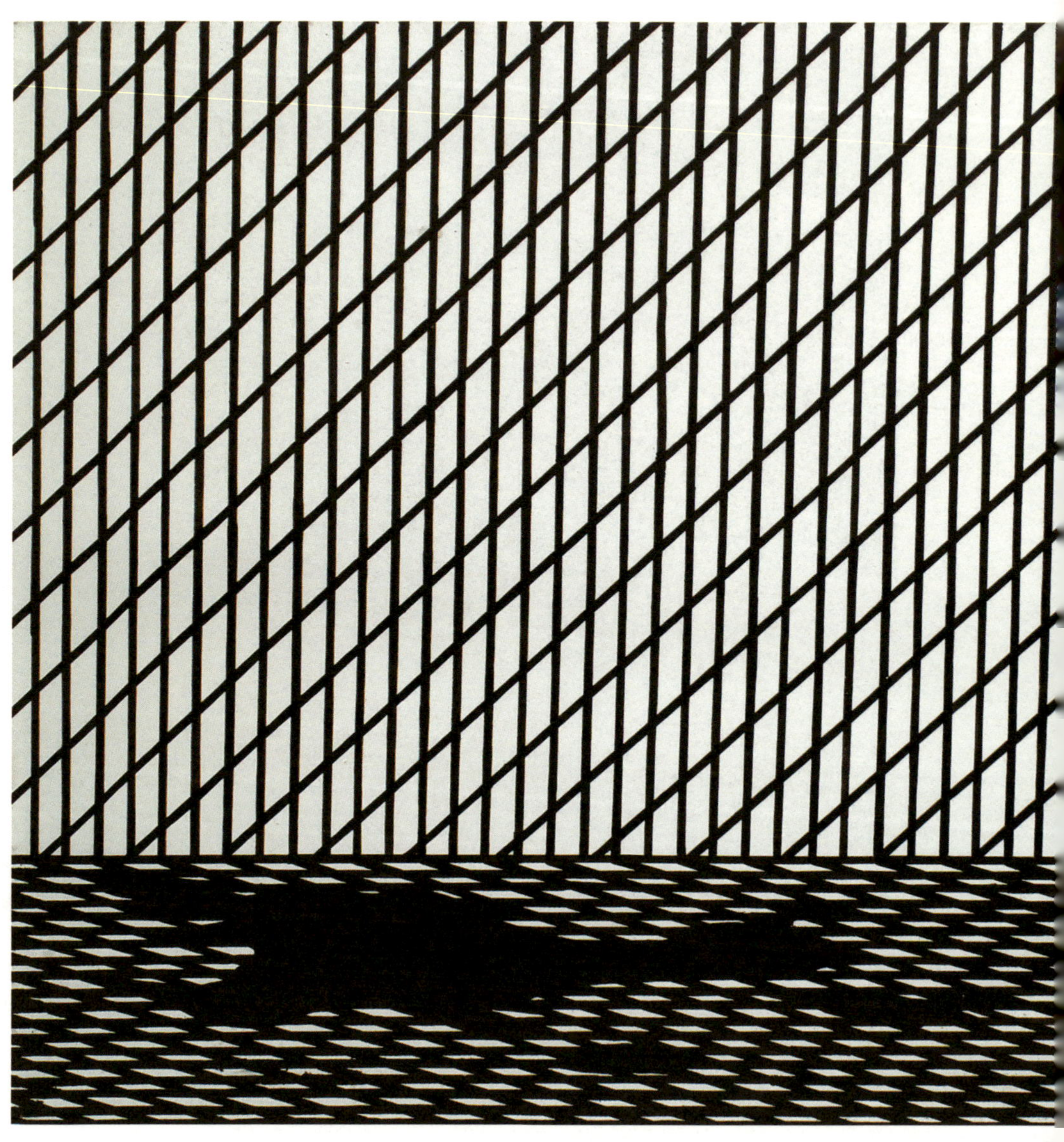

Maus 3, 2001

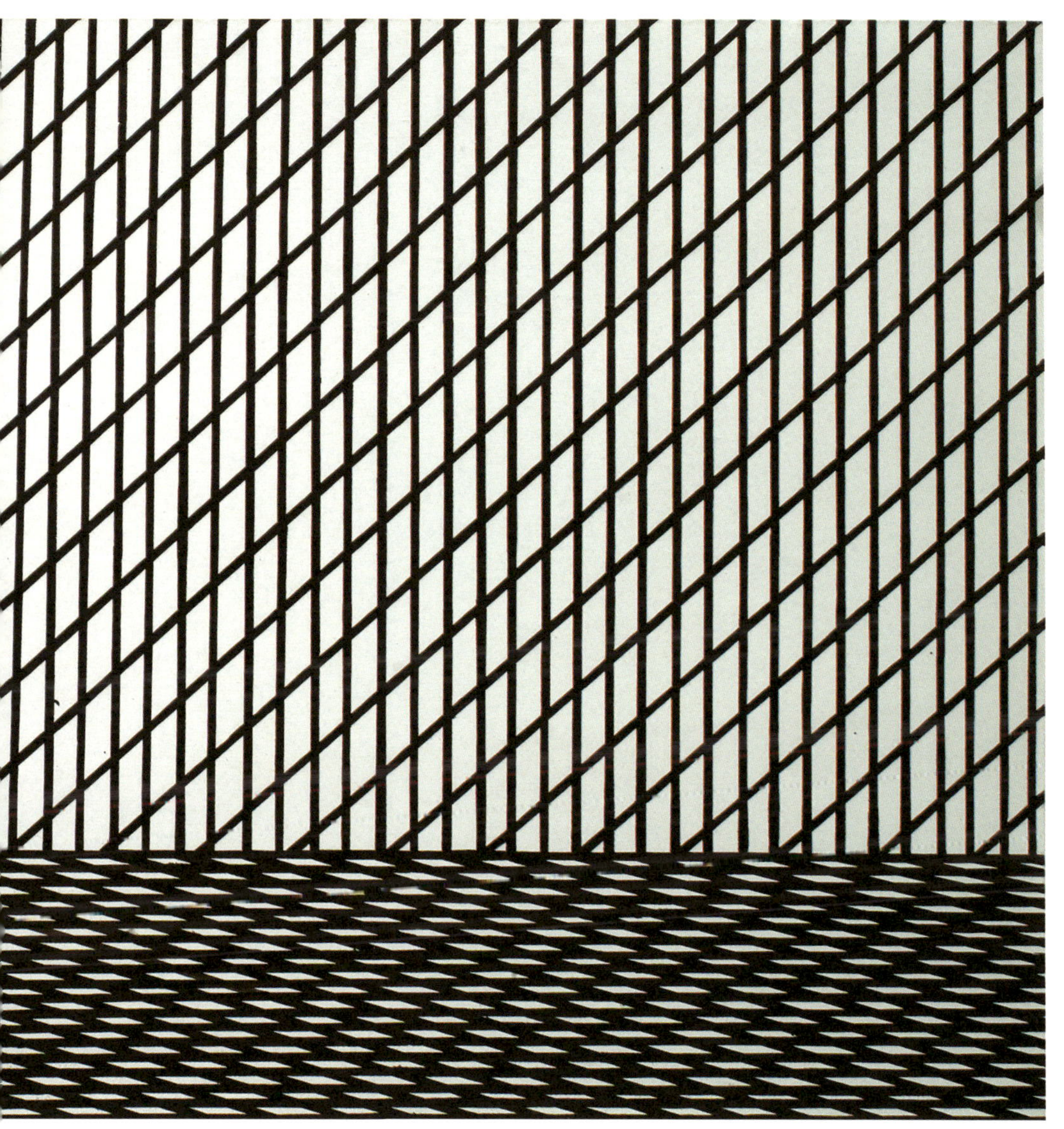

The Negro and the Warsaw Ghetto
By W. E. B. Du Bois

First delivered as a speech in 1952 at *Jewish Life* magazine's 'Tribute to the Warsaw Ghetto Fighters' at the Hotel Diplomat in New York

I *have* been to Poland three times. The first time was fifty-nine years ago, when I was a student at the University of Berlin. I had been talking to my schoolmate, Stanislaus Ritter von Estreicher. I had been telling him of the race problem in America, which seemed to me at the time the only race problem and the greatest social problem of the world. He brushed it aside. He said, 'You know nothing, really, about real race problems.' Then he began to tell me about the problem of the Poles and particularly of that part of them who were included in the German Empire; of their limited education; of the refusal to let them speak their own language; of the few careers that they were allowed to follow; of the continued insult to their culture and family life.

I was astonished; because race problems at the time were to me purely problems of colour, and principally of slavery in the United States and near-slavery in Africa. I promised faithfully that when I went on my vacation that summer, I would stop to see him in his home at Kraków, Poland, where his father was librarian of the university.

Discovery of the Jewish Question

I went down to South Germany through Switzerland to Italy, and then came back by Venice and Vienna and went out through

Austria, Czechoslovakia and into German Poland and there, on the way, I had a new experience with a new race problem. I was travelling from Budapest through Hungary to a small town in Galicia, where I planned to spend the night. The cabman looked at me and asked if I wanted to stop 'unter die Juden'. I was a little puzzled, but told him 'Yes'. So we went to a little Jewish hotel on a small, out of the way street. There I realised another problem of race or religion, I did not know which, which had to do with the treatment and segregation of large numbers of human beings. I went on to Kraków, becoming more and more aware of two problems of human groups, and then came back to the university, not a little puzzled as to my own race problem and its place in the world.

Gradually I became aware of the Jewish problem of the modern world and something of its history. In Poland I learned little because the university and its teachers and students were hardly aware themselves of what this problem was, and how it influenced them, or what its meaning was in their life. In Germany I saw it continually obtruding, but being suppressed and seldom mentioned. I remember once visiting on a social occasion in a small German town. A German student was with me and when I became uneasily aware that all was not going well, he reassured me. He whispered, 'They think I may be a Jew. It's not you they object to, it's me.' I was astonished. It had never occurred to me until then that any exhibition of race prejudice could be anything but colour prejudice. I knew that this young man was pure German, yet his dark hair and handsome face made our friends suspicious. Then I went further to investigate this new phenomenon in my experience.

Thirteen years after that I passed again through Poland and Warsaw. It was in the darkness, both physically and spiritually. Hitler was supreme in Germany where I had been visiting for five months and I sensed the oncoming storm. I passed through Warsaw into the Soviet Union just three years before the horror fell upon that city.

But in Berlin, before I left, I sensed something of the Jewish problem and its growth in the generation since my student days. I went to the Jewish quarter one day and entered a bookstore. It was quiet and empty.

After a time a man came into the room and very quietly he asked me what I was looking for. I mentioned certain books and browsed among those he pointed out. He said nothing more nor did I. I felt his suspicion and at last I wandered out. I went that night to a teacher's home. There were a few Americans and several Germans present. The curtains were carefully drawn and then the teacher spoke. He defended the nazi programme in the main - its employment, its housing and roads; but he frankly confessed that he was ashamed of the treatment of the Jews or at least some of them. He blamed some severely but he had friends among them and he was ashamed of their treatment.

Then, at midnight I entered Poland. It was dark - dark not only in the smoke, but in the soul of its people, who whispered in the night as we rode slowly through the murk of the railway yards.

Then finally, three years ago I was in Warsaw. I have seen something of human upheaval in this world: the scream and shots of a race riot in Atlanta; the marching of the Ku Klux Klan; the threat of courts and police; the neglect and destruction of human habitation; but nothing in my wildest imagination was equal to what I saw in Warsaw in 1949. I would have said before seeing it that it was impossible for a civilised nation with deep religious convictions and outstanding religious institutions; with literature and art; to treat fellow human beings as Warsaw had been treated. There had been complete, planned and utter destruction. Some streets had been so obliterated that only by using photographs of the past could they tell where the street was. And no one mentioned the total of the dead, the sum of destruction, the story of crippled and insane, the widows and orphans.

The astonishing thing, of course, was the way that in the midst of all these memories of war and destruction, the people were rebuilding the city with an enthusiasm that was simply unbelievable. A city and a nation was literally rising from the dead. Then, one afternoon, I was taken out to the former ghetto. I knew all too little of its story although I had visited ghettoes in parts of Europe, particularly in Frankfurt, Germany. Here there was not much to see. There was complete and total waste, and a monument. And the monument brought back again the problem of race and religion, which so long had been my own particular and separate problem. Gradually, from looking and reading, I rebuilt the story of this extraordinary resistance to oppression and wrong in a day of complete frustration, with enemies on every side: a resistance, which involved death and destruction for hundreds and hundreds of human beings; a deliberate sacrifice in life for a great ideal in the face of the fact that the sacrifice might be completely in vain.

Enlarged View of the Negro Question

The result of these three visits, and particularly of my view of the Warsaw Ghetto, was not so much clearer understanding of the Jewish problem in the world as it was a real and more complete understanding of the Negro problem. In the first place, the problem of slavery, emancipation and caste in the United States was no longer in my mind a separate and unique thing as I had so long conceived it. It was not even solely a matter of colour and physical and racial characteristics, which was particularly a hard thing for me to learn, since for a lifetime the colour line had been a real and efficient cause of misery. It was not merely a matter of religion. I had seen religions of many kinds – I had sat in the Shinto temples of Japan, in the Baptist churches of Georgia, in the Catholic cathedral of Cologne and in Westminster Abbey. No, the race problem in which I was interested cut across lines of colour and physique and belief and status and was a matter of cultural patterns, perverted teaching and human hate and prejudice, which reached all sorts of people and caused endless evil to all men. So that the ghetto of Warsaw helped me to emerge from a certain social provincialism into a broader conception of what the fight against race segregation, religious discrimination and the oppression by wealth had to become if civilisation was going to triumph and broaden in the world.

I remembered now my schoolmate, Stanislaus. He has long been dead and he died refusing to be a stoolpigeon for the nazis in conquered Poland. He gave his life for a great cause. How broad it eventually became! How much he realised that behind the Polish problem lay the Jewish problem and that all were one crime against civilisation, I do not know.

I remember now one scene in Poland over a half century ago. It was of worship in a Catholic church. The peasants were crowded together and were grovelling on their knees.

They were in utter subjection to a powerful hierarchy. And out of that, today, they have crawled and fought and struggled. They see the light.

Path to the Future

My friend, Gabriel D'Arboussier, an African, recently visited Warsaw and wrote:

> At the entrance to the city rises an imposing mausoleum erected to the memory of the 40,000 soldiers of the Red Army who fell for the liberation of Warsaw and who are all buried there. This is no cemetery, cut off from the living, but the last resting place of these glorious dead, near whom the living come to sit and ponder the sacrifice of those to whom they owe life. Had I seen nothing else, that mausoleum alone would have taught me enough to understand the Polish people's will to peace and its attachment to the Soviet Union. But there is more to tell and it cannot be too often told: of Poland's thirty-two million inhabitants six and a half million died. There is also Warsaw, 83 per cent destroyed and its population reduced from over a million to 22,000, and the poignant spectacle of the flattened ghetto.

But where are we going - whither are we drifting? We are facing war, taxation, hate and cowardice and particularly increasing division of aim and opinion within our own groups. Negroes are dividing by social classes, and selling their souls to those who want war and colonialism, in order to become part of the ruling plutarchy, and encourage their sons to kill 'Gooks'. Among Jews there is the same dichotomy and inner strife, which forgets the bravery of the Warsaw Ghetto and the bones of the thousands of dead who still lie buried in that dust. All this should lead both these groups and others to reassess and reformulate the problems of our day, whose solution belongs to no one group: the stopping of war and preparation for war; increased expenditure for schools better than we have or are likely to have in our present neglect and suppression of education; the curbing of the freedom of industry for the public welfare; and amid all this; the right to think, talk, study, without fear of starvation or jail. This is a present problem of all Americans and becomes the pressing problem of the civilised world.

First of January (Side), 2021

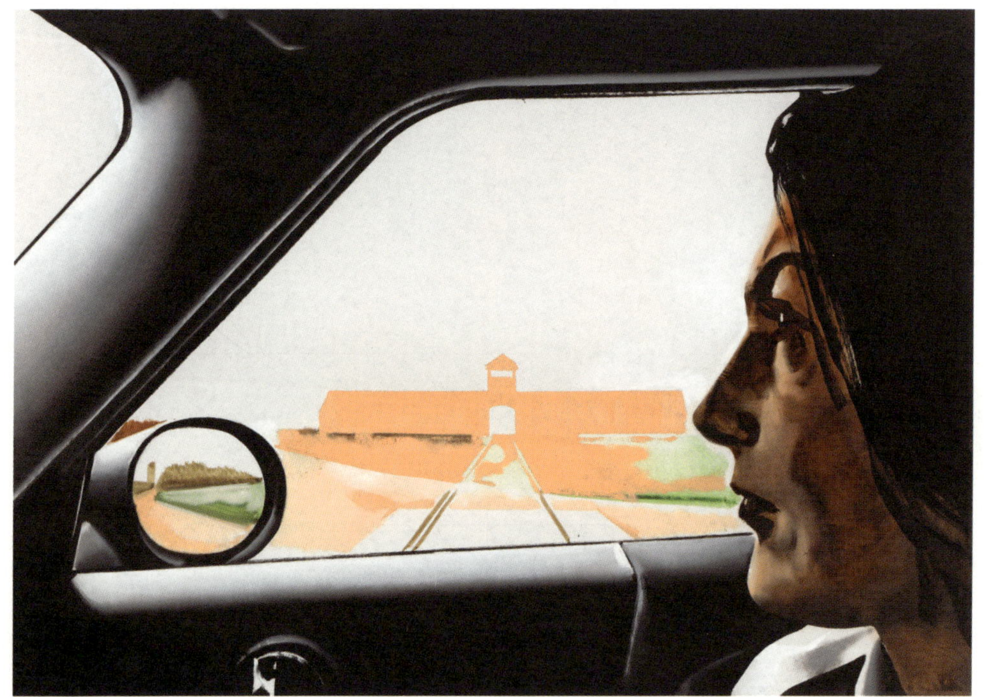

First of January (Back), 2021

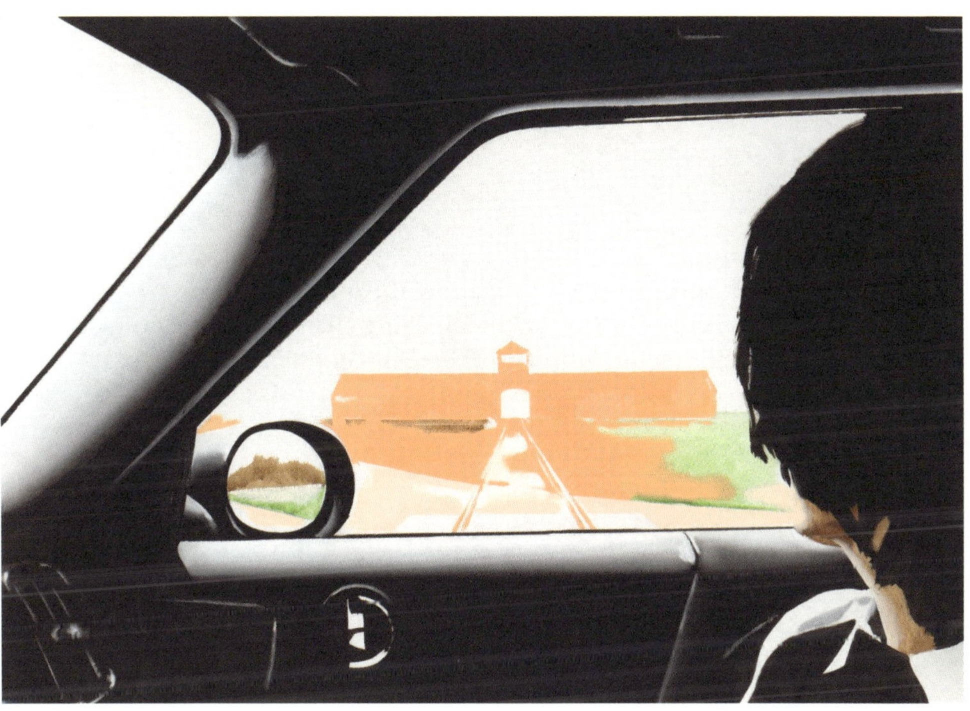

Distancing from Participation: If Auschwitz Were in Switzerland - On Not Acknowledging Historical Guilt and the Long Slumber of the Self-Righteous

By Adolf Muschg

First published in 1997 in *Die Zeit*,
translated from the German by Andrew Boreham

Mr Delamuraz has said: Auschwitz is not in Switzerland.[1]

With my stepchildren's digital globe, which can also measure distances, I have fact-checked this sentence. The globe tells me that Auschwitz is in Poland, 897 kilometres from Bern. When asked for more information on Auschwitz, the globe reports: Town. CET +00:00. Location: 50 degrees 0' N, 19 degrees 15' E. Sights: None. At least the globe knows that there is an old city and the Church of the Holy Ghost in Bern.

If Auschwitz is not in Switzerland, as Mr Delamuraz has quite rightly said, why has this met with such a curious silence? The response bears no comparison to that received when he used the word 'blackmail' - the global echo probably shocked no one more than the person who said it.[2]

1 Editor's note: the author refers to the statement 'Auschwitz is not in Switzerland' made by former Swiss President Jean-Pascal Delamuraz during a 1997 interview with the Swiss papers *24 Heures* and *Tribune de Genève*, 'in which he commented on the Nazi gold affair. ... [that] the issue was not about historical truth but about the American intention to destabilize Switzerland and destroy the "Finanzplatz Schweiz" (Switzerland as financial location)'. Mariatte Denman, '"If Auschwitz Were in Switzerland. . . . :" German Swiss Intellectuals Respond to the Nazi Gold Affair', *New German Critique*, no. 85, 'Special Issue on Intellectuals', Winter 2002, 169.

2 Editor's note: earlier in the year on 1 January 1997, to global outcry, Delamuraz had 'dismissed as "blackmail" calls to set up a compensation fund for Jews who might be entitled to money left in Swiss banks during the Holocaust'. 'Swiss President Says Pleas for a Holocaust Fund are "Blackmail"', *New York Times*,

He had not wanted that thought to come across quite so loudly. He was extremely sorry! In Japan, there are many ways of twisting and turning an apology, so it sounds more like a reproach. If you have the nerve to interpret me that way, then very well, here's your apology, eat that!

That sentence resulted in an international outcry that is now so familiar. Afterwards the unknown Switzerland could no longer be mistaken for Sweden, it was also no longer the same as it had been. Switzerland was now on the map.

The little sentence about Auschwitz, however, was met by an almost piercing silence. Auschwitz is not a place from which one can still draw arguments and counterarguments. No matter how far we go, it is always there, accompanying us like the ground under our feet.

Naming it means both silence and non-silence. To say there could be no more poetry after Auschwitz is an ascertained fact, yet this does not mean no poems were written after Auschwitz - where would German poetry be without the works of Paul Celan, Rose Ausländer or Nelly Sachs. It only means that, for Auschwitz, there is no afterwards, just as there is no elsewhere. The most prominent books by survivors testify to the camp as a place of distancing from participation not previously seen in the history of humanity, not only for the victims, but also among the victims themselves. Everyone had a share in this disconnect: those who knew something of Auschwitz, and those who knew nothing of it, those administering Auschwitz, those 'cleansed' to death there and those refraining from bombing it (to save, but to save what?).

The horror of Auschwitz is not that it lies at the unimaginable end of every civilisation, but that it lies in the now imaginable centre of all civilisations - and hence the silent response to Delamuraz's defiant little sentence. In its execrable protestation of innocence, his statement suddenly collapsed the distance between the two places (897 km). And it no longer needs the evil eye to see in the once real Auschwitz something of the façade of a Switzerland no longer quite real today: the decorative

1 January 1997, https://www.nytimes.com/1997/01/01/world/swiss-president-says-pleas-for-a-holocaust-fund-are-blackmail.html.

geraniums in front of the windows, the meticulous cleanliness where it mattered (on our side of death), the tender emotion of Höß[3] - the good family father, who merely felt sorry for the young people as they passed under the blossoming trees into his gas.

The days we spin into history regularly contain places that construct a moral topography. This is the benchmark against which nations will be measured - and it is no use for them to appeal to geographical distance. The heart of Europe, forged back then by a few old men, was neither a coal and steel treaty, nor was it a defence alliance against the Soviet Union (and covertly against the United States). This Europe was also no longer a territory, but the inception of a consciousness, a coalition against a distancing from participation, the Europeans' reciprocal assurance against their historical enmity between themselves. This enmity's export is the clamour of wars, while antisemitism, genocide, is its internal excess, inflicted on the body of those peoples. Saying that after all Auschwitz is not in Switzerland also has another meaning: Switzerland does not belong to Europe, it does not participate in that civilisation that starts with ourselves.

Before the Second World War, there were Swiss people who knew their Switzerland could not first be defended at its borders. They fought in the international brigades for the legitimate Spanish Republic - and when they came back, their own republic declared them dishonourable; Guernica is another place that, as is well known, is not in Switzerland. When the war came, Switzerland had to stoop to whatever means necessary to keep the war from its borders, including those means that appal it today, fifty years on.

If certain places that a federal council still believes lie far away had been close to Switzerland earlier, then Auschwitz would have become a place of Swiss history - at any rate, if we could have known how many people we had banished there, we could have started feeling shocked sooner.

3 Editor's note: Rudolf Franz Ferdinand Höß was a German SS officer during the Nazi era who, after the defeat of Nazi Germany, was convicted for war crimes. Höß was the longest-serving commandant of Auschwitz concentration and extermination camp. See 'Rudolf Höss', Wikipedia, https://en.wikipedia.org/wiki/Rudolf_H%C3%B6ss.

Certainly, it was not a disgrace to remain out of the war at any cost and with every means available. But when we knew that cost - after all, it came with a human face - we should have called it by its name. These people had names. What we accepted to save ourselves was their lives and then their gold, including the gold in their teeth. For that, we demanded innocuous stamps, after we had demanded unequivocal identification in the passports of those bearing these teeth. We had a part in murdering a people and made money out of it. When it could no longer be denied, we still treated this fact as a footnote to a heroic legend. This is what we are guilty of, and it has become unpardonable by our failure to recognise it.

It is true - and a fortunate thing - that Switzerland survived the war in one piece, but it is not true that it emerged vindicated. And binding its identity to this lie was not just unfortunate, it was sheer foolishness. Switzerland located itself in a legend not just setting itself apart from the history of others, but also from its own history.

Since 1989, its real self-deception has become thinner and thinner and the holes have started to show. Now the moral self-deception has caught up with Switzerland and comes back to haunt it. With the lifting of the state of siege - that also made the Cold War profitable for the country - the last border fell where there was anything left for this country to defend with its hedgehog-like protective reflexes. Without self-pity, one has to recall just how far Switzerland's organised self-delusion went back into previous decades, how far it was prepared to go, how much democratic substance it squandered, and how little it generated in the process. Even at that time, there was a glaring contrast with the rest of Western Europe, which occupied itself with its far more serious things, and a palpable gap between its liberalism and that of Switzerland, to the latter's disadvantage.

Yet Switzerland continued to profit from its moral self-deception never being a topic of discussion (except among its un-Swiss citizens). Now this self-deception has become an issue - and overnight, as people must believe who, even in the last decades, preferred belief to knowledge. Nearly as quickly, the convictions of this credo are exposed in such an abhorrent light that Switzerland not only seems to have taken leave of its senses but has also been deserted by its own faith in itself.

Today, in far from clandestine delight, a world of spectators enjoys the sight of how easily this unmasked model of virtue can be kept on its toes, how ineptly it covers up the fortune it has earned through the misfortune of others; half Tartuffe,[4] half Adam-the village judge - Switzerland protests the idea that it clouded the waters now up to its neck. In any case, one must wait for a thorough investigation. The Swiss model knows nothing of a broken jug,[5] and anyway others were also present when it happened. The model is an abject *Gong Show*,[6] except its entertainment value is shocking enough for no one to want to put a stop to it. For the first time in decades, Switzerland is news, though unfortunately on the scandal page - the model of perfection, a dealer in murder, goody two-shoes as a pimp, truly that's not what we wanted. Is anyone still waiting for Switzerland to make a strong, courageous gesture? One is only waiting for its ineffectualness, its belatedness.

Are we dreaming? That dream is over, and we awaken in the middle of reality. Shame may now squeeze a few tears out of us, yet these are the ones we did not cry when we must have realised Auschwitz is not just everywhere, but in Switzerland as well. 'Stehn wir den Felsen gleich, nie vor Gefahren bleich, froh noch im Todesstreich' (We stand like the rocks, never pale before danger, happy even at the lethal stroke).[7] Yes, as a child when I sang along with these words at the Swiss National Day celebrations, then I had tears in my eyes - tears of pride that I was Swiss.

These tears were not false, even if they did not align with Switzerland's actions in the war, or what it had omitted. They only became false when

4 Editor's note: Tartuffe, the protagonist of the eponymous 1664 play by Molière, is a hypocritical religious devotee whose criminal past is revealed after many twists and turns.

5 Editor's note: here and above the author refers to Heinrich von Kleist's 'The Broken Jug', an 1811 play in which Adam as judge, who acts suspicious throughout the trial, must settle who broke a jug late one night in the room of a young woman named Eve.

6 Editor's note: the American amateur talent programme *The Gong Show* ran on television from 1976–80. The term is also a euphemism for an event that proves to be disastrous in a fun or memorable way.

7 Editor's note: from the first Swiss national anthem, replaced in 1961. See 'Rufst du, mein Vaterland', Wikipedia, https://en.wikipedia.org/wiki/Rufst_du,_mein_Vaterland.

they were preserved as 'diamonds', now, almost fifty years later having become rock-hard and only serving to dazzle.

It was not wrong for Switzerland to muddle its way through the war, just as it could and must; it only became fundamentally wrong when justified opportunism was falsely rewritten as a heroic tale, and everyone who did not parrot the story was berated as a good-for-nothing. The really terrible thing is how after the war without good cause - truly without good cause! - Switzerland made itself guilty of just that distancing from participation that was a feature of the camps and only to be excused by the most extreme plight. All of Switzerland's neighbours saw a world collapse and perish in the war - and we thought it sufficed to only note that our world had remained intact. When it comes to empathy for others, we have substituted - for a long time successfully - sensitivity to our own affairs.

No, surely one could never believe that others now bear a grudge against us for the way we played along with Hitler. Or disparage us for not taking part in what inevitably had to follow Hitler. Or declare we had adopted the business acumen we needed to survive during the war as our guiding principle for the next fifty years, even when the only issue was the lives of others and, first and foremost, life in Europe and ensuring it was secure enough to resist relapses.

We did not drop one single bomb, destroyed nothing, we were not to blame - so why should we now take up responsibility for rebuilding Europe? In that way, we have not only isolated ourselves, but also impoverished ourselves.

Although we have come to feel this impoverishment in our affluence, we could cope with it, just as much as with offering the world the spectacle of our embarrassment and confusion. The unbearable thing is that we have not only distanced ourselves from Auschwitz (or Sarajevo) so much so that we are beyond recognition but have simultaneously distanced ourselves from our own rich sources of history, also full of conflict, which defy legend and could have empowered us to counter inane readings of ourselves.

Do we seriously desire the nonsense of not wanting to know about ourselves in the years 1939-45? Or of how, across our entire history, we find a Switzerland,[8] which in its real - not legendary - form is younger than Belgium and would hardly have existed without a French invasion,[9] without its civil war,[10] and without the imaginative Swiss confederate foreign policy that ensured a bold exchange with Europe?[11] The refugees living and fighting here to ensure Switzerland,[12] thanks to its successful

8 Editor's note: Switzerland has been a state in its present form since 1848. Precursors established a defensive alliance in 1291 forming a loose confederation of states for centuries. In 1798, the revolutionary French government invaded Switzerland and imposed a unified constitution effectively abolishing the cantons, making Switzerland nothing more than a French satellite state. The Nidwalden Revolt in September 1798 showed Switzerland's resistance to occupation. In 1803 following a meeting organised by Napoleon, Swiss autonomy and the cantons' tradition of self-rule within a central government was largely restored, and fully so in 1815 with the Congress of Vienna. See 'Switzerland', Wikipedia, https://en.wikipedia.org/w/index.php?title=Switzerland&oldid=1087075808.

9 Editor's note: Belgium became an independent state in 1830.

10 Editor's note: during the twenty-seven-day Sonderbund (separate alliance) civil war in 1847, the Catholic cantons Lucerne, Fribourg, Valais, Uri, Schwyz, Unterwalden and Zug fought against the centralisation of power in Switzerland. The defeat of the Sonderbund saw the drafting of a new constitution in 1848 whereupon Switzerland became a federal state. Swiss people, whether Catholic or Protestant, realised that the cantons would profit more if their economic and religious interests were merged. Thus, while the rest of Europe saw revolutionary uprisings, the Swiss drew up a constitution that provided for a federal layout. See 'Switzerland', Wikipedia, *ibid.*

11 Editor's note: 'One of the driving forces behind the economic boom were the foreign pioneers who brought their expertise and liberal economic ideas. ... The federal state used its new powers to create favourable conditions for the development of ... industries and service sectors.' See the website of the Federal Department of Foreign Affairs, Swiss Confederation, https://www.eda.admin.ch/dam/PRS-Web/en/dokumente/der-bundesstaat-im-19-jahrhundert_EN.pdf.

12 Editor's note: 'Even prior to 1848 Switzerland had been an attractive haven for political refugees, ... [n]ot only its avowal to democracy and free trade but also its resistance against despots and an almost mythical notion of a tradition of granting asylum reaching back to the Middle Ages increasingly shaped the country's political understanding of self.' Peter Colmer, 'Switzerland as Haven of Political Asylum', blog, Swiss National Museum, 4 April 2017, https://blog.nationalmuseum.ch/en/2017/04/a-haven-of-political-asylum/. 'In the early 1830s a wave of refugees ... arrived following the defeat of the revolutionary movements in neighbouring countries.' Yet the policy did not include fair treatment for all, and working conditions were often precarious. 'Swiss Jews were considered as foreigners and the Swiss Constitution of 1848 denied them the freedom of establishment, trade and worship. Thanks to foreign pressure, particularly from France, the Jewish community in Switzerland was finally granted unlimited civil rights in 1866, and a provision was added to the Federal Constitution of

1848 revolution,[13] did not remain an exception in Europe as they were an inherent part of that policy. It was this Switzerland that, by his own admission, gave the Prussian king sleepless nights, as its heart also beat in those of his subjects who had fled.[14]

That was a long time ago. Today, we are paying for the sleepless nights we never had over Auschwitz, now in the slumber of the self-righteous, where we have also run out of tears, we are overtaken by all those worries we never had about rebuilding Europe.

Ultimately, the shock we are experiencing today offers us a chance - to compare the country we were with the one we could be.

The disdain we sense and begin to confront ourselves with is most likely to disappear when we see that not only do we have something to make amends for, but at last, we now also have something to do.

Postscript: I shouldn't have been surprised at the unequivocal reactions - one way or another - after this intervention appeared in Zurich's *Tages-Anzeiger*. The *Neue Zürcher Zeitung*, in keeping with its style, offered a differentiated response. Martin Meyer, head of the arts pages, considered I would have done better to treat my subject historically rather than morally.

In fact, with Auschwitz before my eyes, the recommended relativisation would have been beyond my means. Of course, in the meantime this also has its history - as the *Historikerstreit* (historians' dispute) - and the traces of it must have shocked me more than the risk of offending the likewise relative innocence of my country. Over the past decades, there has been no shortage of undifferentiated advocates of that.

1874.' See the website of the Federal Department of Foreign Affairs, *ibid.*

13 See n. 8.

14 Editor's note: the 'romanticist on the throne' King Friedrich Wilhelm IV of Prussia reigned from 1840 to 1861. He was also named Prince of Neuchâtel, a Swiss canton, in 1940, a title he maintained even after Swiss independence in 1857 for which he was subject to some ridicule. See Andrej Abplanalp, 'The Neuchâtel Deal', blog, Swiss National Museum, September 2020, https://blog.nationalmuseum.ch/en/2020/09/neuchatel-deal.

What was missing - and still is today - was the general shock of an insight into one's own entanglement that should have resulted in deeds - precisely those 'the world' finds lacking in Switzerland today.

Admittedly, my concern was less the image problem of 'Switzerland as a location' than our readiness to be truthful on our own account. My critic also took exception to this use of the 'we' form. Here, particularly, he may not have reckoned with patriotism, which, as a rule chooses places not quite so dark. 'We' certainly do not need to shoulder the insinuation of a collective guilt, just as little as other nations. Yet when making distinctions, one can also be too obliging. I could accept the sermon on the difference between the 'ethics of conviction' and the 'ethics of responsibility' (in Max Weber's terms) more easily if there had not been a cheap edition of a neutral policy in Switzerland's more recent history.[15] Switzerland did want to be rebuked officially for its 'convictions of neutrality', but only shifted its ground to a more easy-going 'political neutrality' when those convictions came at a price, or their opposites brought a benefit. Besides, the *Neue Zürcher Zeitung* will also have plenty of opportunities to practice the due ethics of responsibility today by naming those responsible: for the blood money business in those days and the blood money business today as with Ferdinand Marcos and Mobutu Sese Seko.[16]

15 Editor's note: the 'ethics of conviction' is based on an accepted hierarchy of values, while the 'ethics of responsibility' acknowledges that the conflict of values is the context for moral endeavour and political action. See Max Weber, *Max Weber: Essays in Sociology*, ed. and trans. H. H. Gerth and C. Wright Mills, New York: Oxford University Press, 1946, pp. 77–128.

16 Editor's note: dictators Ferdinand Marcos, President of the Philippines from 1975 to 1986 and Mobuto Sese Seko, President of then named Congo (as of 1971, Zaire) from 1965 to 1997, were known for their brutality and extreme kleptocracy that impoverished millions during their times in government.

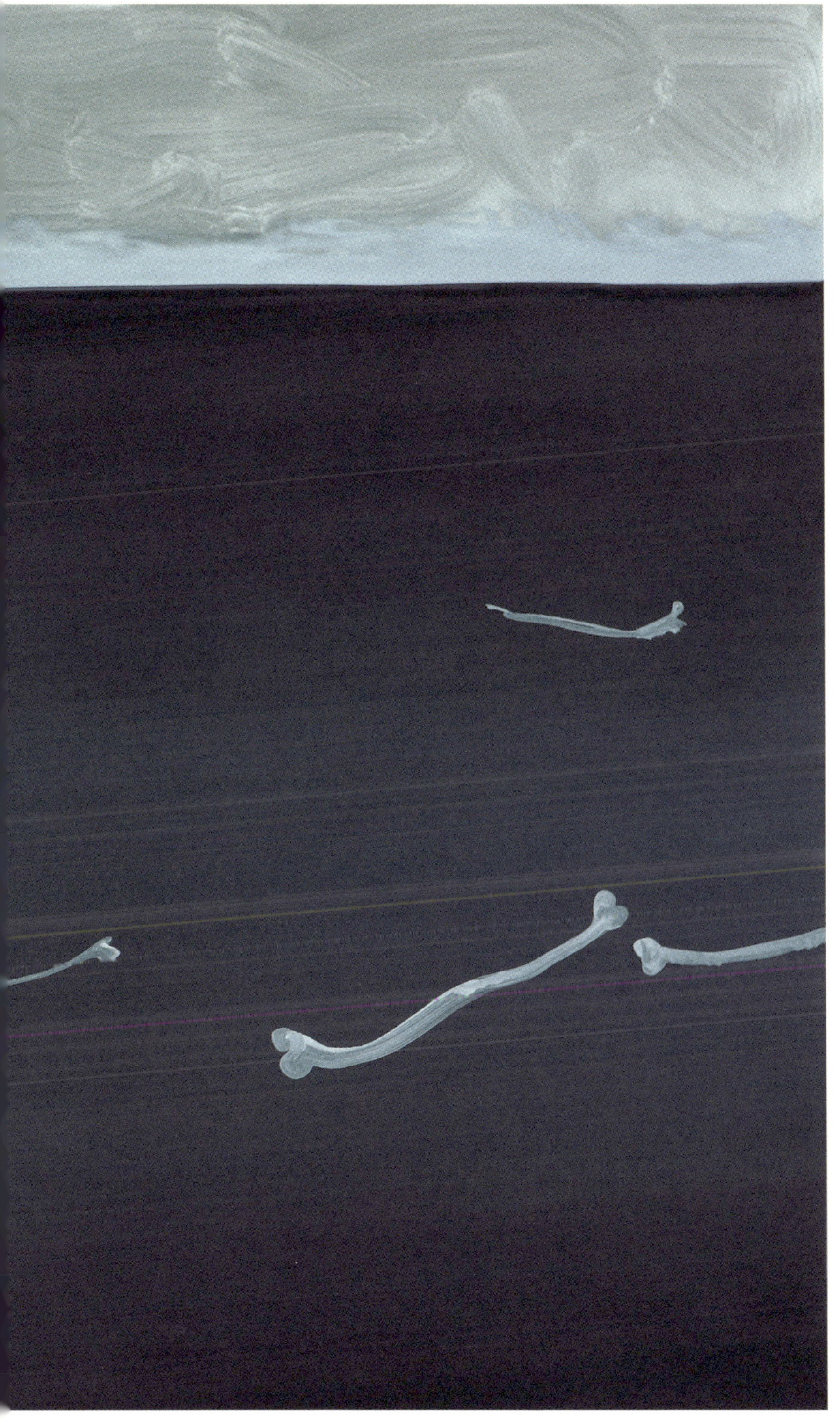

Skeleton of Water, 2008

The Spectres of Comparison: On the Mbembe Affair
By Michael Rothberg

First published in 2020 online in *Zeitgeister*, Goethe-Institut

Germany is haunted by the spectre of comparison. This spectre represents an unintended consequence of one of post-war German society's most laudable achievements: the development over the course of several decades of a culture of memory premised on taking responsibility for the Nazi genocide of European Jews. As Holocaust memory became a linchpin of Germany's official public culture in the post-unification period - with the opening of the Memorial to the Murdered Jews of Europe a concrete symbol of that centrality - the Holocaust also began to occupy a quasi-sacred place as a unique event in the nation's memorial landscape. Defining the Holocaust as unique - in official memory culture if not in scholarship - removes it from the field of ordinary historical understanding, which necessarily relies on comparison and relative commensurability between different events. This sacralisation of the Holocaust's uniqueness is not unique to Germany, but it has come to take a particular - and particularly extreme - form in the Federal Republic in recent years. Mainstream German public discourse assumes that comparing the Holocaust to other events minimises this German-initiated crime and thus undermines the seriousness of German claims to responsibility, an assumption that has led to a determined policing of both public and scholarly expression.

Many Histories of Violence

The insistence on the Holocaust's uniqueness in the German commemorative landscape has resulted in haunting spectres that cluster around two autonomous, but frequently linked hot-button issues: the question of how to relate the Holocaust to other histories of violence, especially the history and aftermath of European colonialism; and the question of what constitutes a legitimate critique of the State of Israel, a state whose self-conception is, like Germany's, also closely tied to the events of the Holocaust.

These two haunting spectres have returned in the most recent intellectual-political scandal to emerge out of Germany: the accusations of antisemitism and Holocaust 'relativisation' against the South Africa-based, Cameroonian scholar Achille Mbembe. A world-renowned scholar of colonialism and its legacies, Mbembe was already well known in Germany before this recent affair; some of his books have been rapidly translated into German and he has received a number of awards, accolades and distinguished visiting positions in the German academy. The accusations against Mbembe, initiated by Lorenz Deutsch, a Free Democratic Party politician from North Rhine-Westphalia, and given greater visibility by Felix Klein, Germany's Commissioner for Jewish Life in Germany and for the Fight against Antisemitism, have left Mbembe's reputation in Germany in tatters, although it seems unlikely that they will have the same effect beyond the Federal Republic. What does this affair teach us about the current status of German public culture?

Comparison and Relativisation

The German establishment's accusations against Mbembe derive from passages in his essay 'The Society of Enmity', which appears in German in his book *Politik der Feindschaft* (Politics of Enmity, 2017). The first passage concerns a comparison (but not an equation, as Deutsch claims) between South African apartheid and the Israeli occupation of Palestinian territories. In Germany, it is simply taken for granted that such a comparison is intrinsically antisemitic. Without interrogating this assumption – as I would, along with dozens of former Knesset members and many other Israeli citizens and Jews around the world who have spoken out about what they see as apartheid-like policies in the occupied territories – there are no grounds for discussion. I turn instead to the second passage, which involves a juxtaposition between apartheid and the Nazi genocide: 'The apartheid system in South Africa and the destruction of Jews in Europe – the latter, though, in an extreme fashion and within a quite different setting – constituted two emblematic manifestations of [a] phantasy of separation.'[1] I find neither equation nor 'relativisation' in this passage, as Mbembe's critics claim. Instead, Mbembe clearly describes the Holocaust as both 'extreme' and as the product of a different historical context from the one that produced apartheid. Mbembe's claim is also less a comparison than a speculative claim about the underlying conditions that make racist systems possible. His focus is on their common construction of an enemy and the concomitant desires and fantasies of separation and destruction that accompany that construction.

This construction, along with these desires and fantasies, is what Mbembe means by the 'society of enmity'. One can contest this approach as an explanation of the Holocaust (or apartheid), but in fact much scholarship on the Nazi genocide investigates just this: the ideological construction of the 'Jew' as an enemy of the *Volksgemeinschaft* who must be eliminated.

Competitive versus Multidirectional Memory

The Mbembe case reveals significant fault lines in German society. The rapidity with which Mbembe has become a *persona non grata* in some official circles reveals that a powerful consensus remains in Germany concerning the incommensurability of the Holocaust. It also suggests that that consensus about the commemoration of Jewish suffering under the Nazis can be collapsed into an uncritical defence of Israel and to the censure of perspectives sympathetic to the Palestinians.

1 Achille Mbembe, 'The Society of Enmity', in *Politik der Feindschaft* (Politics of Enmity), trans. Michael Bischoff, Frankfurt am Main: Suhrkamp, 2017, p. 25.

At the same time, numerous intellectuals - both within Germany and beyond, both Jewish and non-Jewish - have come to Mbembe's defence. The defence of Mbembe from such prominent German scholars as Aleida Assmann and Micha Brumlik suggests that the ruling consensus in Germany has become open to contestation. Today's Germany is caught between two models of cultural memory: a dominant model of competitive memory and an emergent model of what I have called 'multidirectional memory'.

In the model of competitive memory, collective memories are seen as crowding each other out of the public sphere. Understanding collective memories according to the logic of the zero-sum game, this model derives from the fear that bringing memory of the Holocaust into contact with other memories of violence - through comparisons with colonialism, apartheid or occupation - will lead to the diminution, dilution and even denial of the Holocaust. Those concerned with the memories of slavery and colonialism often articulate a similar fear: that an over-emphasis on the Holocaust is depriving other histories of visibility. But does public memory work like this? And, to address German fears directly, must Holocaust comparisons lead to relativisation and the evacuation of responsibility?

My theory of multidirectional memory suggests that - even when memory cultures are subject to impassioned, even angry, conflict - memory does not obey the logic of the zero-sum game. Rather, all memory cultures develop dialogically - through borrowing, appropriation, juxtaposition and echoing of other histories and other traditions of memory. The result of memory conflict is not less memory but more, even if the field of public memory remains unequal. Part of what we see in the Mbembe affair is the well-known fact that as Holocaust memory became globalised it came to serve as a platform for the articulation of other memories of violence - especially those touching on slavery and colonialism. But the now familiar form of Holocaust memory that circulates globally itself emerged out of the earlier era of decolonisation and out of dialogue with other histories that now seem to be competitively pitted against it.

Mbembe's writings grow out of a multidirectional tradition that has, for the past seventy years, reflected on the relationship between the

Holocaust and the racist violence that emerged from centuries of the enslavement, colonisation and segregation of African and African diaspora peoples by Europeans and their descendants.

This tradition includes Aimé Césaire's polemical *Discourse on Colonialism* (1950), in which he described Nazi brutality as a 'crime against the white man' that 'applied to Europe colonialist procedures which until then had been reserved exclusively for the Arabs of Algeria, the "coolies" of India, and the "niggers" of Africa'.[2] It also includes the writings of the African American intellectual W. E. B. Du Bois, who visited the ruins of the Warsaw Ghetto and wrote movingly about how it had transformed his understanding of racism. The visit, Du Bois wrote from the midst of Jim Crow America, led him to realise that 'the problem of slavery, emancipation and caste in the United States was no longer...a separate and unique thing as I had so long conceived it'.[3] Revising his own understanding of race does not, however, lead Du Bois to erase all differences between diverse forms of racism; rather, he remarks that 'nothing in my wildest imagination was equal to what I saw in Warsaw in 1949'.[4] Neither 'separate and unique', nor 'equal' - this is the multidirectional tradition of thinking comparatively about racist violence that one finds across the era of decolonisation and that lives on in thinkers such as Mbembe.

The theory of multidirectional memory does not presuppose that all articulations of public memory are equally valid; we certainly need an ethics of comparison to distinguish the valences of multidirectional articulations. Some comparisons deserve to be taken seriously; some do not. Some comparisons lead to greater solidarity among victims; some lead to increased conflict. Some comparisons may turn into forms of facile equation, but comparison usually involves distinctions of genre and scale. In this context, the theory of multidirectional memory suggests, above all, that the fear of comparison that currently reigns in

2 Aimé Césaire, *Discourse on Colonialism*, trans. Joan Pinkham, New York: Monthly Review Press, 2000, p. 36.

3 See W. E. B. Du Bois, 'The Negro and the Warsaw Ghetto', *The Negro and the Warsaw Ghetto*, New York: Orthodox Jewish Congregations of America, 1952 reprinted in this book, with this passage on p. 56.

4 See *ibid.*, and p. 55 in this book.

Germany could itself be productively rethought. Instead of seeing every juxtaposition of the Holocaust with colonialism or apartheid as a threat to Germans' responsibility-based identity, Germans might instead reflect on the broader histories and responsibilities that come into view when we pause to take multidirectional comparisons seriously. While engagement with the Holocaust is and should remain a touchstone of German identity, there is also a pressing need to engage with the legacies of German and European colonialism and with Germany's implication in the structural racism and economic inequality of the present. Because of how closely linked the aftermath of the Nazi genocide is to the occupation of Palestine, Germans would also do well to reflect on their implication in that ongoing injustice. Instead of targeting Mbembe because of the uncomfortable issues he raises, all of us who are invested in coming to terms with injustices past and present might turn to his writings as a source of insight.

Writing in the 1960s, the Austrian-Belgian Auschwitz survivor Jean Améry argued that the proper attitude of post-Holocaust Germans was that of 'self-mistrust' (*Selbstmisstrauen*). I believe Améry's caution is even more crucial today, precisely because Germany has accomplished so much in the realm of 'working through the past' (*Vergangenheitsäufarbeitung*). It seems to me that, instead of positioning itself as the arbiter of antisemitism and the unquestioning defender of Israeli policy, Germany might return to the practice of 'self-mistrust': it might welcome the spectres of comparison and view them through a multidirectional lens.

Maus 4, 2001

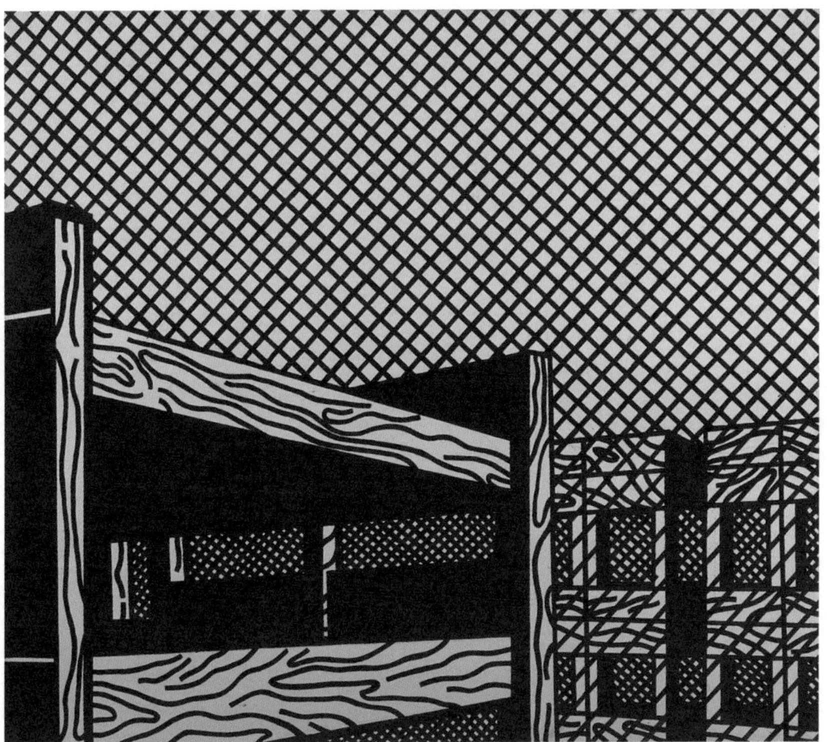

Untitled (Majdanek), 2016

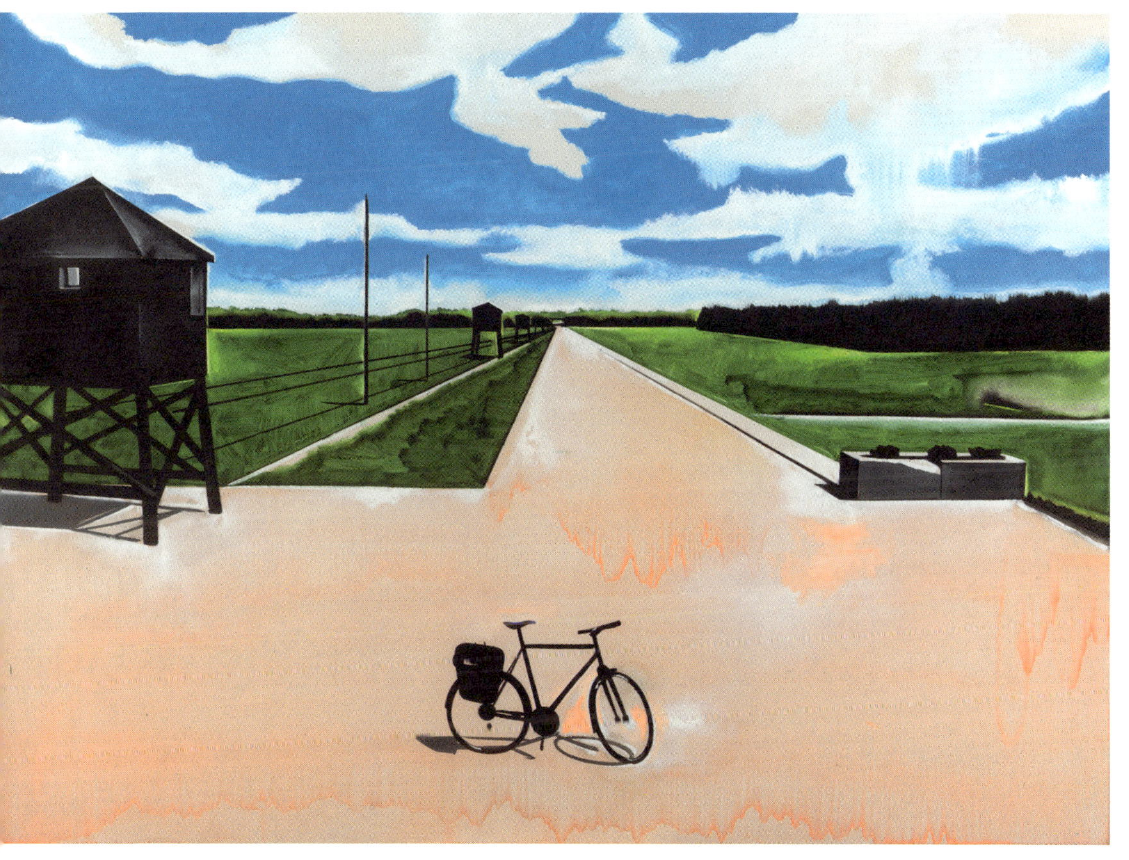

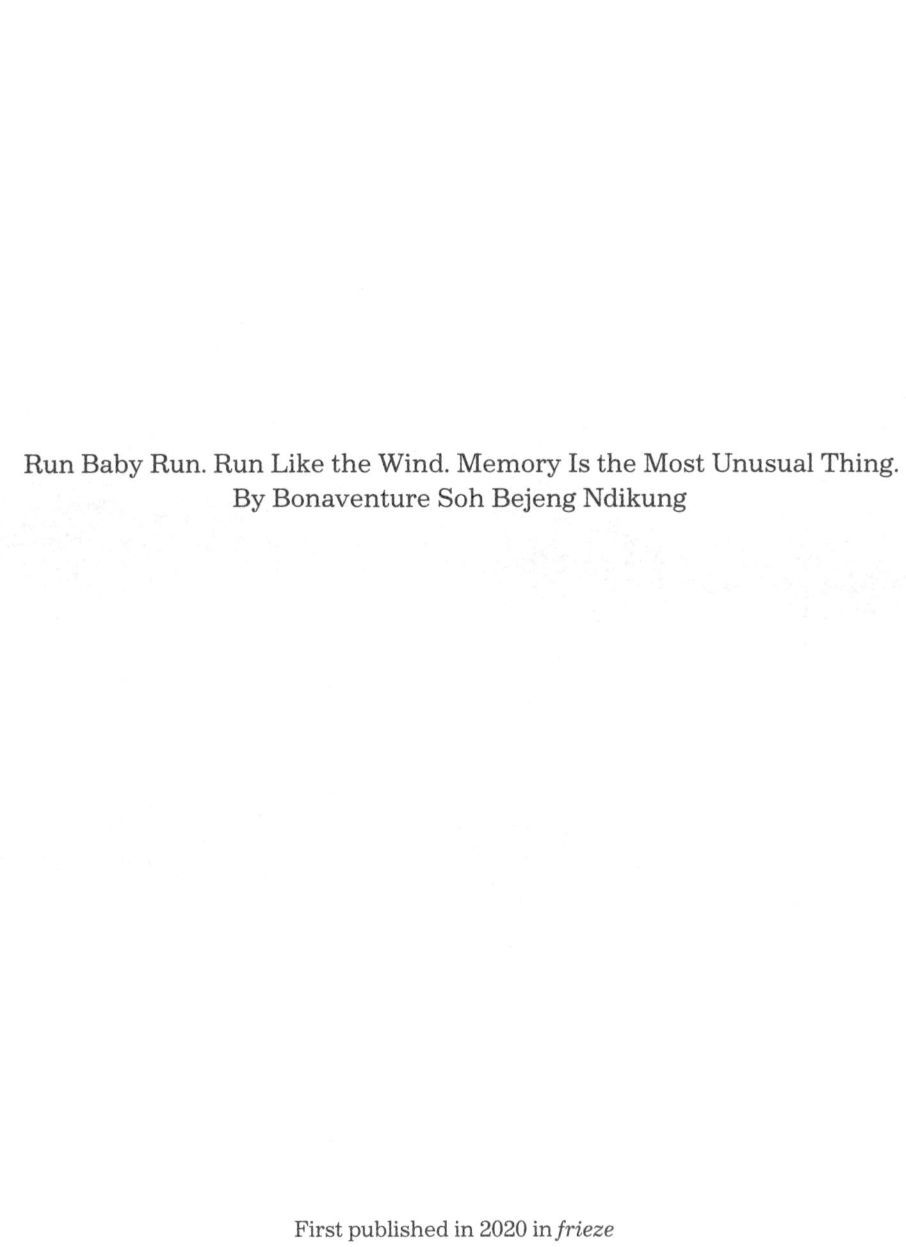

Run Baby Run. Run Like the Wind. Memory Is the Most Unusual Thing.
By Bonaventure Soh Bejeng Ndikung

First published in 2020 in *frieze*

The day after an estimated 40,000 people - driven by neo-Nazi and proto-fascist slogans and carrying fascist and imperial insignia - marched on the streets of Berlin, supposedly in protest at the current Covid-19 measures prescribed by the German government, my nine-year-old Black son cornered me with an almost checkmate question: 'Papa, what is a *Reichsflagge* (imperial flag) and why are all these people waving it?'

On our way to the playground that Sunday afternoon in late August 2020, he had seen the covers of several newspapers on newsstands depicting a sea of people carrying black, white and red flags - some bearing the Prussian eagle, the *Reichsadler*. While on the playground, he had eavesdropped on multiple conversations between adults expressing shock at the number of people who had attended the demonstration neither wearing masks nor practising social distancing in the middle of the Covid-19 pandemic, and dismayed by the violence that had erupted. But it was the symbolism of the imperial flag that had most caught his attention.

How can you explain to a nine year old why, in 2020, thousands of people would flock to the capital of one of the strongest democracies in the world, carrying the insignias of monarchy, to advocate a return to some form of empire? Essentially, these people are attacking the democratic structure that allows them to protest freely, calling to abrogate the system that has enabled their privileges, while putting themselves and others at risk. The images that come to mind instantly are people biting the hands that feed them, or sawing off the branch on which they sit.

How can you explain to a nine year old that varying constellations of the imperial flag's black, white and red can be found as far back as the coats of arms of several member states of the Hanseatic League during the late Middle Ages? Or that those same colours were adopted not only by Prussia but as a tricolour for the North German Confederation (1867-70) and, later, the German Reich, from 1871 until its fall in 1918? Or that, despite the imperial flag being banned during the Weimar Republic (1919-33), it was still used as a Naval war insignia and by the nationalist, right-wing German National People's Party, which was a conglomeration of monarchists, nationalists, antisemites and xenophobes? Or that the Nazis banned the flag of the Weimar Republic and reinstated the colours of the Empire when they first rose to power in 1933, before ceding to the swastika in 1935? Or that it is exactly these same sentiments of xenophobia, nationalism and antisemitism that remain the lubricants of the machinery that propagates the carrying of the imperial flag today? In fact, a variation of the imperial flag was still occasionally hoisted on Wehrmacht buildings, Navy vessels, military aircraft and other war machines until 1945.

Although the imperial flag is not officially banned in Germany today, it remains an open secret that this tricolour symbolises the affiliation of neo-Nazis (and old Nazis) to monarchist and national-socialist ideologies, as much as it is a display of absolute contempt for the democratic system in which its promoters live. At every demonstration by right-wing extremists, at every concert of proto-fascist music, at any *völkisch* festival or other nationalist and identitarian manifestations in Germany, the air is desecrated by the many imperial and Reich war flags. Along with the confederate flag and the swastika, the imperial flag has been a symbol of white supremacy and white oppression for years, but can be paraded without discretion anywhere in Europe and America. Why this flag isn't officially banned in current-day Germany for its ideological affiliations remains a mystery and begs the question of whether Germany is any more enlightened today than the Weimar republic, which saw in the imperial flag an eminent threat to democracy.

When Otto von Bismarck, the chancellor who masterminded German unification in 1871, orchestrated the Congo Conference of 1884–85 – to which he invited fourteen of the world's so-called great nations to Berlin to discuss the partitioning, conquest, colonisation and plundering of Africa – he did so under the auspices of the imperial flag. After the conference, Germany claimed for itself my homeland, German Kamerun (current-day Cameroon and part of Nigeria), Togoland (current-day Togo and part of Ghana), German South West Africa (current-day Namibia) as well as German East Africa (current-day Rwanda, Burundi and part of Tanzania). When the ships of the German merchants and, later, soldiers arrived on the shores of these colonised territories, the first thing they did to mark their newly 'acquired' lands was to plant the imperial flag. Yes, that same flag so proudly brandished during the demonstration against the German government's Covid-19 policies.

How do you explain to a nine year old that his great-grandfathers, again under the rule of the imperial flag, were forced into indentured labour, working on plantations to produce goods for the European market or building the railroad that facilitated the shipping of raw materials and other items from Cameroon to Germany? The wealth that was extorted from these colonies was crucial in building the current German economic and social system from which those marching on the streets with their imperial flags are still profiting today. A century later, the descendants of some of those indentured labourers continue to suffer from the violence and wrath of the colonial enterprise.

The second Saturday after the big *Querdenker* ('lateral thinking') demonstrations in Berlin and many other German cities, thousands of anti-vaxxers, neo-imperialists, proto-fascists, hippies and Christian fundamentalists were still flocking to the streets in protest. That same week, the Moria detention/refugee camp on the Greek island of Lesbos was set ablaze. Originally intended to house 3,000 migrants, by summer 2020 there were an estimated 20,000 occupants from 70 countries subsisting in conditions so inhumane that most people wouldn't allow their dogs to live there. Now, Moria has been erased, yet its destruction appears to have provoked barely a flicker of indignation within the political clans around Europe.

As people who fled wars and famine with their children to seek refuge in Europe now find themselves sleeping rough on the streets and being tear-gassed by Greek police, European governments play political games and make hypocritical gestures by taking in just a few hundred child refugees. I ask myself why this cause hasn't inspired 40,000 people to take to the streets to fight for the rights of fellow human beings whose humanity has been completely stripped away, who have lost the little they had in an arson attack, and who are unable even to receive NGO donations of food, water and medication because the residents of Lesbos have blocked off the roads. The second Saturday after the big *Querdenker* demonstrations in Berlin, I took my nine-year-old son to his first Holy Communion class at St Clara's Church in Neukölln, where he was baptised soon after he was born. As we sat there, masked up, listening to the priest's sermon about finding a home in Jesus, I couldn't help but think of the millions of displaced people around the world who were promised to find a home in Christ, while their homes were taken away. I also thought about how little time it took for laypeople, companies and business tycoons to pledge more than €750 million to rebuild Notre Dame in Paris when it was destroyed by fire in 2019. It is difficult not to be struck by the yawning disparity between the calls to EU member states from French President Emmanuel Macron and European Council President Donald Tusk to support the rebuilding of the cathedral – not to mention offers of help from US President Donald Trump and even some African presidents – in contrast to the deafening silence in relation to the Moria fire, which has thrust tens of thousands of humans, who were already living in purgatory, into hell.

But this is precisely where these two seemingly divergent threads intertwine, because the violent forces that led to the attempted storming of the Reichstag during the *Querdenker* demonstrations in August are the exact same forces that enabled Moria to exist in the first place. And, while some may still think of Moria as happening elsewhere, in reality it is already here.

Memory may be a curse as much as it is a blessing, but our ability to recall past events, and our consciousness in relation to creating future memories, could save us from repeating the mistakes of our ancestors. On 30 January 1933 – the day power was handed over to the National

Socialists in Germany – the artist Max Liebermann leaned out of the window of his home on Pariser Platz to watch a torchlight procession of Nazis at the Brandenburg Gate, and is said to have exclaimed in his Berlin dialect: 'Ick kann jar nich soville fressen, wie ick kotzen möchte' (I can't eat as much as I want to throw up). We do remember that. We do have a recollection of how things ended. As we nurture memories past and cultivate those yet to come, we must be on our toes and be prepared to run like the wind. As Matana Roberts sings on her 2019 album *Coin Coin Chapter 4*: 'I am a child of the wind [...] Run baby run. Run like the wind. Memory is the most unusual thing.'

Population, 2000

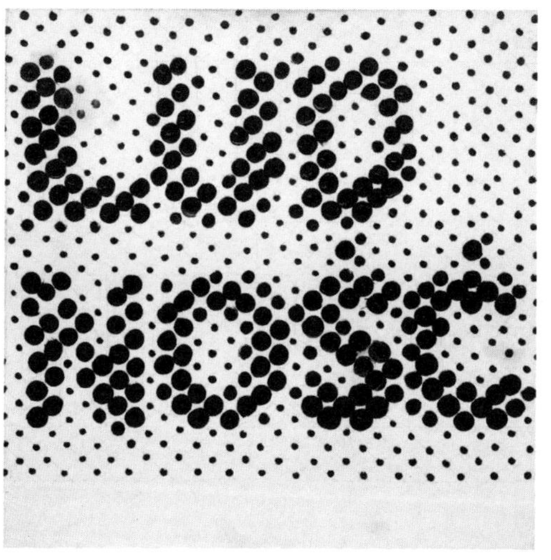

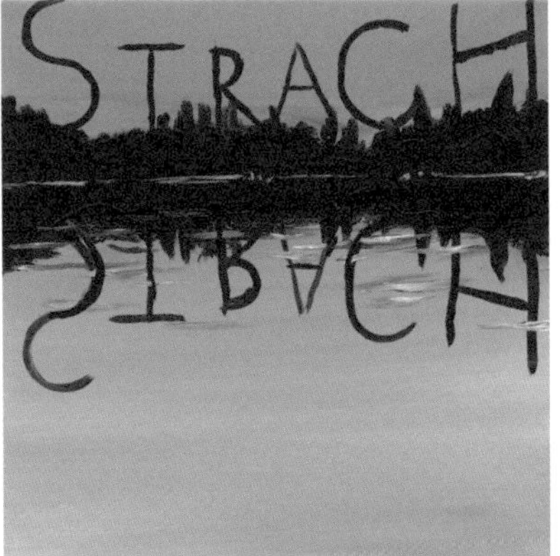
STRACH

We Cannot Escape Our Own History
By Jan Tomasz Gross

First published in 2015 on *Project Syndicate*

I wrote the essay 'Eastern Europe's Crisis of Shame' - reprinted below - in the autumn of 2015, at a time when large numbers of refugees were arriving in Europe from war-ravaged countries in Africa and the Middle East. The piece appeared in thirty-four mostly European newspapers, but was also reprinted in China, Mauretania, Kuwait and a few other equally unexpected places. It owed its worldwide distribution to the American platform for which it was written, *Project Syndicate*, which commissions and publishes opinion pieces on current events by intellectuals and politicians and makes them available to the world press. And even though not a single newspaper in Poland wanted to put it out, the article provoked an intense discussion in the Polish media.[1] In fact, it triggered less of a discussion than a wave of angry voices of protest. Eventually, this led to the prosecutor's office initiating an investigation, with the aim of bringing charges against me for insulting the 'good name' of the Polish nation - a 'lèse-nation', as it were.

What provoked the ire was a statement - tangential to the central argument elaborated in the piece - that in Poland during the Second World War, under German occupation, Poles had killed more Jews

1 Until the editor of *Krytyka Polityczna* Sławomir Sierakowski, irritated by the way that journalists both from the left and the right of the political spectrum had hung me out to dry without bothering to inform the public about the content of the incriminating article, printed a Polish translation of the essay in his journal.

than they had killed Germans (which, unfortunately, had been the case). My other alleged 'offence' was having written the piece for the German newspaper *Die Welt* - which was false, but was nevertheless stressed repeatedly in virtually every article written to disparage me. The prosecutor quashed the proceedings against me twice and was twice ordered to resume the investigation by his superiors until he was removed from the case. After a few years, and despite pressure from above, the judicial procedure was finally dropped.

Since the essay came out in 2015, a number of new historical studies have been published, documenting murders and denunciations by non-Jewish Poles, which led to the deaths of Jewish Poles (I prefer using such terms rather than the customary dichotomy - Poles and Jews - because these murdered Jews were, after all, also Polish citizens). No one who is even remotely familiar with Polish-language historical publications about Polish-Jewish relations during the German occupation can still have any doubts regarding the massive volume and widespread occurrence of anti-Jewish violence on the part of non-Jewish Poles. This included murders as well as pillage of material property. Pointing out that Poles had killed more Jews than they had killed Germans during the war is merely one way of indicating the scale of Polish society's participation in the crimes committed by the German occupiers. Evidently, until today, the scope of these crimes evokes incredulity among the Poles - which reflects well on us, because it is truly horrifying - as well as a refusal to acknowledge the truth, which does not reflect well on us at all, because it goes against a simple rule that people cannot escape from their own history. We know this at least since the time when Abraham Lincoln spoke these words in the American Congress: 'Fellow citizens, we cannot escape history.'[2]

2 In Lincoln's address on 1 December 1862, he said:

> Fellow-citizens, we cannot escape history. We of this Congress and this administration, will be remembered in spite of ourselves. No personal significance, or insignificance, can spare one or another of us. The fiery trial through which we pass, will light us down, in honor or dishonor, to the latest generation. We say we are for the Union. The world will not forget that we say this. We know how to save the Union. The world knows we do know how to save it. We - even we here - hold the power, and bear the responsibility. In giving freedom to the slave, we assure freedom to the

And this history of ours from which we still cannot run away, I am afraid, is widespread antisemitism in Polish society. It was embedded during the interwar years by the teachings of Catholic priests and writings in the Catholic press, by the propaganda of the largest political movement, the National Democrats, as well as several other political parties. And, as the result of this indigenous antisemitism, the heroic Polish underground courier, Jan Karski, in his 1940 report to the Polish émigré government in London wrote:

> '[T]he solution of the Jewish question' by the Germans [in Poland during the German occupation], I have to state this taking full responsibility for my words, is a serious and rather dangerous tool in the hands of the Germans 'to morally pacify' wide segments of the Polish society. [....] The nation hates its mortal enemy, but this issue creates something like a narrow bridge where Germans meet in agreement with a large part of the Polish society.[3]

And so, the story of Polish-Jewish relations unfolded as it did.

Eastern Europe's Crisis of Shame

As thousands of refugees pour into Europe to escape the horrors of war, with many dying along the way, a different sort of tragedy has played out in many of the European Union's newest member states. The states known collectively as 'Eastern Europe', including my native Poland, have revealed themselves to be intolerant, illiberal, xenophobic and incapable of remembering the spirit of solidarity that carried them to freedom a quarter-century ago.

> free - honorable alike in what we give, and what we preserve. We shall nobly save, or meanly lose, the last best hope of earth. Other means may succeed; this could not fail. The way is plain, peaceful, generous, just - a way which, if followed, the world will forever applaud, and God must forever bless.

Quoted in William E. Gienapp, *Abraham Lincoln and Civil War America: A Biography*, Oxford: Oxford University Press, 2002, p. 124.

3 Jan Karski, 'Zagadnienie żydowskie w Polsce pod okupacjami' (The Jewish Question in Poland Under the Occupation), *Mówią Wieki*, no. 4, November 1992, p. 7. My translation, emphasis in original.

These are the same societies that clamoured before and after the fall of communism for a 'return to Europe', proudly proclaiming that they shared its values. But what did they think Europe stands for? Since 1989 - and particularly since 2004, when they joined the EU - they have benefited from massive financial transfers in the form of European structural and cohesion funds. Today, they are unwilling to contribute anything to resolve the greatest refugee crisis facing Europe since the Second World War.

Indeed, before the eyes of the entire world, the government of Hungary, an EU member state, has mistreated thousands of refugees. Prime Minister Viktor Orbán sees no reason to behave otherwise: the refugees are not a European problem, he insists; they are a German problem.

Orbán is not alone in this view. Even Hungary's Catholic bishops are following Orbán's line, with László Kiss-Rigó, Bishop of Szeged-Csanád, saying that Muslim migrants 'want to take over', and that the Pope, who has called on every Catholic parish in Europe to take in a refugee family, 'doesn't know the situation'.[4]

In Poland, a country of forty million people, the government initially expressed a readiness to accept two thousand refugees - but only Christians (Slovakia proposed a similar stipulation). Refugees are not an Eastern European problem, a Polish journalist told National Public Radio in the United States, because these countries did not participate in the decision to bomb Libya (neither did Germany).

Have Eastern Europeans no sense of shame? For centuries, their ancestors emigrated in droves, seeking relief from material hardships and political persecution. And today their leaders' heartless behaviour and callous rhetoric play to popular sentiment. Indeed, the electronic version of Poland's largest newspaper, *Gazeta Wyborcza*, now publishes a stunning notice at the end of every article about refugees: 'Because of the extraordinarily aggressive content of remarks

4 Quoted in Griff Witte, 'Hungarian Bishop Says Pope Is Wrong About Refugees', *The Washington Post*, 7 September 2015, https://www.washingtonpost.com/world/hungarian-bishop-says-pope-is-wrong-about-refugees/2015/09/07/fcba72e6-558a-11e5-9f54-1ea23f6e02f3_story.html.

advocating violence, contrary to the law, and calling for racial, ethnic, and religious hatred, we will not allow readers to publish comments.'

Not so long ago, in the immediate post-war years, Eastern European Jewish Holocaust survivors fled from the murderous antisemitism of their Polish, Hungarian, Slovak or Romanian neighbours to the safety of displaced persons camps in, of all places, Germany. *Safe Among the Germans* proclaimed the title of an important book by the historian Ruth Gay about these 250,000 survivors.[5] Now Muslim refugees and survivors of other wars, having found no refuge in Eastern Europe, also are fleeing to safety among the Germans.

In this case, history is not a metaphor. On the contrary, the root cause of the Eastern European attitudes now on grim display is to be found in the Second World War and its aftermath.

Consider the Poles, who, deservedly proud of their society's anti-Nazi resistance, actually killed more Jews than they killed Germans during the war.[6] Although Poland's Catholics were cruelly victimised during the Nazi occupation, they could find little compassion for the fate of Nazism's ultimate victims. In the words of Józef Mackiewicz, a conservative, anti-Communist Polish writer with impeccable patriotic credentials: 'During the occupation there was not, literally, a single person who would not have heard the saying - "One thing Hitler has done correctly is to wipe out the Jews." But one should not talk about this openly.'[7]

Of course, there were Poles who helped Jews during the war. Indeed, the number of Polish 'Righteous Among the Nations', recognised by Israel's Yad Vashem for their wartime heroism, is the largest among all European countries (unsurprisingly, given that pre-war Poland had Europe's largest Jewish population by far). But these remarkable individuals typically acted on their own, against prevailing social norms. They were misfits who, long after the war had ended, insisted on keeping their wartime

5 See Ruth Gray, *Safe Among the Germans: Liberated Jews After World War II*, New Haven, CT: Yale University Press, 2011.

6 See the author's note to the article on *Project Syndicate*, https://webapi.project-syndicate.org/library/bebb317a1d5c22b7b68f7634ad8416fc.pdf.

7 Source unknown.

heroism a secret from their neighbours - afraid, it seems, that their own communities would otherwise shun, threaten and ostracise them.

All occupied European societies were complicit to some degree in the Nazi effort to destroy the Jews. Each made a different contribution, depending on country-specific circumstances and conditions of German rule. But the Holocaust played out most gruesomely in Eastern Europe, owing to the sheer number of Jews in the region and the incomparable ruthlessness of the Nazi occupation regimes.

When the war ended, Germany - because of the victors' denazification policies and its responsibility for instigating and carrying out the Holocaust - had no choice but to 'work through' its murderous past. This was a long, difficult process; but German society, mindful of its historical misdeeds, has become capable of confronting moral and political challenges of the type posed by the influx of refugees today. And Chancellor Angela Merkel has set an example of leadership on migrants that puts all of Eastern Europe's leaders to shame.

Eastern Europe, by contrast, has yet to come to terms with its murderous past. Only when it does will its people be able to recognise their obligation to save those fleeing in the face of evil.

Widespread occurrence of criminal behaviour towards their Jewish fellow citizens during the German occupation, embedded in widespread antisemitism in Polish society, has not been worked through in Poland. Or else how could a decent person after the war be an antisemite in a country where three million Jewish citizens were killed during the Shoah in full view of their neighbours?

'Before the war, when people argued that Jews are harmful just by virtue of being Jewish, I thought they are out of their mind, or felt contempt for them as if they were barbarians' - I am quoting the words of a Polish poet, Julian Przyboś, who spent most of the war in his home village near the town of Rzeszów.

> Today, after the horrifying experience, which revealed where this antihuman nonsense and the unconscious murder wish

> lead – I consider an antisemite as a potential murderer. I look into the faces of friends and strangers, I circulate among the people in Poland, I listen to conversations – and many a time I am stricken by horror that I live among the possessed and among potential killers.[8]

Przyboś wrote these words after the Kielce pogrom (forty Jews were killed in Kielce by a Polish mob on 4 July 1946) – the most violent, but by no means the only murderous eruption of post-war Polish antisemitism.

And what specifically could Przyboś have in mind when invoking 'the horrifying experience' from wartime Poland? Perhaps the city of Tarnów, where during the first deportation of Jews to death camps in June 1942, Germans killed around four thousand people *in situ*, that is, in the town and its vicinity? A river of blood flowed into neighbouring streets from the beautiful Renaissance central square, slightly tilted to the south, where several hundred people had been killed. Or perhaps the poet was thinking about Szczebrzeszyn, where Nazis deported nine hundred Jews to death camps in the summer and autumn of 1942, and killed about two-thousand three-hundred *in situ*? In his gripping diary from the years of the German occupation the director of the local hospital, Dr Zygmunt Klukowski, described the Dantesque circumstances of this deportation: 'some people [in the original manuscript Klukowski wrote "many people"] took active part in looking for and ferreting out the Jews. They pointed out where the Jews are hiding, boys ran after small Jewish children, whom the policemen were killing in front of everybody.'[9]

8 Julian Przyboś, 'Hańba antysemityzmu' (The Disgrace of Antisemitism), in *Martwa fala. Zbiór artykułów o antysemityzmie* (Dead Wave: A Collection of Articles on Antisemitism), Warsaw: Wiedza, 1947, p. 225.

9 Entry from 22 October 1942 in Zygmunt Klukowski, *Zamojszczyzna 1918–1959*, Warsaw: Karta, 2017, p. 325. Unfortunately, the printed versions, both in the first edition of Klukowski's *Dziennik* (Diary) from 1958 and in the reprint from 2017 quoted above, contain several such editorial interventions falsifying the full meaning of Klukowski's observations. See Dariusz Libionka, 'Polska ludność chrześcijańska wobec eksterminacji Żydów – dystrykt lubelski' (Polish Christian Population in the Face of the Extermination of Jews – Lublin District), in D. Libionka (ed.), *Akcja Reinhardt. Zagłada Żydów w Generalnym Gubernatorstwie* (Operation Reinhardt: Extermination of Jews in the General Government), Warsaw: Państwowe Muzeum na Majdanku, 2004, p. 311.

These are only examples. Similar scenes played out in the streets of hundreds of Polish towns and villages. I am bringing up these concrete examples so that a contemporary reader might not take Przyboś as the voice of an oversensitive artist full of despair.

A historian always looks on a subject 'from afar'. The beauty of this undertaking consists primarily in the effort to name and comprehend what has happened, and not necessarily in the view that is unveiled as a result. We always address the past with new questions, in part because people who share certain experiences and sensibilities (and thus acquire certain modes of thinking) die out. It may very well be that because the generation of murderers, pillagers and direct beneficiaries of the Holocaust of Polish Jews is passing away - I mean the people among whom we grew up and who raised many of us - we can now finally look more honestly at the history of the German occupation of Poland during the Second World War. But their pedagogical efforts have scarred us deeply.

Contempt for those who think differently ('treacherous mugs' - *zdradzieckie mordy*), contempt for refugees who have a different physical appearance or are feared to transmit diseases ('cholera on Greek islands, dysentery in Vienna, various kinds of parasites, amoebas, which are not injurious to the organisms of these people'), homophobia ('the rainbow pest')[10] - contempt as a kernel of politics in a country where an immediately identifiable social signifier of contempt is a Jew - is but poorly disguised antisemitism. I've written a small book on the subject,[11] and I will only repeat here the words of a great contemporary Polish writer, Szczepan Twardoch, which I quoted there already:

> I am convinced that one of the foundations of what one may call a shared Polish identity or ethnic consciousness is deeply repressed knowledge about all the evil that Poles committed against Jews during the war. [...] False consciousness leads to

10 These are all very well-known quotes from public remarks of leading politicians and church figures of the current Polish regime.

11 Jan Tomasz Gross, *PiS i antysemityzm, czyli pośmiertne zwycięstwo Dmowskiego* (PiS and Antisemitism, i.e. Dmowski's Posthumous Victory), Kraków: Austeria, 2018.

> suffering. What is repressed will come to the surface sooner or later and reveal the shameful quality of invented heroism and sainthood. Poland suffers from false consciousness, and for this reason it is rotting from the inside.[12]

From afar the view may even be beautiful, but up close it turns out that in order to process the tragic and criminal experiences of the Second World War, the present generation still has a lot of work to do.

12 Szczepan Twardoch, 'Co we współczesnej Polsce boli Szczepana Twardocha' (What Hurts Szczepan Twardoch in Contemporary Poland?), a conversation with Aleksandra Pawlicka, *Newsweek*, 30 December 2018, https://www.newsweek.pl/polska/szczepan-twardoch-o-polsce-historii-i-polityce-wywiad/ndk9myd.

Untitled (Borowski), 2002

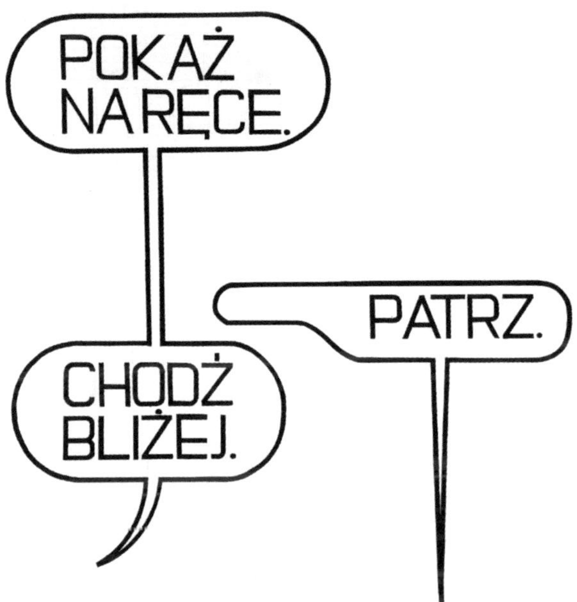

Show your hands – Look – Come Closer
From Tadeusz Borowski, 'Dzień na Harmenzach' (A Day at Harmenz),
Wybór opowiadań (*This Way for the Gas, Ladies and Gentlemen*, 1976), Warsaw:
Państwowy Instytyt Wydawniczy, 1959. Passage translated by Adam Szymczyk.

Reactions, Discussions and Disputes:
Polish Controversies Over the Holocaust
By Dariusz Stola

Translated from the Polish by Zofia Sochańska

The amount of public debate in Poland about the Holocaust distinguishes the country from others in Europe, including other post-communist nation-states in East-Central Europe. The nature and course of these debates speak volumes not only about the dramatic events of the Second World War, but also about present-day Poland and the nature of collective memory. The genocide of Jews perpetrated by Nazi Germany and its collaborators during the Second World War has, since the 1960s, gradually transformed from a marginal topic into a critical part of Western culture. The Holocaust is a point of reference in discussions worldwide - the German *Historikerstreit*, the French dispute over the issue of Vichy collaboration, the Swiss banks' holdings of assets belonging to Holocaust victims, the question in the Anglo-Saxon world as to whether the Allies could have bombed the gas chambers in Auschwitz - stirring international interest and regarded as important steps in the evolution of collective memory. Other debates, albeit less publicised, have been taking place across the whole of Europe, from Portugal to Finland, from Norway to Greece. Against this background, it is rather the absence of debate - for instance, in Russia and in Belarus - that comes as a surprise.

Poland does not stand out solely because Poles continue to fuel public controversies about the Holocaust, but rather due to the volume and intensity of the debates. Triggered by Claude Lanzmann's

1985 documentary *Shoah* and up until the amendment to the Institute of National Remembrance (IPN) Act in 2018, we can track at least a dozen debates in the Polish press (both legal and clandestine) lasting from several weeks to almost two years.[1] The peak was in the early twenty-first century when *Sąsiedzi. Historia zagłady żydowskiego miasteczka* (2000; *Neighbors: The Destruction of the Jewish Community of Jedwabne, Poland*, 2001 [2000]) by Jan Tomasz Gross provoked a debate on the title crime committed in the summer of 1941. The book prompted thousands of texts in the press and TV and radio appearances, including addresses by state leaders and other key figures in Polish public life. Not only was it the biggest Polish debate on the Holocaust, but the biggest Polish debate to date on the past in general, reaching almost all Poles in a short period of time. While its impact on public perception in Polish society remains unclear, it exerted a lasting influence on the development of Polish research into the Holocaust, the Polish intelligentsia and the arts in Poland.

The discussions and their various aspects: historical, moral and psychological, have excited attention also abroad and among scholars in varied disciplines. This has resulted in a substantial and growing secondary literature in which wartime events, and more so, the present-day controversies that these have sparked, are analysed. The first foreign book dedicated to this topic was published as early as 1989. Over a dozen volumes have been published since. The two monographs by Piotr Forecki are the most comprehensive and systematic, and deal with, as the title of the first suggests, 'disputes about the Polish-Jewish past and memory'.[2] Other book-size contributions have been published by Paweł Dobrosielski, Martyna Grądzka-Rejak and Jan Olaszek, Maryla Hopfinger, Elżbieta Janicka and Tomasz Żukowski, Bartłomiej Krupa, Joanna B. Michlic, Lech Michał Nijakowski, Magdalena Nowicka-Franczak, Annamaria Orla-Bukowska and Robert Cherry, Antony Polonsky, Michael Steinlauf, Joanna Tokarska-Bakir

1 See list in this text, pp. 115–16.

2 Piotr Forecki, *'Od Shoah' do 'Strachu': spory o polsko-żydowską przeszłość i pamięć w debatach publicznych*, Poznań: Wydawnictwo Poznańskie, 2010; published in English as *Reconstructing Memory: The Holocaust in Polish Public Debates*, trans. Marta Skowrońska (Frankfurt am Main: Peter Lang, 2013); P. Forecki, *Po Jedwabnem: anatomia pamięci funkcjonalnej* (After Jedwabne: The Anatomy of Functional Memory), Warsaw: Instytut Badań Literackich PAN, 2018.

and Geneviève Zubrzycki.[3] Relevant scholarship also includes several dozen articles penned by the aforementioned scholars and others, too many to be mentioned here by name. These are all publications on

3 Tomasz Żukowski, *Wielki retusz: jak zapomnieliśmy, że Polacy zabijali Żydów* (Airbrushing History: How We Forgot That Poles Had Killed Jews), Warsaw: Wydawnictwo IBL PAN, 2018; Paweł Dobrosielski, *Spory o Grossa. Polskie problemy z pamięcią o Żydach* (Disputes Over Gross: Polish Problems with the Memory of Jews), Warsaw: IBL PAN, 2017; Martyna Grądzka-Rejak and Jan Olaszek, *Holokaust, pamięć, powielacz: Zagłada Żydów i okupacyjne stosunki polsko-żydowskie w publikacjach drugiego obiegu w PRL* (The Holocaust, the Memory, the Mimeograph: The Holocaust and Polish-Jewish Relations in Underground Publications in Communist Poland), Warsaw: Instytut Studiów Politycznych PAN, 2020; Maryla Hopfinger and Tomasz Żukowski (ed.), *Lata czterdzieste: początki polskiej narracji o Zagładzie* (1940s: The Beginnings of Polish Narrative on the Holocaust), Warsaw: IBL PAN, 2019; Elżbieta Janicka and Tomasz Żukowski, *Przemoc filosemicka? Nowe polskie narracje o Żydach po roku 2000* (Philosemitic Violence? New Polish Narratives on Jews After the Year 2000), Warsaw: IBL PAN, 2016; Bartłomiej Krupa, *Opowiedzieć Zagładę: polska proza i historiografia wobec Holocaustu (1987-2003)* (To Narrate the Shoah: Polish Prose and Historiography in the Face of the Holocaust), Kraków: Universitas, 2013; Joanna B. Michlic, *Poland's Threatening Other: The Image of the Jew from 1880 to the Present*, Lincoln: University of Nebraska Press, 2006; Lech Michał Nijakowski, *Polska polityka pamięci: esej socjologiczny* (Polish Politics of Memory: A Sociological Essay), Warsaw: Wydawnictwa Akademickie, 2008; Magdalena Nowicka-Franczak, *Niechciana debata: spór o książki Jana Tomasza Grossa* (The Unwanted Debate: Controversy Over Books by Jan Tomasz Gross), Warsaw: Wydawnictwa Akademickie, 2017; Annamaria Orla-Bukowska and Robert Cherry (ed.), *Rethinking Poles and Jews: Troubled Past, Brighter Future*, Lanham, MD: Rowman & Littlefield Publishers, 2007; Geneviève Zubrzycki, *The Crosses of Auschwitz: Nationalism and Religion in Post-Communist Poland*, Chicago: University of Chicago Press, 2006; Antony Polonsky and J. B. Michlic (ed.), *The Neighbors Respond: The Controversy Over the Jedwabne Massacre in Poland*, Princeton, CT: Princeton University Press, 2004; Joanna Tokarska-Bakir, *Rzeczy mgliste: eseje i studia* (Hazy Things: Essays and Studies), Sejny: Fundacja Pogranicze, 2004; Michael Steinlauf, *Bondage to the Dead: Poland and the Memory of the Holocaust*, Syracuse: Syracuse University Press, 1997 and A. Polonsky (ed.), *'My Brother's Keeper?': Recent Polish Debates on the Holocaust*, London: Routledge, 1989. Studies on the Holocaust within Polish literature and art have also been mentioned such as Grzegorz Niziołek, *Polski teatr Zagłady* (Polish Theatre of the Holocaust), Warsaw: Instytut Teatralny im. Zbigniewa Raszewskiego, Wydawnictwo Krytyki Politycznej, 2013; Marta Budkowska (ed.), *Sztuka polska wobec Holokaustu* (Polish Art Facing the Holocaust), Warsaw: Żydowski Instytut Historyczny, 2013; Sławomir Buryła *et al.* (ed.), *Literatura polska wobec Zagłady (1939-1968)* (Polish Literature Facing the Holocaust), Warsaw: IBL PAN, 2012 and Alina Brodzka *et al.* (ed.), *Literatura polska wobec Zagłady* (Polish Literature Facing the Holocaust), Warsaw: ZIH, 2000. There were also collections of essays/voices raised in the course of debates, published by polish magazines *Znak*, *Więź* and *Fronda*.

Polish debates on the Holocaust rather than studies on the Holocaust itself. The latter are much more numerous.

***

It is worthwhile to look at the Polish debates not just as a collection of unrelated events, but as a chain of events stretched over the years. When we tread back along this chain, we arrive at the earliest, primary reactions to wartime horrors and can see that contemporary disputes appear as successive reactions increasingly distant from the dramatic events, increasingly indirect and mediated. It is no longer 'A Poor Christian Looking at the Ghetto' (to quote the title of Czesław Miłosz's 1943 poem), but a descendant of the poor Christian looking at the movie about the ghetto, or reading Miłosz's poem or an article reacting to it. These are reactions to the projections of the Holocaust, to images moulded by family tales, school education, film and books - sometimes better, sometimes worse. The debates on (an imagined) past that we discuss here modify knowledge of it, and lead to the production of new films and books, or the reinterpretation of old ones, which in turn transform the representation of the past. We are dealing with an endless spiral of reactions that alter the object we react to. Such debates on the past are never definitively over.

The above chain of discussions began with the personal experience of those who 'looked at the ghetto'. Already here we can see substantial differences between Poland (and the western stretches of the USSR) and the rest of the continent. The experience of non-Jews who watched the crimes committed against Jews was much more universal in Eastern Europe than in the West; there were more eyewitnesses, that is, people who saw horrific scenes at close range. Firstly, this was due to the fact that occupied Poland was the main site of the crime: three million Polish Jews constitute the majority of all Holocaust victims. Furthermore, Polish lands were turned into a killing field for Jews from other places - transports from all across Hitler-dominated Europe headed first to the ghettoes, and then to the death camps built in occupied Poland. Secondly, the crimes were much more conspicuous in Eastern Europe - unlike the French, Dutch or Greeks who only saw their Jewish neighbours being deported, the Poles and other inhabitants of 'Bloodlands' east of Germany did see or hear the killings and other acts of unimaginable cruelty towards Jews or smelled the stench coming from the mass graves and crematoria. Thirdly, cruel persecution and extermination of Jews lasted the longest in occupied Poland - it began already in September 1939, in 1940 starvation and disease took a massive toll on the Nazi-established ghettoes, and in 1941 the Holocaust *sensu stricto* began - the systematic extermination of all Jews. The culmination of the mass killing of Polish Jews occurred in 1942, and was followed by a hunt for those who tried to hide in towns, villages and forests, which lasted until the very end of German occupation. Polish lands were therefore not only the main site of the crimes, but also their main scene. Although many of the crimes were committed by perpetrators in hiding, the sights or sounds of the killings reached enough people to make the Poles the largest group of non-Jewish eyewitnesses to encounter the horror of the Holocaust up close, or, as the title of a recent exhibition on the subject suggests, 'from terribly close'.[4]

Furthermore, the combination of the spatial proximity and the system of rule introduced by the Nazis to secure the obedience of the conquered population, blurred the boundary between the 'scene' and the 'audience'. The observers were often just a few steps away from the crime and a step from participating. They could help either the victim or the perpetrator by acting or failing to, by offering words of denunciation or life-saving advice or remaining silent. It is precisely these reactions - actions and failures to take action, spoken and unspoken words in the face of the death and suffering of Jews - that constitute the main subject of contemporary Polish debate on the Holocaust.

Recent research developed over the past two decades suggests that there were more forms of participation in the Holocaust in occupied Poland than historians had previously envisaged (and substantially more than the propaganda of national innocence proclaims). Yet the (non-Jewish) Poles whose actions towards the tragedy of Jews

4 See *Terribly Close: Polish Vernacular Artists Face the Holocaust* curated by Erica Lehrer, Roma Sendyka, Wojciech Wilczyk and Magdalena Zych at the Ethnographic Museum in Kraków, December 2018 - March 2019, http://etnomuzeum.eu/wystawy-czasowe/widok-zza-bliska-inne-obrazy-zaglady.

we can say something about - both 'the helpers of death' and 'the rescuers of life' - were in the minority. The silent majority are those whose actions left no trace - a common occurrence in historical research - or those who remained passive. Interpreting their silence, just as any *ex silentio* reasoning, is difficult and risky.

As Michael Steinlauf noted years ago, if the Holocaust was an unprecedented event, the experience of witnessing it was just as unprecedented. Steinlauf pointed to the need to apply the apparatus of psychology to analysing the experience of (non-Jewish) Polish witnesses. He also introduced the concepts 'death imprint' and 'psychic numbing' coined by Robert Jay Lifton, who diagnosed these in former camp prisoners struggling with the effects of watching the cruel deaths of their fellow inmates.[5] We may add here the notion of 'moral injury', which psychologists diagnose in, among others, witnesses to acts that violate their deep moral convictions. In this context we need to add that Polish lands were not only a scene of thousands of crimes committed against Jews, but also many other crimes and dreadful events, leaving many witnesses with psychological scars.[6] The interest in the experience of Polish 'bystanders' (a much-contested term) of Jewish suffering has yielded more adequate terms and an understanding, but deserves more research.[7]

5 M. Steinlauf, *Bondage to the Dead*, pp. 56-58. See also Robert Jay Lifton, *The Broken Connection: On Death and the Continuity of Life*, New York: Simon and Schuster, 1979.

6 See Hazel R. Atuel *et al.*, 'Exploring Moral Injury: Theory, Measurement, and Applications', *Military Behavioral Health*, vol. 8, no. 3, 2020, pp. 248-55; Brett T. Litz *et al.*, 'Moral Injury and Moral Repair in War Veterans: A Preliminary Model and Intervention Strategy', *Clinical Psychology Review*, vol. 29, no. 8, 2009, pp. 695-706; M. Lis-Turlejska *et al.*, 'Rozpowszechnienie PTSD wśród osób, które przeżyły II wojnę światową w Polsce' (Prevalence of PTSD Among People Who Survived the Second World War in Poland), *Psychiatria polska*, vol. 50, no. 5, 2016, pp. 923-34; Maja Lis-Turlejska *et al.*, 'Aktualny poziom objawów stresu potraumatycznego w próbie osób, które w dzieciństwie przeżyły II wojnę światową' (Current Levels of Post-Traumatic Stress Disorder Symptoms in Sample of Second World War Child Survivors), *Psychiatria Polska*, vol. 46, no. 2, 2012.

7 Ewa Koźmińska-Frejlak, 'Świadkowie Zagłady - Holocaust jako zbiorowe doświadczenie Polaków' (Witnesses to the Genocide - the Holocaust as a Collective Experience of Poles), *Przegląd Socjologiczny*, vol. 49, no. 2, 2000, pp. 181-206; J. Grabowski, 'Biedni Polacy patrzą na warszawskich Żydów i na getto warszawskie' (Poor Poles Look at the Warsaw Jews and at the Warsaw Ghetto), *Zagłada Żydów. Studia i materiały* (The Holocaust: Studies and Materials), no. 10, 2014, pp. 721-67; Roma Sendyka, 'Poświadek, przeciw-postronny i (niczyja) trauma'

Wartime was not only a time of personal experience, but also of a gradual understanding of what was happening to the Jews. No observer alone could have seen the Nazi 'Final Solution', or enough of it to realise what the scenes happening before them would add up to. Through accumulation of fragmentary information, they gained some knowledge - a collective cognitive endeavour based on communication. Beginning in the summer of 1941, the fragmentary and hard-to-believe news of the mass murder of Jews from Poland's eastern lands and in various localities drove activists in the Polish and Jewish underground to try to determine what was happening. In 1942, these bits of information were accompanied by the news of a brutal liquidation of the ghettos in Central Poland and of setting up camps where Jews 'vanished without a trace'. This was followed by first accounts from those who had managed to flee the death factories. Relevant knowledge grew thanks to rumour, underground publications and broadcasts on London-based radio.[8]

In the historical sources of those years: reports from the Polish underground, clandestine press, documents of the Polish government-in-exile in London and thoughts and conversations recorded in diaries and memoirs, one can discern diverse opinions about, for example, the aims and effectiveness of the German policy towards Jews and the reactions of the Polish underground, government and Polish population in various localities. Among them are documents such as the 1942 Protest of the Front for the Rebirth of Poland, which condemned Nazi crimes yet did not call for helping the Jews, the appeal of Prime Minister Władysław

(Post-witness, Counter-Bystander and (Unclaimed) Trauma), *Widok. Teorie i praktyki kultury wizualnej*, no. 18, 2017; R. Sendyka, 'Od obserwatorów do gapiów. Kategoria *bystanders* i analiza wizualna' (From Spectators to Gawkers: The Category of *Bystanders* and Visual Analysis), *Teksty Drugie*, no. 3, 2018, pp. 117-30; Karolina Koprowska, *Postronni? Zagłada w relacjach chłopskich świadków* (Bystanders? The Holocaust in Witness Accounts from Peasants), Kraków: Towarzystwo Autorów i Wydawców Prac Naukowych Universitas, 2018. See also Michael Rothberg, *The Implicated Subject: Beyond Victims and Perpetrators*, Stanford: Stanford University Press, 2019.

8 See D. Stola, 'Early News of the Holocaust from Poland', *Holocaust and Genocide Studies*, vol. 11, no. 1, 1997 and 'Kilka uwag o początkach polskich dyskusji o Zagładzie' (A Few Remarks on the Beginnings of Polish Debates on the Holocaust), in *Od zgonu Ojca Narodów do śmierci Orła Karpat* (From the Death of the Father of Nations to the End of the Eagle of the Carpathians), ed. Włodzimierz Borodziej *et al.*, Warsaw: Wydawnictwo Naukowe Scholar, 2020.

Sikorski to the Poles under occupation to provide such aid or the publications of the right-wing National Armed Forces (NSZ) discouraging Poles from aiding Jews and expressing satisfaction at their 'disappearance'. Soon came reflections about the social, psychological and spiritual effects of the crime, such as Kazimierz Wyka's notes or the already mentioned poem by Czesław Miłosz published in the underground. In these voices, we can spot the first Polish debate on the Shoah. Some of them would recur in subsequent debates - as an inspiration, best exemplified by Miłosz's poem, which became the basis for Jan Błoński's article in 1987, or as the subject of discussion and judgment - for these voices could have influenced the attitudes of readers and listeners, and thus could have contributed to someone's survival or death.[9]

9 D. Libionka, '"Kwestia żydowska" w Polsce w ocenie Delegatury Rządu RP i KG ZWZ-AK w latach 1942-1944' (The 'Jewish Question' in Poland as Assessed by the Government Delegation and the Headquarters of the Home Army in the years 1942-1944), in *Zagłada Żydów. Pamięć narodowa a pisanie historii w Polsce i we Francji* (The Holocaust: National Memory and Writing History in Poland and in France), ed. Barbara Engelking, Lublin: UMCS, 2006; D. Libionka, 'Polska konspiracja wobec eksterminacji Żydów w dystrykcie warszawskim' (Polish Underground in the Face of the Extermination of Jews in the Warsaw District), in *Prowincja noc: życie i zagłada Żydów w dystrykcie warszawskim* (Province of the Night: The Life and Destruction of Polish Jewish in the Warsaw District), ed. B. Engelking and J. Grabowski, Warsaw: Wydawnictwo Instytutu Filozofii i Socjologii PAN, 2007; M. Hopfinger and T. Żukowski (ed.), *Lata czterdzieste* (1940s); Agnieszka Michałowska, 'Postawy wobec Holocaustu Żydów w polskiej prasie konspiracyjnej: analiza wybranych czasopism' (Attitudes Towards the Holocaust in Polish Underground Press: Analysis of Selected Magazines), *Kultura i Społeczeństwo*, vol. 34, no. 2, 1990, pp. 52-64; Adam Puławski, *W obliczu Zagłady. Rząd RP na Uchodźstwie, Delegatura Rządu RP na Kraj, ZWZ-AK wobec deportacji Żydów do obozów zagłady (1941-1942)* (Facing the Holocaust: Polish Government-in-Exile, the Government Delegation and the Home Army in the Face of Deportations of Jews to Extermination Camps), Lublin: Instytut Pamięci Narodowej - Komisja Ścigania Zbrodni Przeciwko Narodowi Polskiemu, 2009; A. Puławski, *Wobec 'niespotykanego w dziejach mordu'. Rząd RP na uchodźstwie, Delegatura Rządu RP na kraj, AK a eksterminacja ludności żydowskiej od 'wielkiej akcji' do powstania w getcie warszawskim* (In the Face of a 'Murder Unprecedented in History': Polish Government-in-Exile, the Government Delegation, the Home Army and the Extermination of the Jewish Population: From the 'Great *Aktion*' to the Warsaw Ghetto Uprising), Chełm: Stowarzyszenie Rocznik Chełmski, 2018; D. Stola, *Nadzieja i Zagłada: Ignacy Schwartzbart jako żydowski przedstawiciel w Radzie Narodowej RP, 1940-1945* (Hope and the Holocaust: Ignacy Schwartzbart as a Jewish Representative in the National Council, 1940-1945), Warsaw: Oficyna Nauk, 1995; Paweł Szapiro, *Wojna żydowsko-niemiecka: polska prasa konspiracyjna 1943-1944 o powstaniu w getcie Warszawy*

The second phase in the history of the Polish debates took place in early post-war years, when several titles of the Polish press became the forum for what was possibly the first European discussion on the Holocaust. The discussion, conducted under conditions of a relative freedom of speech (that is, freedom greater than Poland had in earlier and later years), developed against the background of a wave of anti-Jewish violence, which culminated with the pogrom in Kielce in July 1946. Despite many insightful opinions, the debate soon died down, stifled by the accelerated Sovietization of Poland, and opinions were largely forgotten for several decades.[10]

Since the late 1940s, communist Poland - deprived of freedom of speech - was by no means a good place for sincere public discussions on any topic, and for discussions about the Holocaust in particular. In all communist states, the wartime tragedy of the Jews was subject to official distortion or organised oblivion. In Poland, we can distinguish two tendencies that marginalised or distorted it. The first, common throughout the Soviet bloc and dominant in the 1950s, was a perversion of anti-fascist internationalism. The victims of Nazi Germany and its collaborators were presented as innocent citizens of various nations: Poland, France, the Netherlands, Austria or the Soviet Union, ignoring the fact that the vast majority of these civilian victims (especially from Western Europe) were Jews, killed precisely because of who they were. In this international group of victims of fascism, the Jews receded from view, or were put in a place just like the others, that is, disproportionate to the scale of the crimes committed against them and to the unique nature of Nazi anti-Jewish policy. The second tendency, dominant since the 1960s, was based on a similar treatment of Polish history. Murdered Polish Jews were presented as 'Polish

(Jewish-German War: Polish Underground Press 1943-1944 on the Warsaw Ghetto Uprising), London: Aneks, 1992.

10 D. Libionka, 'Antysemityzm i zagłada na łamach prasy w Polsce w latach 1945-1946' (Antisemitism and the Holocaust as Covered by the Press in Poland in the Years 1945-1946), *Polska 1944/45-1989. Studia i materiały*, vol. 2, 1997; J. B. Michlic, 'The Holocaust and Its Aftermath as Perceived in Poland: Voices of Polish Intellectuals, 1945-1947', in *The Jews are Coming Back: The Return of the Jews to Their Countries of Origin After WW II*, ed. D. Bankier, Jerusalem: Yad Vashem, 2005; H. Datner, 'Tuż po wojnie napisali już wszystko. Radykalni publicyści i pisarze o antysemityzmie' (They Wrote It All Down Right After the War: Radical Journalists and Writers on Antisemitism), in *Lata czterdzieste*.

citizens', 'Polish victims' and sometimes simply as 'Poles'. To be sure, they were Poles in the civic sense of the word, yet the blurring of differences between the wartime fates of ethnic Poles and Jews, the omission of the fact that they had been murdered *because* they were Jews and that they constituted the majority of 'more than six million Polish victims of the war' was a serious misrepresentation, and one with a lasting impact on popular perceptions of the past within Polish society.[11]

Until as late as the 1980s, the fact that the majority of Polish victims of the Second World War were Jews, was concealed or glossed over in public media. The fate of Jews during the war was marginalised, and the attitudes of Poles other than selfless aid provided to Jews were concealed. This does not mean, however, that there was utter silence on the subject of the Holocaust during the forty-year rule of the United Polish Workers' Party: books were written, films were made and monuments were unveiled. Yet it is difficult to speak of the debate as a public exchange of diverse opinions. Where there is no freedom of speech, and the topic alerts censors (and self-censorship, inevitable under censorship), there is no room for any open debate. A glaring expression of this was the year 1968, when many relevant articles appeared in the press, but were merely voices in a government-run antisemitic campaign.[12]

Against the background of these nearly forty years without debate, the density of open and heated discussions about the Holocaust in the next

11 On the politics of memory during the People's Republic of Poland, see Z. Wóycicka, *Arrested Mourning: Memory of the Nazi Camps in Poland, 1944-1950*, Frankfurt am Main: Peter Lang, 2014; Jonathan Huener, *Auschwitz, Poland, and the Politics of Commemoration, 1945-1979*, Athens, OH: Ohio University Press, 2003; Joanna Wawrzyniak, *Veterans, Victims, and Memory: The Politics of the Second World War in Communist Poland*, Frankfurt am Main: Peter Lang, 2015; M. Steinlauf, *Bondage to the Dead*; Renata Kobylarz, *Walka o pamięć. Polityczne aspekty obchodów rocznicy powstania w getcie warszawskim 1944-1989* (Fight for Memory: Political Aspects of the Warsaw Ghetto Uprising Commemorations 1944-1989), Warsaw: Instytut Pamięci Narodowej - Komisja Ścigania Zbrodni przeciwko Narodowi Polskiemu, 2009; Martyna Rusiniak, *Obóz zagłady Treblinka II w pamięci społecznej (1943-1989)* (Treblinka II Extermination Camp in the Social Memory, 1943-1989), Warsaw: Wydawnictwo Neriton, 2008.

12 Looking at the countries of Western Europe, where the many years of silence about the Holocaust cannot be explained away by a lack of freedom of speech, one can ask whether the same would not have been true in non-communist Poland, had it existed at the time.

thirty years appears all the more striking. Researchers might argue which of the numerous public controversies are important enough to be included in an analysis such as this one. This essay takes into consideration the following ones:

1. in reaction to the film *Shoah* by Claude Lanzmann (1985);[13]

2. in response to the article by Jan Błoński, 'Poor Poles Look at the Ghetto' (1987);

3. regarding the Carmelite Convent located at the edge of the Auschwitz-Birkenau State Museum (1989–93, abroad the controversy began a few years earlier);

4. in reaction to Michał Cichy's article 'Poles–Jews: Dark Side of the Uprising' in which the author refers to the killing of Jews by Warsaw insurgents in 1944 (1994);

5. on the subject of location of a church in Brzezinka, next to the site of the Auschwitz-Birkenau State Museum (1995);

6. in relation to the commemoration of the fiftieth anniversary of the liberation of the Auschwitz-Birkenau camp (1995);

7. in relation to the commemoration of the fiftieth anniversary of the Kielce pogrom and the appearance of religious symbols at the side of the former Birkenau death camp (1996);

8. in response to allegations of murdering Jews by Home Army soldiers made by the American historian Yaffa Eliach (1996);

9. in reaction to plans to open a supermarket near the Auschwitz-Birkenau State Museum and a nightclub in another part of the town of Oświęcim (1996–99);

13 Incidentally, the People's Republic of Poland was the only communist country where a film lasting several hours was shown in the cinema and its fragments broadcast on television.

10. on the subject of the crosses installed at the so-called gravel pit, next to the building vacated by the Carmelite sisters following the dispute (see no. 3 in this list) (1998);

11. in connection with a lawsuit filed against Poland in a New York court regarding the estates of murdered Jews (1999 - the discussion was at its peak back then, but the issue kept recurring at other times as well);

12. about the Jedwabne crime (J. T. Gross's book *Sąsiedzi* (*Neighbors*) was published in May 2000, the debate flared up in the autumn, its symbolic conclusion being the two-volume publication of the Institute of National Remembrance titled *Around Jedwabne* in the autumn of 2002);

13. in reaction to the book by J. T. Gross, *Fear: Antisemitism in Poland After Auschwitz - an Essay in Historical Interpretation* (2006; *Strach. Antysemityzm w Polsce tuż po wojnie. Historia moralnej zapaści*, 2008);

14. in reaction to another challenging book by J. T. Gross (written together with Irena Grudzińska-Gross) titled *Złote żniwa* (2011; *Golden Harvest: Events at the Periphery of the Holocaust*, 2012);

15. about the plan to build a monument in Warsaw to commemorate Poles rescuing Jews (2013-16, with varying intensity);

16. in response to the amendment to the Act of the Institute of National Remembrance penalising certain statements about Polish complicity in Nazi crimes (2018). The dispute coincided with attacks on a two-volume collection of studies *Dalej jest noc. Losy Żydów w wybranych powiatach okupowanej Polski* (2018; *Night without End: The Fate of Jews in German-Occupied Poland*, 2022), edited by Barbara Engelking and Jan Grabowski.

Smaller debates were also triggered, for example, by the films *Pokłosie* (*Aftermath*, 2012) by Władysław Pasikowski and *Ida* (2013) by Paweł Pawlikowski awarded an Oscar for Best Foreign Film in 2015; by outrageous statements made by historian Krzysztof Jasiewicz (2009), the Minister of Education Anna Zalewska and the candidate for Chair of the Institute for National Remembrance Jarosław Szarek (2016); or by the desecration of the monument in Jedwabne in 2011.

The aforementioned films may be considered the fruits of discussions on Jedwabne, similarly to Tadeusz Słobodzianek's play *Nasza klasa* (*Our Class*, 2008), which won the 2010 Nike Award, and refers directly to the history of the town. At least several exhibitions in galleries and museums, including the most important Polish exhibition centres as well as high-profile urban spaces, can also be regarded as reactions to the aforementioned discussions, or as voices derived specifically from them. Some were the subject or seeds for further reactions, both personal and public, thus becoming successive links in the chain here - a developing network of statements made with words and other means of expression.

The discussions focused on three main issues. Most concerned Polish attitudes towards the Holocaust - what non-Jewish Poles did (or failed to do) in the face of their Jewish neighbours' tragedies, how these reactions could be evaluated and what conclusions could be drawn. Less numerous, but no less heated, were the controversies over how the victims of the Auschwitz camp should or should not be commemorated and who should decide on that. In their wake, the site was given its current official name, 'the former German Nazi concentration and extermination camp of Auschwitz Birkenau'. The third issue - relatively rarely addressed explicitly but subliminally present in some debates on the Polish reactions to the *Shoah* - concerned the victims' property seized by their non-Jewish neighbours or the Polish state. The question was manifested, for example, in the slander against historians exposing the crimes of ethnic Poles against Jews, that their voices were a preview for Jewish property claims. Controversies from the second and third groups, on the other hand, often drifted towards the question of the reactions, which - from the Polish perspective - constitutes the necessary moral backdrop to the second and the third.

Notably, the words 'a Pole' or 'Poles' used here are shorthand for ethnic Poles, or those ethnic Poles regarded as non-Jews by the Nazis. The German occupation made the racist Nazi phantasmagoria - the conviction that Jews are a race, separate from the rest of humanity (or not a part of humanity in the first place) - a reality. It often found fertile ground, prepared by local antisemites. We mustn't forget that it also included ethnic Poles of Jewish origin: everyone who had Jewish grandparents, even if they themselves were far away from Jewish traditions and identity. We avoid the word 'Aryans', a Nazi legal term of the time, sensing its racist connotation, and yet in our discussions we are entangled in categories created by racists. After all, the paragraphs above dedicated to 'Polish reactions' during the war were, in fact, about the reactions of 'Aryan Poles'.

The discussions from the first group - about Polish reactions to the Holocaust - were not Polish-Jewish but rather Polish-Polish discussions. Some participants went to great lengths to present their opponents as Jews, or at least their voices as Jewish voices, as an expression of the 'Jewish point of view' (which, supposedly, cannot be also a Polish voice), which says more about them that their opponents or the dispute. Putting aside the affinity of such statements with racism, this rhetorical device invalidated the opponents' inconvenient arguments turning them into Aliens while they remained self-appointed spokesmen and defenders of Polishness. The device also falsified the expression of diverse beliefs, values and attitudes within Polish society about the role of memory and who we are as Poles. The disputes about a Polish-Jewish past were in fact disputes among Poles about their understanding of their own identity and their attitude towards their own past.

Some proponents of Jewishness as the inconvenient voice might not have been motivated by cynical calculation or overwhelming prejudice, but rather a sincere - perhaps even unconscious - fear that in thinking on such fundamental questions the Polish nation is deeply divided, which somehow threatened its very existence. Without sharing their fear of diverse opinions, we can agree that among the Poles today there are divisions in attitudes towards the past and the right ways of dealing with it. However, this does not have to be specifically Polish - we might look at it from a broader perspective, as stemming from human nature or European culture. Perhaps Poles, like other Europeans, are divided into spiritual descendants of Spartans and Athenians, to whom the philosopher Rémi Brague attributes opposite approaches to critical thinking about history. The former, according to him, value all that is familiar and tame, and protect it from criticism. The latter are not content with familiarity – they risk confronting the truth that can emerge from the world through thinking.[14]

Unfortunately, a tendency of Polish discussions on the *Shoah* has hindered seeing the past in a broader perspective. We find it in the title of Błoński's famous 1987 essay 'Poor Poles Look at the Ghetto', which came from Miłosz's poem 'A Poor Christian Looks at the Ghetto' but replaced its individual and universal subject with the collective and ethnonational – expressing the tendency towards nationalist de-universalisation of Polish discussion and reflection on the Holocaust. Miłosz's conveyance of a simultaneously universal and personal problem that concerns every Christian (or, every 'uncircumcised' person, as he wrote), changes into a collective problem for Poles. Perhaps without that change, the 1987 and subsequent debates would not have aroused such emotions and acquired the scale it did. The price was that the problem a cruel history posed for humanity (or at least for Christians, or non-Jews) was reduced to a problem for the Poles alone. The systematic superseding of a universalist by a nationalist perspective impairs the ability to convey possible conclusions to Polish experience and limits the cognitive horizon of research and reflection. By assuming *a priori* ethnonational categories of analysis we cannot see what of the past does not fit into them.[15]

14 See Andrzej Leder's reflections on this topic in 'Konsekwencje doświadczenia Zagłady dla polskiej świadomości (i nieświadomości) społecznej' (Consequences of the Holocaust Experience for the Polish Social Consciousness [and Unconsciousness]), *Zagłada Żydów. Studies and Materials*, no. 14, 2018, pp. 503–04, who quotes Brague: 'People's attitude to the past is spontaneously "Spartan".'

15 I thank Professor Andrzej Paczkowski for drawing my attention to this aspect of Błoński's title. The universal dimension of the issues raised during the Polish debates was pointed out by, among others, Marci Shore in 'Conversing with Ghosts: Jedwabne, Żydokomuna, and Totalitarianism', *Kritika: Explorations in Russian and Eurasian History*, 2005, vol. 6, no. 2, pp. 345–74. A universalising perspective was adopted by prominent early texts on the Holocaust by Tadeusz Borowski and Zofia Nałkowska, with the latter's famous sentence 'people have served this fate unto other people'. Today, she could be accused of de-Judaising the Holocaust or concealing who the perpetrators in fact were (see *Lata czterdzieste*).

The last feature of the Polish debates around the Holocaust, even more disturbing than the previous ones, is supplanting discussion with disputes. This is most visible in recent years. According to the Great Dictionary of the Polish Language, a discussion is 'an exchange of opinions between persons of different views', whereas the Polish Scientific Publishers' [PWN] Language Dictionary notes that it is 'an oral or written exchange of opinions on a subject, which is to lead to shared conclusions'. The first definition implies that an exchange of opinions involves a readiness to accept at least some of the opposition's opinions. The second, on the other hand, points to reaching joint conclusions as a goal of the exchange. For the past several years, Polish controversies related to the Holocaust have increasingly met the dictionary definition of a dispute: 'a situation in which two or more persons or groups express different opinions on a subject and *are unwilling* [emphasis added] to accept the opinions of their opponents'. Violent attacks against those who disagree, discrediting *ad personam* arguments with heavy accusations (of anti-Polish activity, betrayal, etc.) do not convince those accused to move towards a shared conclusion but rather invalidate their arguments in the eyes of those who observe. Piotr Forecki noted this tendency in the disputes around Gross's books, which he attributes to a violent reaction (backlash) to those books. Its most dangerous manifestation has been slanderous attacks on the historians of the Shoah, including those launched through public and government-sponsored media, and recently the harassment by means of a lawsuit, behind which stands an organisation sponsored by the ruling party.[16]

This militancy has increased in the past decade with the rise of Facebook, Twitter and YouTube and decline of the press. Public debate - and not only about history - has moved on to these new media platforms where they are governed by algorithms designed to maximise platform owner profits. They favour emotional and controversial content, produce relatively isolated groups of like-minded people ('information bubbles'), and facilitate the spread of fake news and conspiracy theories. If this does not change, the history of Polish

16 D. Stola, 'Miarą dyktatury są nienapisane książki' (Unwritten Books Are the Measure of a Dictatorship), *Kultura Liberalna*, no. 6 (631), 2021; Michał Okoński, 'Dobre imię' (Good Repute), *Tygodnik Powszechny*, 9 February 2021.

discussions about the Holocaust will turn into a history of disputes – pointless without shared conclusions, producing liars as winners, and promoting the conviction that we cannot establish anything for certain, and that there isn't anything to unite us, not even a difficult past.

Shoah (Forest-Ner River), 2003

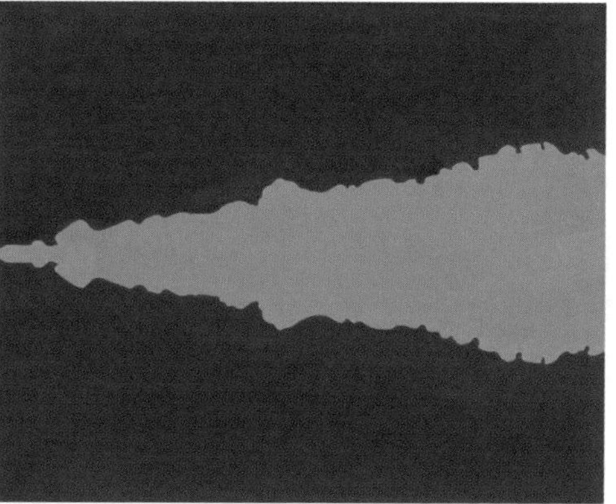

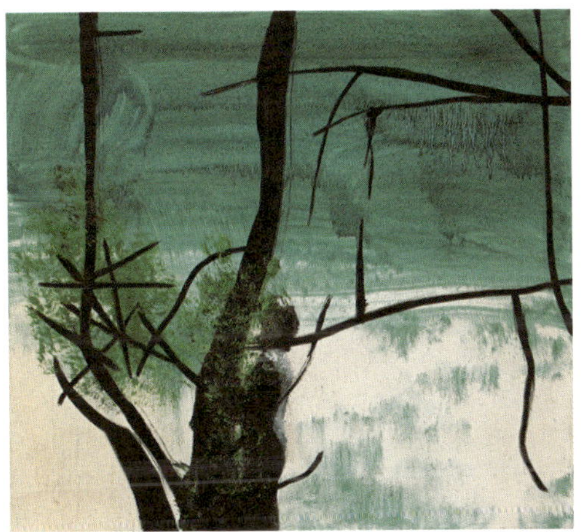

Untitled, 2003

Formlessness Versus Formalisation:
Towards a Post-National Culture of Remembrance

By Noit Banai

'The past is never dead. It's not even past'
- William Faulkner, *Requiem for a Nun*, 1953

Let us consider a few disturbing public spectacles from 2021, the year of Wilhelm Sasnal's exhibition *Such a Landscape* at the POLIN Museum of the History of Polish Jews in Warsaw. Among the protesters who stormed the US Capitol on 6 January was a man wearing a sweatshirt with the words 'Camp Auschwitz' emblazoned above a skull and crossbones and, above that, the perverse phrase *Arbeit Macht Frei* (Work Brings Freedom), which greeted prisoners when they entered the concentration camp in Poland. There he stood, posing for the camera with a group of revellers holding up the Speaker of the House - Nancy Pelosi's vandalised name plate - while wrapped in the American flag. Barely a month later, on 31 January, demonstrators in Belgium took to the streets to protest the Covid-19 quarantine and vaccination policies that have regulated social and economic life since the pandemic began. In Brussels, with some draped in the yellow and black flag of Flanders, the far-right carried a banner depicting a herd of sheep heading towards the entry-gate to Auschwitz. Now replacing *Arbeit Macht Frei*, a rainbow with two crossed syringes and the phrase *Ça va bien aller* (It's going to be fine) above the portal. More recently, in July and August 2021, thousands of protesters representing a wide spectrum of political affiliations, wore Stars of David as they marched against the 'Health Pass' in Italy and 'Green Pass' in France. Their claim: the vaccination card, required to participate in public life, would create a two-tier system of citizenship akin to the oppression of Jews in Nazi Germany. These moments of populist rage and their viral media distribution, of which there are many other examples, raise the urgent question of what it means to inhabit our contemporary post-Holocaust (Shoah) paradigm and how to assess role of artistic practices that confront antisemitism and the constitutive role of the Holocaust in our present moment. Taking seriously Wilhelm Sasnal's claim that 'I constantly get the feeling that we are not living in the post-1989 but the post-1945 period'[1] means recognising that the Holocaust still plays a structural and epistemological role in the complex articulations of a global post-war public sphere even as it is systematically minimised, relativised, repressed or denied in both personal accounts and official narratives.[2] In this essay, I inscribe

1 Wilhelm Sasnal quoted in interview with Andrzej Przywara, 'Always Return by Another Route', *Wilhelm Sasnal*, London and New York: Phaidon, 2011, p. 39.

2 It is crucial to recognise the important contributions of scholars grappling with

Sasnal's oeuvre as part of the physical, emotional and mental 'lieux de mémoire'[3] that accompanies both the Polish experience of the Holocaust and, more broadly, its persisting global aftermaths. Specifically, I am thinking about Sasnal's practice as one that moves through the category of mimesis into formlessness in order to build the foundations for a post-national, multidirectional culture of remembrance that does not abide by the limited orthodoxies and regulations installed by the nation-state.

Representation: Between Silence and Silencing

The terms of the discussion can no longer be couched in Theodor W. Adorno's pronouncement that 'to write a poem after Auschwitz is barbaric' but need to be embedded in our present material conditions.[4]

this situation in various disciplines, including art history. Luiza Nader and Piotr Słodkowski write:

> One might sum up the current situation by saying that the history of art in Poland, when facing the Holocaust, has remained unmoved, untroubled, indifferent. [...] [W]e seek, on the one hand, to emphasize existing research that has worked towards the visibility of the Holocaust in both art and the history of art in Poland, as well as to move (in the emotional and physical sense of the word), perhaps even shake up, our somewhat fossilized discipline, breaking down historical-artistic discourses, dissembling familiar epistemes, opening up new vistas for research. [...] [O]ur intention is to treat the Holocaust as the epicenter of a transhistorical and transgenerational experience in Poland's history of art, while at the same time remaining sensitive to the distinctions involved in the many positions occupied by witnesses, bystanders, observers, viewers, onlookers and, finally, perpetrators...

Luiza Nader and Piotr Słodkowski, 'The History of the Art in Poland and the Holocaust. Introduction', *Miejsce*, no. 6, 2020, https://www.doi.org10.48285/8kaewzdo3p.

3 According to Nora, *lieux de mémoire* are 'created by a play of memory and history'; they are 'mixed, hybrid, mutant, bound intimately with life and death, with time and eternity, enveloped in a Möbius strip of the collective and the individual, the sacred and the profane, the immutable and the mobile'. Invested with 'a symbolic aura' *lieux de mémoire* can hope to 'block the work of forgetting'. Pierre Nora, 'Between Memory and History: Les Lieux de Mémoire', *Representations*, vol. 26, 1989, pp. 7–24, https://doi.org/10.2307/2928520.

4 'Kulturkritik findet sich der letzten Stufe der Dialektik von Kultur und Barbareigegenüber: *nach Auschwitz ein Gedicht zu schreiben ist barbarisch*, und das frißt auch die Erkenntnis an, die ausspricht, warum es unmöglich ward, heute Gedichte zu schreiben' (Cultural criticism finds itself faced with the final

Writing in the wake of the Second World War, Adorno was deliberating on the transformations that led to the irrevocable breakdown of the Enlightenment's foundational basis of rational knowledge, or, in his words, to the 'final stage of the dialectic of culture and barbarism'.[5] What he was grappling with in those years was how to hold two thoughts in dialectical tension, namely, the claim for art's necessity and its inadmissibility under such corroded epistemological conditions.[6] The subsequent decontextualisation of Adorno's statement from a dialectical matrix has led many to understand it as an outright interdiction: silence - or the impossibility of cultural representation - as the only conceivable response to the unthinkable catastrophe of the Shoah. Paradoxically, in the almost eighty years since the end of the Second World War, the debates around the limits of the 'representability' of the Holocaust never subsided in critical circles even as new visual iterations have proliferated in the sphere of mass culture. In the field of art history, scholars have continued to debate the merits and inadequacies of trying to give the Holocaust form via figurative or abstract pictorial conventions;[7] interrogated the ethics of 'imagining' oneself in the camps by ways of photographic images;[8] and examined the filmic possibilities of confronting the traumas of the 'concentrationary complex'.[9] At the same time, the silencing of the Holocaust by national governments and their proxies follow the pattern delineated by Michel-Rolph Trouillot in *Silencing the Past: Power and the Production of History*: 'Silences enter

---

stage of the dialectic of culture and barbarism: to write poetry after Auschwitz is barbaric; and this corrodes even the knowledge of why it has become impossible to write poetry today). Theodor W. Adorno, 'Kulturkritik und Gesellschaft', *Prismen. Kulturkritik und Gesellschaft*, Munich: Suhrkamp Verlag, 1963 [1955], p. 26. Emphasis mine. Translation from T. W. Adorno, *Prisms*, trans. Samuel and Shierry Weber, Cambridge, MA: MIT Press, 1981, p. 34. Adorno's 1949 essay titled 'Kulturkritik und Gesellschaft' was initially published in *Soziologische Forschung in unserer Zeit. Leopold von Wiese zum 75. Geburtstag*, Wiesbaden: VS Verlag für Sozialwissenschaften, 1951.

5 *Ibid.*

6 See Klaus Hofmann, 'Poetry After Auschwitz - Adorno's Dictum', *German Life and Letters*, vol. 58, no. 2, April 2005, pp. 182-94.

7 See Mark Godfrey, *Abstraction and the Holocaust*, New Haven, CT: Yale University Press, 2007.

8 See Georges Didi-Huberman, *Images in Spite of All: Four Photographs from Auschwitz*, Chicago: University of Chicago Press, 2008.

9 See Griselda Pollock and Max Silverman, *Concentrationary Imaginaries: Tracing Totalitarian Violence in Popular Culture*, London: Bloomsbury, 2015.

the process of historical production at four crucial moments: the moment of fact creation (the making of sources); the moment of fact assembly (the making of archives); the moment of fact retrieval (the making of narratives); and the moment of retrospective significance (the making of history in the final instance).'[10]

Embedded in the ethical, political and legal realms as much as the channels of the social and sensory, the Holocaust is caught between the strictures of silence and silencing, on the one hand, and the proliferation of its signs and symbols, on the other. What once may have been a repressed, unspoken or un-articulable memory by those who lived through the events is now actively manufactured, revised, censored, or legislated by governments, institutions or populations who are the inheritors of the post-Holocaust world.[11]

From 'Images of Images' Towards the Shudder

In the case of Wilhelm Sasnal, a discourse about the creation of 'images of images' gained momentum around the early 2000s.[12] That earlier discussion, framed by the broader concerns over 'representability', centred on the possibility of using found images to encounter historical trauma and brought Sasnal (b. 1972) into an artistic conversation with

10 See Michel-Rolph Trouillot, *Silencing the Past: The Power and Production of History*, Boston: Beacon Press, 1995, p. 26.

11 While each European nation-state went through its own process of confronting its role in the Second World War and thus assimilating or rejecting its complicity with the Nazi plans to annihilate World Jewry, there are a number of common factors in the immediate post-war period (1945–48) that have fostered specific myths and memories that are still active in the contemporary public sphere. These include the wholesale assignment of responsibility for the war, its sufferings and its crimes on Germany; the incomplete de-Nazification of both Axis and Allied powers and incorporation of Nazis into post-war governments; the formulation and amplification of 'resistance myths' by native populations against Fascism and the German occupation. See Tony Judt, 'Epilogue: The Past is Another Country: Myth and Memory in Post-War Europe', in *The Politics of Retribution in Europe: World War II and its Aftermath*, ed. István Deák, Jan Tomasz Gross and Tony Judt, Princeton, NJ: Princeton University Press, 2000, pp. 293–323.

12 See Susie Rushton, 'The Polish Painter Mr. Sasnal and His Cosmopolitan Life on the Out-skirts of Cracow', *Fantastic Man*, April 2008, pp. 56–63.

Gerhard Richter (b. 1932) and Luc Tuymans (b. 1958).[13] A recurrent point of comparison revolves around transformation of Holocaust images, taken from personal archives, press photographs, films and television, comics, and internet sources, into a painterly language limning the boundaries of abstraction and figuration by artists of three different generations.[14] Perhaps more fruitful, the conversation has been extended to the growing tension between the evidentiary pursuits of historians and their reliance on archival sources (i.e. the primacy of the document) and the more speculative contributions of writers, theorists and artistic and cultural practitioners (i.e. the primacy of aesthetics). These frictions make visible the challenges posed by memory as a conflicted site that negotiates the objectivity of historical facts and the contingencies of representation. At the intersection of these two poles, one of the central questions animating current debates is whether 'those victims who experienced and survived the Holocaust [are] the prime emissaries of its meaning' and, by extension, whether we might simultaneously attend to the 'testimony of [non-Jewish] populations whose lives were also marked by the experience'.[15] Circa 2021, it seems difficult to resuscitate the same

13 Ulrich Loock, 'Sasnal's Nominalism', in Carina Plath and Beatrix Ruf (ed.), *Wilhelm Sasnal: Night Day Night*, exh. cat., Berlin: Hatje Cantz, 2003, pp. 96-109; Ulrich Wilmes, 'Painting History', in *Wilhelm Sasnal*, exh. cat., London: Whitechapel Gallery, 2011, pp. 88-92; Matthew Collings, 'The Difference between Wilhelm Sasnal and Luc Tuymans', *Modern Painters*, Autumn 2004, pp. 26-29.

14 Carina Plath aptly encapsulates Sasnal's choice of subjects and generational position, here in particular:

> Sasnal's choice of subjects is not arbitrary, but grounded in a personal encounter with specific themes, like the contemporary discussion of Poland's role in the Holocaust. The various groups of images that reflect on this history demonstrate, in their appeal to other media, that an unmediated encounter with the events has long since ceased to be possible. Because they draw on earlier evidence in order to react to the discussion of the standpoint of the Poles during the Nazi regime - a conversation that only began in critical form with the 1990s - it becomes vividly clear that the discussion is a historically belated one. *The disparity of the images demonstrates the dilemma of the generation of those born after the 1960s, who can no longer lay hold of history and yet are compelled to seek an encounter with it in order to discover a new identity...*

C. Plath, 'Mościce', *Wilhelm Sasnal. Night Day Night*, p. 14. Emphasis mine.

15 Noit Banai, 'Violent Topographies: Multidirectional Post-Memory and the Production of the Present', in *Natural Histories, Traces of the Political*, ed. Rainer Fuchs, Vienna: Museum moderner Kunst Stiftung Ludwig, 2017, pp. 237-38. In the case of Poland:

polemics that grounded previous discussions as the survivors of the Holocaust are vanishing while contemporary processes of subjectivisation are consolidated via new technologies, materials, objects and image systems of mass (re)production. Without diminishing or distorting the specific logic and singularity of the Holocaust, our challenge is to situate it as a collective trauma that cuts across nations, populations and individual bodies and that continues to permutate into new symbolic and sensory formations.

In the last thirty years, these concerns have gone hand in hand with the elaboration of two important concepts - *postmemory* and *multidirectional memory* - that have enlarged the Holocaust's temporal and spatial scope as well as its archival parameters. In the 1990s, in an article on Art Spiegelman's *Maus*, the scholar Marianne Hirsch coined the term 'postmemory'[16] to characterise an ever-widening

> As part of the policy to destroy the Polish resistance, the Germans killed many of the nation's political, religious, and intellectual leaders. They also kidnapped children judged racially suitable for adoption by Germans and confined Poles in dozens of prisons and concentration and forced labor camps, where many perished. [...] Poles were prisoners in nearly every camp in the extensive camp system in German-occupied Poland and the Reich. A major camp complex at Stutthof, east of Danzig, existed from September 2, 1939 to war's end, and an estimated 20,000 Poles died there as a result of executions, hard labor, and harsh conditions. The Polish scholar Franciszek Piper, the chief historian of Auschwitz, estimates that 140,000 to 150,000 Poles were brought to that camp between 1940 and 1945, and that 70,000 to 75,000 died there as victims of executions, of cruel medical experiments, and of starvation and disease. Some 100,000 Poles were deported to Majdanek, and tens of thousands of them died there. An estimated 20,000 Poles died at Sachsenhausen, 20,000 at Gross-Rosen, 30,000 at Mauthausen, 17,000 at Neuengamme, 10,000 at Dachau, and 17,000 at Ravensbrueck [Ravensbrück]. In addition, victims in the tens of thousands were executed or died in the thousands of other camps - including special children's camps such as Lodz [Łódź] and its subcamp, Dzierzazn [Dzierżązna] and in prisons and other places of detention within and outside Poland.

See *Poles*, Washington DC: United States Holocaust Memorial Museum, 2002, pp. 1-28.

16 Marianne Hirsch, 'Family Pictures: Maus, Mourning, and Post-Memory', special issue, 'The Emotions, Gender, and the Politics of Subjectivity', *Discourse*, vol. 15, no. 2, Winter 1992-93, pp. 3-29. While initially, Hirsch spelled the term with a hyphen, she has now adopted the non-hyphenated form. We may wish to consider the difference produced by this hyphen and its removal: an embedded caesura versus the entanglement of temporalities and spaces.

generational distance from the historical event, in which the memories of the children of Holocaust survivors are 'mediated not through recollection but through an imaginative investment and creation'.[17] For Hirsch, postmemory describes

> the relationship that the 'generation after' bears to the personal, collective, and cultural trauma of those who came before – to experiences they 'remember' only by means of the stories, images, and behaviours among which they grew up. But these experiences were transmitted to them so deeply and affectively as to seem to constitute memories in their own right.[18]

Today, writing from the globally dispersed perspective of the third and fourth generations, we understand the importance of analysing how postmemory continues to animate our contemporary relationship to the Holocaust through creative appropriation of and a libidinal attachment to events that we have not lived through ourselves. A citation of Art Spiegelman's depiction of his parents' survival of the Holocaust in comic book form (serialised between 1980 and 1991), Sasnal's *Maus 4* (2001) is a black and white graphic rendering of the wooden bunk beds in which concentration camp prisoners were quartered. Such images of bunk beds, barbed wire, train tracks and watch towers among others have become paradigmatic for the memorialisation of the Holocaust and continue to become a site for the construction of multiple vectors of postmemory. They function as 'memory knots on the social body' – or, following Steve J. Stern's more colloquial formulation, as 'sites where the social body screams' – that connect between personal memories and collective imaginaries.[19] This is not only the case in the genealogy of Jewish survivors and their kin – who pass on stories of genocide and survival with each generation. It is also in the case of global collective memory – in which future generations may accept or resist the knowledge that their families were implicated in the

17 M. Hirsch, 'Mourning and Postmemory' (1997) first published in *Family Frames: Photography, Family, and Postmemory*, Cambridge, MA: Harvard University, 2012 and reprinted in *The Holocaust: Theoretical Readings*, ed. Neil Levi and Michael Rothberg, Edinburgh: Edinburgh University Press, 2003, p. 416.

18 M. Hirsch, 'Postmemory', *Postmemory.net*, https://www.postmemory.net/.

19 Steve J. Stern, 'From Loose Memory to Emblematic Memory: Knots on the Social Body', *Remembering Pinochet's Chile: On the Eve of London 1998*, Durham, NC: Duke University Press, 2004, p. 120.

Holocaust in frequently overlapping roles, including bystanders, witnesses, enablers, perpetrators, beneficiaries, victims, rescuers or collaborators.

Mimeticism and Alterity: Releasing the Formless

According to Katarzyna Bojarska, the publication of the Polish translation of *Maus* in 2001 incited protests in front of the office of Piotr Bikont, the graphic novel's translator.[20] This resistance to accepting the entanglement between Jewish and Polish histories and memories was so powerful that a copy of the book was destroyed and the publisher was sued for defamation of the Polish nation.[21] In the same year, as part of a group exhibition *Painters' (dis)Appointments*, curated by Adam Szymczyk, Sasnal rendered a scene from *Maus* as a mural on the back wall of the Galeria Bielska, an art space in the town of Bielsko-Biała that occupies the site of a former synagogue that was destroyed by the Nazis. In the selected episode, Spiegelman's father - Władek - pays Polish blackmailers (*szmalcowniks*), represented as pigs, to help him escape, only to be betrayed and handed over to the Nazis.[22] This happens just as the train he is fleeing in passes through the town of Biała where he used to own a factory.[23] After being detained, he is

20 Katarzyna Bojarska, 'Wilhelm Sasnal's Transitional Images', *Miejsce*, no. 6, 2020, http://miejsce.asp.waw.pl/en/english-wilhelm-sasnals-transitional-images/.

21 *Ibid.*

22 The derogatory term *szmalcownik* ('blackmailer') comes from the German word *Schmalz* ('lard') and expresses the blackmailer's financial motive, i.e. the bribe to be paid by the victim. *Szmalcowniks* would bribe Jews in hiding for money and valuables or promise to smuggle them out of danger while often denouncing them to the German authorities or the Polish Blue Police for a bounty; they would also extort Poles who were helping Jews. From the summer of 1943, *Szmalcowniks* faced punishment by death from the Polish underground courts. See Wiktoria Sliwowska, Jakub Gutenbaum and Agnieszka Latała, *The Last Eyewitnesses: Children of the Holocaust Speak*, Evanston, IL: Northwestern University Press, 1998, p. 329; Gunnar S. Paulsson, 'Secret City: The Hidden Jews of Warsaw, 1940-1945', New Haven, CT: Yale University Press, 2002, p. 5; Dariusz Libionka, *ZWZ-AK i Delegatura Rządu RP wobec eksterminacji Żydów polskich* (ZWZ-AK and the Delegation of the Government of the Republic of Poland Against the Extermination of Polish Jews), in ed. Andrzej Żbikowski, *Polacy i Żydzi pod okupacją niemiecką 1939-1945. Studia i materiały* (Poles and Jews Under the German Occupation 1939-1945: Studies and Materials), Warsaw: Instytut Pamięci Narodowej, 2006, p. 123.

23 Bielsko-Biała is composed of two former towns on two sides of the Biała River - Bielsko in the west and Biała in the east - which merged in 1951.

sent to Auschwitz.[24] Originally meant for the walls of the Museum of Technology and Textile Industry in Bielsko-Biała, which is located in a former factory (i.e. Spiegelman's factory), Sasnal portrays this scene of blackmail and double-dealing by reproducing the speech bubbles from Spiegelman's book while excluding the images. In this decision, the artist creates a performative situation with each contemporary reader bringing the scene to life in their own voice. In the span of a single page from *Maus*, they became the victimised Jewish townspeople, the Polish *szmalcowniks* and the German *Gestapo*. As Bojarska recounts, the mural and exhibition incited protests and legal complaints on the grounds that 'they were based on a false premise that "Poles denounced and turned in Jews to Germans", a premise which it has been known for a while now is a historical fact'.[25] Indeed, around the year 2000, with Jan Tomasz Gross's ground-breaking publication *Sąsiedzi. Historia zagłady żydowskiego miasteczka* (2000; *Neighbors: The Destruction of the Jewish Community in Jedwabne, Poland*, 2001), the complicity of the Polish population in annihilating their Jewish neighbours, with whom they had lived together for generations, was supported by ample historical evidence.[26] Gross's contribution altered the terrain of Holocaust studies because it questioned 'the conviction that the destruction of Polish Jewry happened to "them" and not to "us" - or, to put it in other words, the externalization of the

---

> Bielsko ... was a part of the Czech Kingdom [from the fourteenth century], and later, from 1526, it became a part of the Franco-Habsburg Dynasty. Małopolska Biała ... was a small hamlet, part of the village Lipnik; it was situated on the west frontier of Poland. After the First Partition in 1772, Biała was also situated in Austria, in a newly established province - Galicia. Just in 1918 both cities came back into the re-formed Republic of Poland .... The characteristic of the people of Bielsko-Biała and its surroundings before World War II was multinational.

See 'Bielsko-Biała: History of the City', Miejskie Centrum Informacji Turystycznej w Bielsku-Białej, http://it.bielsko.pl/history-of-the-city/.

24 Polish artist Erna Rosenstein (1913-2004) lost her parents Anna (née Schrager) and Maksymilian Rosenstein to a *szmalcownik* who organised their escape from Warsaw to a countryside hideout that did not exist and mugged and murdered them both in 1942. She returns to this traumatic event, to which she was witness, numerous times in her paintings.

25 Bojarska, 'Wilhelm Sasnal's Transitional Images'.

26 See Jan Tomasz Gross, *Neighbors: The Destruction of the Jewish Community in Jedwabne, Poland*, Princeton, NJ: Princeton University Press, 2001.

Holocaust...' [27] With Gross's assertion that the dichotomy between 'us' and 'them' is false and that the Holocaust, rather than being a strictly 'Jewish subject', implicates the entire Polish population,[28] I would like to return to Bielsko-Biała in 2001: how do we account for the visceral response that led to public acts of iconoclasm and grievance in the face of Sasnal's *Maus*? It may be useful to consider the connection between the mimetic faculty and what Adorno has characterised as the aesthetic category of the 'shudder': 'a reaction to otherness... [that involves] the subject being overwhelmed or shocked by an experience that [he or she does not know] how to characterize, conceptualize or properly represent.'[29] In this shudder, which resonates with both the romantic and psychoanalytic notions of the uncanny, autonomy and critical distance are cancelled and the individual is compelled to somatically encounter a form or feeling of alterity that reason cannot readily comprehend. What has been cast out from one's sense of sovereign-rational self as unfathomable or un-articulable is now animating it. At various times, this alterity might be conceived as 'the Jew', 'the Negro', 'the Savage', 'the Gypsy' - or any other type of figure that has been vital to the constitution of European modernity within its geographical borders and beyond its frontiers. In the case of the book burning and outcry over Sasnal's mural, this sudden identification with a habitually exteriorised alterity - the Jewish victim, Polish double-dealer and German occupier - was accompanied by a violence against the very object that triggers such sensual reverberation in the individual and collective body. As there was no representational

27 J. T. Gross, '"Making History": My Intellectual Journey into the Hidden Polish Past', *Social Research*, vol. 86, no. 1, Spring 2019, p. 418.

28 J. T. Gross, 'Introduction', *East European Politics and Societies*, vol. 25, no. 3, August 2011, pp. 391-92.

29 Justin Neville Kaushall, 'On Adorno's Aesthetic Category of the Shudder', *The Telos Press Podcast*, 12 January 2021. For a more comprehensive etymology and genealogy see Kaushall's article on the subject in which he writes:

> Adorno uses two different German terms for 'shudder': *Erschütterung* and *Schauer*. The former term has various meanings: physical tremor or vibration (as in an earthquake), convulsion, traumatic breakdown, concussion, or shock (both physical and psychological). Hence the term *Erschütterung* is associated with both objective and subjective experience. The latter term, *Schauer*, might be translated as shudder, shiver, or thrill. Hence, it is associated with cold and with fear - with both physical and emotional experience.

J. N. Kaushall, 'Natural Spontaneity, or Adorno's Aesthetic Category of the Shudder', *Telos*, no. 192, Fall 2020, p. 125, n. 1.

mimetic rendering, only a speech act performed by each member of the public, the relationship between self and other was actualised through singular voices that momentarily embodied each of the figures in *Maus*. Here the paradox becomes untenable: while it is possible to defile a figurative mural - iconoclasm against an iconography - how do you lash out at the mimetic function when it is your own voice that is unleashing the return of the repressed within you? When no externalisation is possible, there is only a choice between speaking and silence.

Sasnal has continuously drawn on the mimetic faculty to complicate the viewer's subject position, as, for example, in *Untitled* (2010), a realistic portrait of Hitler painted from a photograph; *Untitled* (2007), a painting of (Eastern European) orthodox Jews counting money; *Jews (after Degas)* (2014), a depiction of (Western European) assimilated Jews participating in commerce;[30] and *Murzynek Bambo* (2014), a Sambo-like representation of a black boy.[31] What does it mean to be situated vis-à-vis the leader of the Third Reich or in relation to enduring tropes of Jewish and Black otherness in the European public sphere? If we consider the function of the shudder, then we understand that Sasnal activates the somatic register in ways that elide between various subjects and their alterities and disturbs any claim to moral privilege or cultural superiority. Circulating transnationally, the portrait of Hitler poses the question of whether it is possible to identify a single perpetrator who can be charged with the extermination of the Jews: Can the guilt be associated only with one man or solely with the German nation? What about the Poles? French or Dutch? British or the Americans? The Catholic Church? Were no other nation-states, institutions and individuals also complicit with betraying their Jewish population, delivering them to the Nazis and actively blocking their safe passage out of Europe? A similar process occurs with the portraits of Jews, which may elicit reflections on how diverse European protagonists construct the object of their racism. Sasnal situates the viewer before the 'Shtetl Jew' - the

30 The painting is a copy of a segment of Edgar Degas's *Portraits at the Stock Exchange* (1878-89), which has been extensively analysed by Linda Nochlin in 'Degas and the Dreyfus Affair: A Portrait of the Artist as an Anti-Semite', in *The Dreyfus Affair: Art, Truth, and Justice*, ed. Norman L. Kleeblatt, Los Angeles: University of California Press, 1987, pp. 96-116.

31 *Murzynek* is a diminutive of the Polish N-word 'Murzyn'. For more on the term see pp. 17 and 139, n. 41 in this book.

adherent of Orthodox Judaism who lived in Central and Eastern Europe for centuries before the Holocaust - as well as the 'Cosmopolitan Jew' - who had largely assimilated within Western European modernity and secularism. As both portraits draw on the negative stereotypical attributes and signifying systems that constitute 'Jewishness' - prominent noses and money counting - they raise the question of their intended audience.[32] Here, for example, we might want to consider the intersection of Sasnal's paintings with popular figurines of 'Lucky Jews' (*Żyd na szczęście*) that began to be sold in Poland in the 1960s, in the aftermath of the biggest Jewish emigration from the country and that are still ubiquitous today. These good luck charms, sometimes in the form of beeswax candles, depict an Orthodox Jew holding a gold coin and come in various sizes, including the 'Big Jew' (17 cm) and 'Little Jew' (10 cm).[33] According to Erica Lehrer,

> It could be said that in Poland today there are more Jewish figurines than Jews. Indeed, most people living in Poland today have never met a Jew. But they are living in towns and cities where Jews once made up 30% or more of the population. In many places, not a trace is left of the Jewish community that once lived there. That blank space is filled today with images of Jews - figurines, pictures, magnets, postcards, and more...[34]

With Jews living in Poland for more than a thousand years, the Jewish past is a vital part of Polish history and, perhaps to state

32 Max Horkheimer and T. W. Adorno:

> [Anti-Semites] detest the Jews and imitate them constantly. There is no anti-Semite who does not feel an instinctive urge to ape what he takes to be Jewishness. The same mimetic codes are constantly used: the argumentative jerking of the hands, the singing tone of voice, which vividly animates a situation or a feeling independently of judgment, and the nose, that physiognomic *principium individuationis*, which writes the individual's peculiarity on his face.

M. Horkheimer and T. W. Adorno, *Dialectic of Enlightenment: Philosophical Fragments*, ed. Gunzelin Schmid Noerr and trans. Edmund Jephcott, Stanford, CA: Stanford University Press, 2002, p. 151.

33 Cnaan Liphshiz, 'Latest "Lucky Jew" figurines in Poland: Candles that Promise "financial success"', *The Times of Israel*, 16 March 2021, https://www.timesofisrael.com/latest-lucky-jew-figurines-in-poland-candles-that-promise-financial-success/.

34 Erica Lehrer, *Lucky Jews: Poland's Jewish Figurines*, Kraków: Korporacja Halart, 2014, p. 24.

the obvious, Polish culture was in part Jewish and vice versa. Before the Second World War, there were 3.5 million Jews in Poland, thus 10 per cent of Poland's total population and more than 50 per cent of many small towns. In Warsaw, one in three people were Jewish while, in Tarnów – where Sasnal was born in 1972 – they represented nearly half the population (or 25,000 people) in 1939.[35] Just ten per cent of Poland's Jewish population survived and many left the country in the following years.[36] Following the 1968 purge, in which more than 15,000 Jews – half of the Jewish population – were stripped of their Polish citizenship by the Communist state and forced to leave, less than 10 per cent of those who had survived the Holocaust remained.[37] While there has been a modest revival of Jewish life,[38] Sasnal's paintings of Jews urge the Polish population to consider their own multilayered projections vis-à-vis these missing or *formless* neighbours who were once in their midst.[39]

35 The figures about Poland and Warsaw can be found in Erica Lehrer, '"Shoah-business", "Holocaust culture", and the repair of the world in "post-Jewish" Poland: A quest for ethnography, empathy, and the ethnic self after genocide', PhD dissertation, University of Michigan, Minneapolis, 2005; the figures about Tarnów are available at 'Tarnów History in Brief', https://www.inyourpocket.com/tarnow/history. 'On June 14th 1940, 728 Tarnów residents (mostly Poles, in fact) became the first victims of Auschwitz; of 40,000 Jews crammed into Tarnów's ghetto, over 10,000 were executed and the rest deported to the Bełżec death camp.'

36 'Approximately 1,000 Jews per month left Poland between July 1945 and June 1946, immediately after the [Kielce] pogrom [July 1946, 42 Jewish survivors who had returned from the camps were murdered by Polish residents] the numbers spiked dramatically: in July 1946, almost 20,000 fled; in August 1946 that number swelled to 30,000, and in September 1946, 12,000 Jews left Poland.' See 'Anti-Jewish Violence in Poland After Liberation', Yad Vashem: The World Holocaust Remembrance Center, https://www.yadvashem.org/articles/general/anti-jewish-violence-in-poland-after-liberation.html#footnoteref1_i7c7o93.

37 Stanisław Krajewski, activist and leader of the Jewish community in Poland, quoted in Yardena Schwartz, 'Forty Miles from Auschwitz, Poland's Jewish Community is Beginning to Thrive', *Time Magazine*, 27 February 2019, https://time.com/5534494/poland-jews-rebirth-anti-semitism/.

38 'As of 1 January 2016, the core Jewish population of Poland was estimated to be 3,200 (0.008 per cent of the wider population), and the enlarged Jewish population was estimated at 7,500 (0.02 per cent of the wider population).' See 'Poland', Institute for Jewish Policy Research, https://www.jpr.org.uk/country?id=244.

39 According to Erica Lehrer,

> inquiries revealed in and around the figurines unseen layers of cultural intimacy and emotion on the part of makers and buyers, Jews and non-Jews alike. They embody not only timeworn stereotypes, but also traces of history, traumatic memory, and unspoken nostalgia. They are bought and displayed as gestures of superstition, and as touchstones for identity, belief, cultural

Entangled Performativity

To return to Sasnal's *Maus* mural, Bojarska argues that '[the artist] does not seem to be interested in or devoted to shameless exposure of collective guilt, rather he intertextually reworks visual motives already present in the public sphere, in an act of self-imposed civic and artistic duty'. She writes: 'Sasnal does not accuse, he rather spins a visual reflection on the position of the bystander, on the role of the one who comes after and on the condition of this belatedness.'[40] While he may not be literally pointing a finger in this instance - the vehement 'J'Accuse...!' of Émile Zola who denounced the French government for antisemitism in 1898 in response to the Dreyfus Affair - Sasnal becomes a generator of intertextual, intersubjective intensities that produce an aesthetic shudder and, indeed, implicates the performative reader of the *Maus* mural both *in situ* and in subsequent mediums of reproduction. Taking this a step further, I propose that Sasnal releases the formless that is at the very core of antisemitism and fuses it with the somatic register of his public. This broadens and multiplies the field of reception towards the generations of postmemory in Poland and other national contexts and thus connects those who accept and reject historical complicity with their nation's troubled past to those who have been at the brunt of it.

Yet we are not simply in a world of binary identifications and disidentifications between Poles and Jews but more complicated entanglements as is evident in Sasnal's rendering of the black protagonist of the children's poem 'Murzynek Bambo'.[41] Written by the Jewish-Polish author Julian Tuwim in 1923 or 1924 and published in 1934 in the *Reader for Elementary Schools*, it uses rhyming couplets to recount the adventures

aspiration, or politics. They provoke by turns curiosity, amusement, anger, anxiety, and an aura of magic. They reveal the presence of the Jewish past in Polish consciousness, even in the most intimate spaces of Polish domesticity: on kitchen tables, bookshelves, side-boards, mantels.

E. Lehrer, *Lucky Jews*, p. 25.

40 K. Bojarska, 'Wilhelm Sasnal's Transitional Images'.

41 Although many still claim that the word *Murzyn* is neutral and does not carry racial bias, its etymology is connected to the German word *Mohr*, an outdated and racist word for people of African descent. See Agnieszka Wądołowska, '"Stop Calling me Murzyn": Black Lives Matter Sparks Linguistic Debate in Poland', *Notes from Poland*, 12 June 2020, https://notesfrompoland.com/2020/06/12/stop-calling-me-murzyn-black-lives-matter-sparks-linguistic-debate-in-poland/.

of a young black boy in Africa who enjoys reading, but can also be naughty: climbing a tree instead of drinking his milk, and refusing to take a bath out of fear that he will turn white.[42] As in 1934 Poland pulled out of the Little Treaty of Versailles, also known as the Polish Minority Treaty, which protected ethnic minorities, Tuwim's poem was a rare and radical call for tolerance and inclusion.[43] The treaty was geared primarily towards the Jewish, German, Ukrainian and White Russian minorities within Poland's new borders, situating Tuwim's poem as a progressive expansion beyond those populations. The impact of 'Murzynek Bambo' extends much farther, well into the 1970s and Wilhelm Sasnal's childhood, as he, too, owned a copy of the book and recalls its imagery during a period when Socialist Poland admitted allies from non-European socialist bloc countries to study and live in the country. Solidarity with African countries in the imperialist struggle meant that, beginning in 1955 on the occasion of the 5th World Festival of Youth and Students and ending in 1989 with the transition from socialism to a liberal democracy, Polish society became more visibly diverse. Although often exoticised in the press, 'for Polish citizens, it was one of the first opportunities to interact with non-white people after the destruction of the multicultural Second Polish Republic during the Second World War'.[44]

Taken from the book's illustrations, which were rendered by Ignacy Witz in 1948, Sasnal reproduces the poem's imagery in the featureless, black silhouette, individualised only by his white underpants and the

42 The poem was first published (with texts by other authors and including Tuwim's other two poems) in M. Falski, *Czytanka dla II klasy szkół powszechnych miejskich* (A Reader for the 2nd Grade City Public Schools), rys. (drawings by) K. Mackiewicz, K. Sopoćko, Lviv: Książnica-Atlas, 1934, p. 15 and later in February 1935 in the progressive literary magazine *Wiadomości Literackie*.

43 The Little Treaty of Versailles was signed on 28 June 1919, the same day as the Treaty of Versailles, with the League of Nations and formally established Poland as a sovereign and independent state after one hundred and twenty-three years of partitions. It declared that 'Poland undertakes to assure full and complete protection of life and liberty to all inhabitants of Poland without distinction of birth, nationality, language, race or religion' (article 2). Poland renounced the treaty at the League of Nations forum in Geneva on 13 September 1934. See http://ungarisches-institut.de/dokumente/pdf/19190628-3.pdf.

44 Richard Greenhill, 'Afro-Poland: a revolutionary friendship, captured in rare photos from 1955–1989', *The Calvert Journal*, 30 June 2021, https://www.calvertjournal.com/features/show/10455/poland-africa-rare-photos-race-bartosz-nowicki.

white book in his hand.[45] In this 'primitivist' rendering, the figure is surrounded by green foliage, accented by red birds and flowers. The white painterly stain hovering above his head and melding with his body operates like other such instances in Sasnal's oeuvre as a zone where mimetic faculty is intertwined with formlessness. Produced in 2014, at a time when minority populations in Poland have dramatically diminished, Sasnal's gesture points to an entanglement between the visible loss of difference and the amplification of antisemitism and racism in the public sphere.

Forms of Formlessness: Antisemitism and Amnesia

This mandate of examining the processes of postmemory by animating the mimetic faculty towards formlessness is linked to a profound recognition: picturing the Holocaust and giving form to the structural antisemitism at its core cannot be thought apart from the instability of an index that fuses with a host of other signs without any inherent logic. This, I argue, was already all too clear to Franz Kafka when, writing to the publisher of *The Metamorphosis* in 1915, he stipulated that the 'monstrous vermin' (in German, the doubly negated 'ungeheures Ungeziefer') to which Gregor Samsa transforms should never be depicted: 'the insect itself cannot be drawn. It cannot even be shown at a distance.'[46] In the twilight years

45 The poem was first included in the book edition of Tuwim's poems for children *Słoń Trąbalski* (with illustrations by Janina Jankowska), published by J. Przeworski in 1938. Drawings by I. Witz were made for the post-war edition, first published in 1948 (the year, in which Tuwim and Witz worked on the book) or 1949. Earlier illustrations (by Mackiewicz and Sopocko, 1937 and Jankowska, 1938) were similarly stereotyped in how they portrayed the black boy.

46 Franz Kafka in a letter to Kurt Wolff publishing company, 1915 in Franz Kafka, *The Metamorphosis*, ed. Stanley Corngold, New York: Norton, 1996, p. 70. Iris Bruce has interpreted Kafka's directive as a desire to 'maintain the ambiguity of the "vermin" signifier' at a time when modern artists were often called to augment a book's marketability through graphic flourishes; she understands the repetition of the prefix 'un' in 'ungeheure[s] Ungeziefer', as an evocation of the Freudian 'uncanny' [das Unheimliche] '...which produces feelings of fear, terror, or even humorous disbelief'. She further suggests that '"ungeheures" can be translated as "monstrous," "incredible," or "outrageous," while "Ungeziefer" [vermin] carries notions of uncleanliness with religious overtones, identifying Gregor as something unholy bringing disaster [Unheil].' See I. Bruce, 'The

of the Habsburg Monarchy, Kafka's evocation of the trope of the 'Jew parasite' became one of the most obvious allusions to antisemitic stereotypes in his work and resonates with the contexts, practices and discourses of his day, including rising nationalism, emergent Zionism and a wave of antisemitic events across Europe.[47] Exceeding one signification, the vermin metaphor has nevertheless been understood as 'a symbol of modernity par excellence' and Gregor's 'opaque body' as a *form of formlessness* through which to maintain him 'without speech or intelligible gesture, in the solitude of an indecipherable sign'.[48] More than a century later, this indexical volatility at once implicated those who are engaging with the production of memory for critical or commemorative purposes as well as those who are marshalling antisemitism and the Holocaust for reactionary objectives.[49]

Cultural and Historical Context of Kafka's *Metamorphosis*: Antisemitism, Zionism, and Yiddish Plays', in *Critical Insights: The Metamorphosis*, ed. James Whitlark, Pasadena, CA: Salem Press, 2012.

47 Alexander Bein, 'Der jüdische Parasit', *Vierteljahrshefte für Zeitgeschichte*, vol. 13, no. 2, 1965, pp. 121-49; most notably, the Zionist poet Chaim Nachman Bialik wrote the poem 'In Schchite Stot' (In the City of Slaughter) (1904) - as a response to the Kishinev Massacre in Russia (April 1903):

antlofen, wi die majss, bahalten sich, wi wanzen
un, wi di hint, gestorben
(they ran away like mice
they stayed and hid like vermin
and they died like dogs)

Translated by I. Bruce in, 'The Cultural and Historical Context of Kafka's *Metamorphosis*', p. 73. Not only did Kafka know the poem, he also knew that Bialik himself had translated it from the 'original Hebrew [...] into Yiddish' as a call for resistance (Franz Kafka, *The Diaries of Franz Kafka, 1910-1913*, ed. Max Brod, New York: Schocken, 1948, pp. 101-02). All three animals - mice, vermin and dogs - appear in Kafka's work; vermin, bedbugs and cockroaches would become some of the most dominant antisemitic tropes in Nazi propaganda.

48 F. Kafka, *The Metamorphosis*, p. 89.

49 This includes the recent revival of the vermin and parasite metaphor to mark migrants as unclean and un-European, thus as a 'contagion' that threatens the majority public sphere. In Poland, Jarosław Kaczyński, a former prime minister and leader of the Law and Justice party, stated that migrants have brought 'all sorts of parasites and protozoa, which ... while not dangerous in the organisms of these people, could be dangerous here'. *Reuters*, 15 October 2015, https://www.reuters.com/article/us-europe-migrants-poland-idUSKCN0S918B20151015. In Austria, the Freedom Party of Austria (FPÖ), which was part of the governing coalition between 2017 and 2019, published a poem titled 'The City Rat' (*Die Stadtratte*) comparing migrants to rats. Penned by the Braunau chapter, where Nazi leader Adolf Hitler was born, the poem includes the lines:

In Poland, the Law and Justice party's passing of the 2018 Amendment to the Act on the Institute of National Remembrance, is an emphatic signal that both history and memory are, indeed, contested sites and that the debates around the representability of the Holocaust are now also accompanied by legislation to prohibit and criminalise its representation. The outcome of such governmental enacted amnesia bore fruit in February 2021, when a court ruling of libel was issued by a Polish judge for a two-volume academic study by historians Barbara Engelking (Polish Academy of Sciences in Warsaw) and Jan Grabowski (University of Ottawa) on the topic of complicity by individual Poles in the murder of Jews during the Holocaust.[50] Engelking and Grabowski cited the testimony of survivors to investigate a claim that Edward Malinowski, the late mayor of Malinowo - a village outside of Warsaw - had collaborated with German soldiers, resulting in the execution of a group of eighteen Jewish people in a forest in eastern Poland. The late mayor's niece, assisted by the government-backed nationalist organisation, the Polish Anti-Defamation League, used the 2018 Amendment to the Act on the Institute of National Remembrance as the basis for her case. The verdict, which included a stipulation that Engelking and Grabowski issue a public apology for including 'inaccurate information', set an ominous

As we live down here,
so must the rats,
as guests or migrants,
even those we did not know yet,
share our way of life,
or hurry away!
(So, wie wir hier unten leben,
müssen and're Ratten eben,
die als Gäst' oder Migranten,
auch die, die wir noch gar nicht kannten,
die Art zu leben mit uns teilen!
Oder rasch von dannen eilen!)

See 'FPÖ verbreitet Hetz-Flugblatt mit rechtem Gedicht: Migranten mit Ratten gleichgesetzt' (FPÖ Distributes Hate Leaflet with a Right-Wing Poem: Equating Migrants with Rats), *Focus*, 23 April 2019, https://www.focus.de/politik/ausland/linz-wien-fpoe-provoziert-mit-ratten-gedicht-kanzler-kurz-abscheulich_id_10619347.html.

50 Barbara Engelking and Jan Grabowski (ed.), *Dalej jest noc. Losy Żydów w wybranych powiatach okupowanej Polski* (*Night without End: The Fate of Jews in German-Occupied Poland*, 2022), Warsaw: Polish-Jewish Studies, Institute of National Remembrance, 2018.

precedent for all future scholarly work on the topic.[51] Following Marina Gržinić, it becomes clear that the contemporary moment is characterised by constructed silences and the institutionalisation of processes of de-historicisation.[52] Governments seize and confiscate both history and memory, transforming them into a terrain for revision: in the case of Engelking and Grabowski, the late-mayor's niece demanded that he be officially classified as a 'Jew Saving Hero' while the authors had described him as a 'thief and Nazi collaborator'.[53] In Poland, as in many other former Eastern European nation-states, we recognise a specific type of erasure that is predicated on both a denial of responsibility and an active rewriting of the genocidal past on an individual, collective and national level. These processes of amnesia are simultaneously amplified through displays of nationalism by the state and its representatives, which include cultural, artistic, archival, political and economic institutions. It should come as no surprise, therefore, that the new federal law passed in Poland in August 2021, which sets a thirty-year time limit on each restitution case, will make it harder for Jewish survivors and their descendants to regain art or property stolen by Nazi Germany and confiscated by the former Communist regime.[54] This is only one aspect of a systematic

51 Andrew Higgins, 'Polish Court Orders Scholars to Apologize Over Holocaust Study', *New York Times*, 9 February 2021.

52 Marina Gržinić, 'Introduction: Burdened by the Past, Rethinking the Future. Eleven Theses of Memory, History, and Life', in *Opposing Colonialism, Anti-Semitism, and Turbo-Nationalism: Rethinking the Past for a New Conviviality*, ed. M. Gržinić, Jovita Pristovšek and Sophie Uitz, Newcastle-upon-Tyne: Cambridge Scholars, 2020.

53 This demand was rejected by Judge Ewa Jonczyk along with the request for $27,000 in damages. A. Higgins, 'Polish Court Orders Scholars to Apologize Over Holocaust Study'. As of August 2021, an appellate court rejected the lawsuit against Engelking and Grabowski but the plaintiff, Filomena Leszczyńska, said she would appeal to Poland's Supreme Court. Leszczyńska passed away on 8 November 2021 at the age of eighty-one. See 'Polish appeals court dismisses case against Holocaust book historians', *Reuters*, 16 August 2021, https://www.reuters.com/world/europe/polish-appeals-court-dismisses-claims-against-holocaust-book-historians-2021-08-16/.

54 The law, which passed on 14 August 2021, sparked an outcry from both the United States and Israeli governments. Israel's Prime Minister Naftali Bennett called its passage, 'a shameful decision and disgraceful contempt for the memory of the Holocaust'. See Raoul Wootliff, 'Bennett slams Polish restitution law: "Disgraceful contempt for the memory of the Holocaust"', *Times of Israel*, 14 August 2021, https://www.timesofisrael.com/liveblog_entry/bennett-slams-polish-restitution-law-disgraceful-contempt-for-the-memory-of-the-holocaust/.

logic of capture, which extends as much to property as to the archive of memory. The goal is to 'systematically change and alter a certain group's political past' and thus to 'modify and alter our concepts of the future'.[55] The Holocaust, antisemitism and the archive of memory are identified as disrupting Polish national unity, increasingly associated with a smaller, ever-more homogenised image of the 'people' (free of migrants, non-Catholics, non-heterosexual groups and other minorities).

The Double Exorcism: Separating Modernity from Coloniality

Extension of the analysis beyond Poland's frontiers reveals that contemporary Europe is performing a double exorcism as a way to maintain its façade of being the modern force of 'civilisation': as the vilification and 'cancellation' of the Cameroonian historian and philosopher Achille Mbembe in Germany has made clear, accusations of antisemitism are used to muzzle postcolonial subjects and thus separate between the two genealogies of racialisation that were produced within Europe and projected outwards onto other bodies.[56] Following the passing of legislation in Germany in March 2019 that brands the Boycott, Divestment and Sanctions movement (BDS) as antisemitic, a lecture by Mbembe that was supposed to take place at the opening of the Ruhrtriennale was cancelled on the grounds that he had 'relativized the Holocaust and denied Israel's right to exist'.[57] Revealing the current instrumentalisation of antisemitism by all parts of the political spectrum is the fact that, among those who attacked Mbembe, were Felix Klein, the German government's antisemitism commissioner, and Lorenz Deutsch, Germany's right-wing Free Democratic Party spokesperson. As Michael Rothberg has shown, the singularity of the Holocaust remains an essential cornerstone around which memory culture has been historically shaped and maintained in Germany and, thus, to compare it to any other event is to damage its quasi-sacred status.[58]

55 M. Gržinić, 'Introduction: Burdened by the Past, Rethinking the Future. Eleven Theses of Memory, History, and Life', p. 18.

56 For a rigorous analysis of the mechanisms through which capitalism produces this racialised divide, see Š. Tatlić and M. Gržinić, 'Global Capitalism's Racialization/s'.

57 Peter Kuras, 'Germany's Holocaust Remembrance Is Turning Upside Down', *Foreign Policy*, 20 February 2021.

58 Michael Rothberg, 'The Specters of Comparison', *Zeitgeister: International*

In the 2016 essay 'The Society of Enmity', Mbembe's comparison - which was not an equation - between South African apartheid and the Israeli occupation of Palestinian territories was sufficient to have him branded an antisemite. While this policing of antisemitism may at first glance appear as a cause that should justly be spearheaded by Germany, as the main perpetrator state of the Holocaust and a nation-state that has historically accomplished the most 'work' of 'coming to terms with the past' (*Vergangenheitsbewältigung*), such hyper vigilance is actually one way through which the contemporary archive of amnesia is implemented.

In the Mbembe case, accusations of antisemitism - linked to the critique of the State of Israel - are used as prime mechanisms of suppression: Germany, as a perpetrator state, regains control over discourses surrounding the Holocaust by demoting and delegitimating a postcolonial critique. Simultaneously, in this twisted logic, even as Germany takes on the moral obligation of defending Jews as the historical 'other' and supporting the existence of the State of Israel, a population of mostly Muslim migrants that arrived as guest workers or refugees lives as second-class citizens within Germany's own borders. The projection of antisemitism outward - its externalisation onto mostly Muslim minority groups - has become a way to suppress debates about the latent structural antisemitism in the majority European society. According to Helga Embacher and Jan Rybak, 'It allows the majority society to "prove" its new, enlightened, anti-antisemitic self-image, while the Muslim minority serves as the despicable "Other" enabling the moral self-reassurance of German nationalism.'[59] Thus, the permutation of antisemitism in the contemporary Euro-sphere is now organised through a paradigm in which the Jew's unique status as a historical victim is threatened by the postcolonial subject's call for a multidirectional critique that extends to other crimes and traumas.[60] Though

Perspectives from Culture and Society, Goethe-Institut, May 2020, https://www.goethe.de/prj/zei/en/pos/21864662.html. Reprinted in this book, pp. 74–80.

59 Helga Embacher and Jan Rybak, 'Antisemitism in Muslim Communities and Islamophobia in the context of the Gaza War 2014: Austria and Germany', *openDemocracy*, 1 October 2015, https://www.opendemocracy.net/en/anti-semitism-in-muslim-communities-islamophobia-gaza-war/.

60 The Herero and Namaqua genocide, occurring between 1904 and 1908, was waged by the German Empire in what was then German South West Africa (Namibia).

they are positioned as competitors for the scant space of identity and memory, the lives of both Jews and postcolonial subjects have been historically organised according to the internal processes of racialisation and 'othering' that govern the constitution of European nation-states along the dual paradigm of modernity/coloniality.

Performing Memory Knots in a Multidirectional Archive

While nation-states may use the legislative process to regulate history and memory and to try to separate modernity from coloniality, Sasnal's work points to the fact that the phantom signifier of antisemitism and racism continues to flow and mutate through the body of the post-Holocaust and postcolonial nation-state - conceived as a nervous system - and is prone to erupt both publicly and privately at any time. This is not a one-way process as both Michel Foucault and Frantz Fanon make clear; rather, the structural racism of the nation-state - linked to bio- and necro-politics - simultaneously produces racialised 'others' while also infecting the body politic of the majority in ambiguous ways. Rather than targeting the nation-state as an administrative entity, however, many of Sasnal's paintings become memory knots for the shared experience of the Shoah as it implicated and continues to inhabit the bodies, psyches and habitats that Poles and Jews shared for centuries. What do we make of the clouds of blurry smoke that swirl above a barren field in *Kraków-Warszawa (Cracow-Warsaw)* (2006)? Moving from the mimetic to the formless, we may be witnessing the everyday life of farmers working the land; or, more ominously, observing the smoke that was permanently hovering over certain environments, produced by the systematic murder of Jews, neighbours, human beings. What is a beloved territory for some, remains a landscape of trauma for others.

It was the first genocide of the twentieth century and saw the ethnic extermination of between 24,000 and 100,000 Hereros and 10,000 Namaqua. According to the 1985 United Nations's Whitaker Report, some 65,000 Herero (80 per cent of the total Herero population) and 10,000 Nama (50 per cent of the total Nama population) were killed between 1904 and 1907. See also *Walter Nuhn, Sturm über Südwest. Der Hereroaufstand von 1904*, Koblenz, DEU: Bernard & Graefe-Verlag, 1989.

Michael Rothberg's concept of 'multidirectional memory', which he developed approximately two decades after Hirsch, helps us map out the stakes of this ongoing mutation and intersectionality beyond the claims of nation-states through a creative appropriation. It enables us to make dialogical, intercultural connections between diverse archives of memory that are 'subject to ongoing negotiation, cross-referencing, and borrowing'.[61] According to Rothberg, we must remain attentive to the entanglement of various traditions of genocide and gestures of remembrance as, he argues, public memory is not under the sole ownership of any one people or nation-state and it is impossible to try and keep it static, fortified, or under sanction. Rather, the mobility and dynamism of memory means that the Nazi genocide of European Jews needs to be considered transnationally and transculturally, in its ever-growing multiplicity and crosspollination with other histories and memories, including those of slavery, colonialism and apartheid. This is not an equalising gesture, on Rothberg's part, but rather an attempt to think comparatively and lay the ethical groundwork for justice.[62] He writes:

> an ethics of multidirectional memory involves creating fidelity... with the multiple events and historical legacies that define any situation. *A politics built on that ethical foundation will require a notion of transnational, comparative justice that can negotiate conflicting and something mutually exclusive demands made on an unstable and shifting terrain.*[63]

61 M. Rothberg, *Multidirectional Memory: Remembering the Holocaust in the Age of Decolonization*, Stanford, CA: Stanford University Press, 2009, p. 3; Mikhail Bakhtin has offered the most sustained concept of the dialogic in *The Dialogic Imagination: Four Essays*, ed. Michael Holquist and trans. Caryl Emerson and M. Holquist, London and Austin: University of Texas Press, 1981.

62 M. Rothberg, 'The Spectres of Comparison', pp. 79–80 in this book:

> The theory of multidirectional memory does not presuppose that all articulations of public memory are equally valid; we certainly need an ethics of comparison to distinguish the valences of multidirectional articulations. Some comparisons deserve to be taken seriously; some do not. Some comparisons lead to greater solidarity among victims; some lead to increased conflict. Some comparisons may turn into forms of facile equation, but comparison usually involves distinctions of genre and scale. In this context, the theory of multidirectional memory suggests, above all, that the fear of comparison that currently reigns in Germany could itself be productively rethought ... .

63 M. Rothberg, *Multidirectional Memory*, p. 22. Emphasis mine.

Is this an easy or clearly delineated process? Choosing to embrace multidirectional memory is one of the most burdened, strenuous and fraught options, as the gulf between different archives of memory become evermore polarised and the bandwidth of identity politics becomes ever narrower and reductively articulated around the bastion of the nation-state. Here, Sasnal's *Arab I* and *Arab II* (both 2006), along with *Palestinian* (2008), perform an opening up to such a difficult linking. It is not only the inclusion of these subjects in the artist's repertoire but the sensorial connectivity that Sasnal forges, via a transversal shudder, between the genocide of Jews in the Holocaust, the establishment of the Jewish State in 1948 and the Palestinian trauma of the *Nakba* (The Catastrophe) of the same year.

There is a particular resonance between the grouping of three figures in *Shoah (Forest)* (2003) and the woman holding tomatoes in *Palestinian* (2008). In both works, the green background, with its varied modulations, creates an almost impossible spatial framework for its protagonists. In the one, this green non-site communicates the intrinsic fear of extermination (by Jews who escaped to the forests) while, in the other, it provokes a reflection on the impossibility of becoming a subject (for Palestinians under conditions of Israeli Occupation). Sasnal elides the non-sites of background and foreground as Jewish bodies and Palestinian faces dissolve into painterly gestures. They are both equally *dis-figured* and *un-figured*, loosened and unbounded from the strictures of mimesis towards the threshold of the formless and often beyond it. Without any explicit indexicality, we are led to consider the loss of legal status, sovereignty and the disintegration into conditions of bare life that made possible the genocide of European Jewry as much as the unattainability of legal status and sovereignty for the Palestinian people when they are effectively transformed into bare life. These are not uniquely Polish, Jewish or Palestinian histories or collective memories of extreme violence that haunt our contemporary public space but mutually entangled ones. As Rothberg reminds us, 'even if it were desirable - as it sometimes seems to be - to maintain a wall, or *cordon sanitaire*, between different histories, it is not possible to do so. Memories are mobile; histories are implicated in each other.'[64] Through

64 *Ibid.*, p. 313.

formlessness, Sasnal is showing us a path towards multidirectional memory and beyond the zero-sum game of contemporary agendas of nation-states and their formalisation and instrumentalisation of identity politics. Yet this project is far from an abstract aesthetic proposition or an objective scientific method; on the contrary, it requires the participation of a situated spectator, one who implicates their embodied knowledge in a long-term process and is willing to experience and negotiate feelings of confusion, pain and anger along the way. In the words of Donna J. Haraway: 'the only way to find a larger vision is to be somewhere in particular.'[65] Towards a multidirectional memory, we engage with the formless from our limited locations and partial perspectives, grounded in a body that is constituted by violent and traumatic histories and post-memories while navigating their reconfiguration as sites of amnesia in the age of neoliberal global capital.

Communities of Implication

Sited within these overlapping contexts, Sasnal's paintings affirm and accept the burden of future generations. Is it possible to build bridges between remembrances so that a memory culture does not remain exclusive, competitive or delineated by the agendas of the nation-state? As Europe - writ large and small - continues to expose its own mechanisms of internal constitution via the social fabrication of race, and as Poland grapples with the censored trauma of the Holocaust through palimpsests of post-socialism and neoliberal global capitalism, we need to consider Sasnal's oeuvre as an urgent proposition on how to shape 'communities of implication'.[66] This term has been proposed by anthropologist Erica Lehrer in her study on 'orphaned objects' that entered Polish museum collections after the extermination of their Jewish owners. Lehrer draws on the writings of anthropologists Ivan Karp and Corinne Kratz to foreground multiple 'relations of implication'

65 Donna J. Haraway, 'Situated Knowledges: The Science Question in Feminism and the Privilege of Partial Perspective', *Feminist Studies*, vol. 14, no. 3, Autumn, 1988, p. 590.

66 E. Lehrer, 'Material Kin: "Communities of Implication" in Post-Colonial, Post-Holocaust Ethnographic Collections', in Margareta von Oswald and Jonas Tinius (ed.), *Across Anthropology: Troubling Colonial Legacies, Museums, and the Curatorial*, Leuven: Leuven University Press, 2020.

towards these objects, which bear the historical traces of a multi-ethnic, multi-religious pre-war Polish society in which Jewish and Catholic neighbours lived side by side. The 'proximity, exchange, and hybridity' of these communities was accompanied by 'cultural boundary maintenance via mutual endogamy and prejudice, as well as anti-Jewish symbolic (and real) violence'.[67] Lehrer is not only foregrounding the positive memories of pre-war Poland's multiplicity, but also the role of the Polish citizenry as 'implicated subjects' in the destruction of their indigenous Jewish community. This notion, also inspired by Michael Rothberg, attempts to expand the experience of the Holocaust to intersectional subject positions. 'Implicated subjects,' he writes, are the 'large and heterogeneous collection of subjects who enable and benefit from traumatic violence without taking part in it directly.' The category, 'helps direct our attention to the conditions of possibility of violence as well as its lingering impact and suggests new routes of opposition... implication draws attention to how we are entwined with and folded into ("im-plicated in") histories and situations that surpass our agency as individual subjects.'[68] By reframing these orphaned objects in Poland's museums as part of previously entangled communities that were separated by a genocide, which left traumatic wounds in different populations, Lehrer argues that one can also 'allow for (or encourage) a future oriented community'.[69]

In Sasnal's oeuvre, implication is often embedded in the prosaic, as suggested in *Cabbages* (2013). In this heaping of vegetables, Jews and Catholics - and anyone else with familial roots in Poland - may recollect the prime staple of the Polish kitchen. Such intimacy extends across religious affiliations, as much as generations, and beyond Poland's borders with recipes that have been shared and recreated in various Diasporas. Filling a landscape marked by a foreboding sky, the cabbages may conjure associations with the mounds of objects or body parts that remained after the extermination of Jewish concentration camp prisoners. In this visual and mental leap - from cabbages to corpses - Sasnal

67 *Ibid.*, pp. 297–98.
68 M. Rothberg, 'Trauma Theory, Implicated Subjects, and the Question of Israel/ Palestine', *Profession*, May 2014, https://profession.mla.org trauma-theory-implicated-subjects-and-the-question-of-israel-palestine/.
69 E. Lehrer, 'Material Kin', pp. 302–03.

performs both the implication (in a shared culinary culture) and the separation (by genocide) of Poland's various indigenous communities. He initiates a similar process in *Section Through Poland* (2014), a triangulation between a potato plant taking root in the (Polish) soil, an elevation rendering of a church and white horizontal strokes suggestive of barbed wire. This was once a shared land of collective traditions, ingredients and eating habits cutting across different faiths (...the love affair with *ziemniaki* or *kartofel* being only one example of this shared habitus); yet the fact that three million Polish Jews were exterminated in their own land suggests that it was also an environment permeated by antisemitism, propagated in part by the deeply ingrained structures and broad reach of the Catholic Church.[70] With Sasnal, we might ask: what would it take for Poland to become a community of implication once again?

Broadening Lehrer's concept beyond the Polish context, we realise that there are orphaned objects, implicated subjects and possibilities for communities of implication in all countries that have gone through modern processes of nation-state formation. At the crux of these processes are the twin dynamics of modernity and coloniality that sustain biopolitical and necropolitical techniques that manufacture forms of life that matter and bare life that does not. In various places at different times, the genocide, ethnic cleansing and occupation of people has been accompanied by the orphaning, pillaging and protection of objects. It is easy to think of all those paintings and artefacts in European museums that are the result of colonisation, Aryanisation, Nazi looting and Communist expropriation as well as the souvenirs of

70 According to historian Dariusz Libionka, we must remain attentive to the complexity of the Catholic Church's attitude towards the destruction of Jews in Poland. Nevertheless, he writes that, particularly in the 1930s, the Catholic Church largely assimilated the widely held belief that Jews were a 'problem' and that they posed 'an economic and a cultural threat, and a threat to Polish national identity. The Jews, according to right-wing ideology, had given birth to Bolshevism and were the reason for its successes. This approach was warmly adopted by many members of the Catholic Church, who supplemented and enriched right-wing anti-Jewish rhetoric with traditional elements taken from Church doctrine.' See D. Libionka, 'The Catholic Church in Poland and the Holocaust, 1939 - 1945', in *The Holocaust and the Christian World*, ed. Carol Rittner, Stephen D. Smith and Irena Steinfeldt, London: Paulist Press, 2000, p. 74, https://www.yadvashem.org/download/about_holocaust/christian_world/libionka.pdf.

conquest and dispossession that have entered private homes. Yet there are also stories of individuals guarding the objects of their expatriated or disappeared neighbours, like the case of the *Sarajevo Haggadah*, which escaped destruction during the Second World War and the Yugoslav Wars;[71] or more quotidian incidents where Jewish families entrusted photographs to gentile neighbours as they were about to be deported.[72]

Enfolded within modernity, we are all implicated subjects who belong to the post-Holocaust paradigm as much as to post-colonialism. This means that there is an urgency to communicate - and also control - the vast network of 'memory knots' that resonate in the public sphere as unfinished legacies. From the current perspective, the struggles of how and what to remember and commemorate intersect with a surge in nationalism, populism and an ever-intensifying neoliberal capitalism that has spawned a new wave of antisemitism while recycling familiar tropes. In other words, the symbology and processes of racialisation that led to the necropolitics of the Holocaust returns as a perverse symptom of necro-capitalism. We have seen how this upsurge - that irrationally elides between the Holocaust and novel forms of economic, social and cultural dispossession - has been routinely weaponised by various actors to stigmatise issues and individuals and create borders between 'us' and 'them' as much as to single out Jews in particular. In tandem to this rearticulation, memory is in the process of being *formalised* by nation-state through laws, memorials, exhibitions and other sanctioned outputs that effectively revise, silence and instrumentalise histories towards extreme right- and left-wing ideologies and political ends.

It has never been simple to confront - let alone visually represent - the Holocaust and the antisemitism that enabled the categorical

71 The Haggadah was hidden in a countryside mosque in the region of Bjelasnica after Derviš Korkut, a Muslim librarian at the National Museum, managed to smuggle it out of Sarajevo after the occupation of the Kingdom of Yugoslavia by the Axis powers and the Ustashe in 1941. During the Yugoslav Wars, it was discovered on the floor of during a break-in at the National Museum. The inspector Fahrudin Čebo moved it to an underground bank vault where it survived the Siege of Sarajevo and returned to the Jewish community in 1995.

72 Joseph Berger, 'The Things They Left Behind: Photographs from Poland's Lost Jews', *New York Times*, 28 February 2007, https://www.nytimes.com/2007/02/28/arts/design/28yesh.html.

transformation of so many millions of people into bare life. Yet what Wilhelm Sasnal has developed in the last twenty years is an oeuvre through which to encounter a specific Polish history of cohabitation and genocide that still animates the present. It is a contemporary practice of postmemory that blurs boundaries between mimeticism and abstraction in order to unleash a discomforting *formlessness* that is at once the precinct of antisemitism, bare life and the general equivalent of capital. Through formlessness he creates a multidirectional landscape where memory knots reveal historical relations between Jews and Poles and interweave with other nationalities, ethnicities and peoples. It is a proposal for a global community of dialogical implication in which the post-1945 and post-1989 worlds cannot be separated.

Kraków-Warszawa (Cracow-Warsaw), 2006

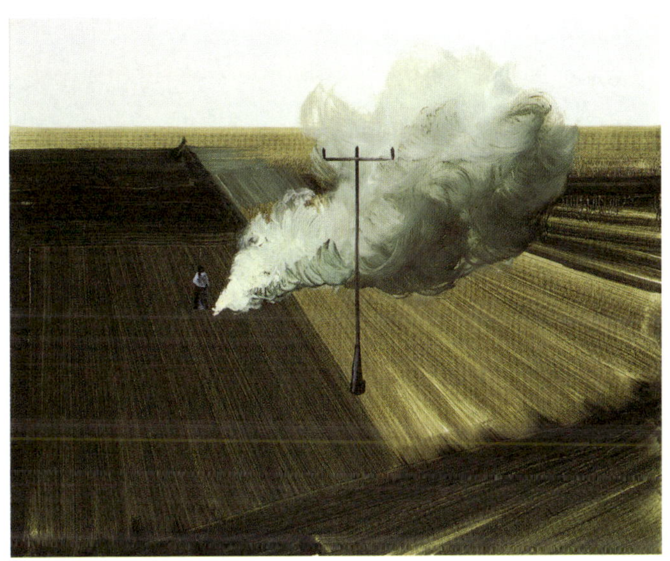

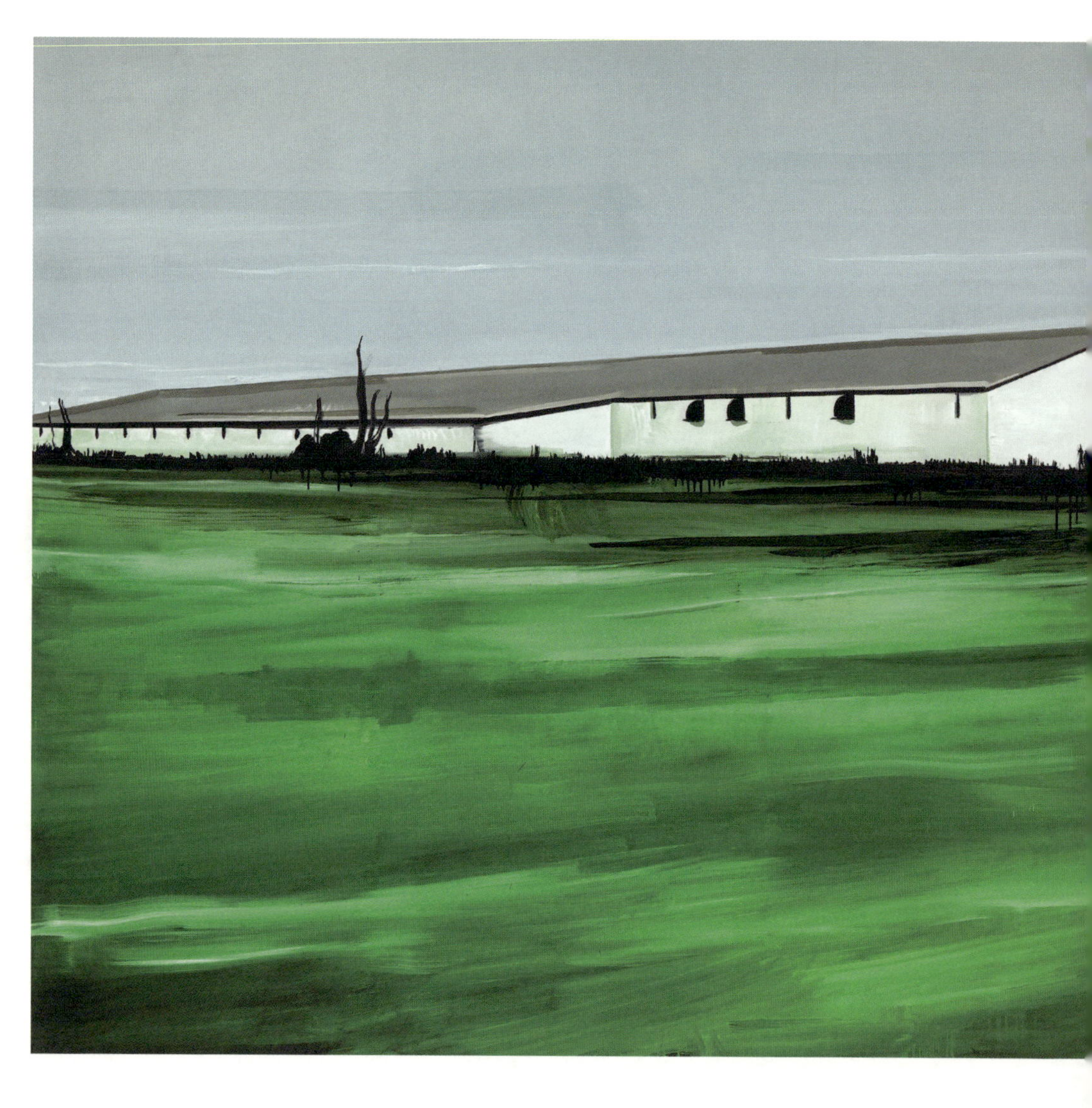

Pigsty, 2011

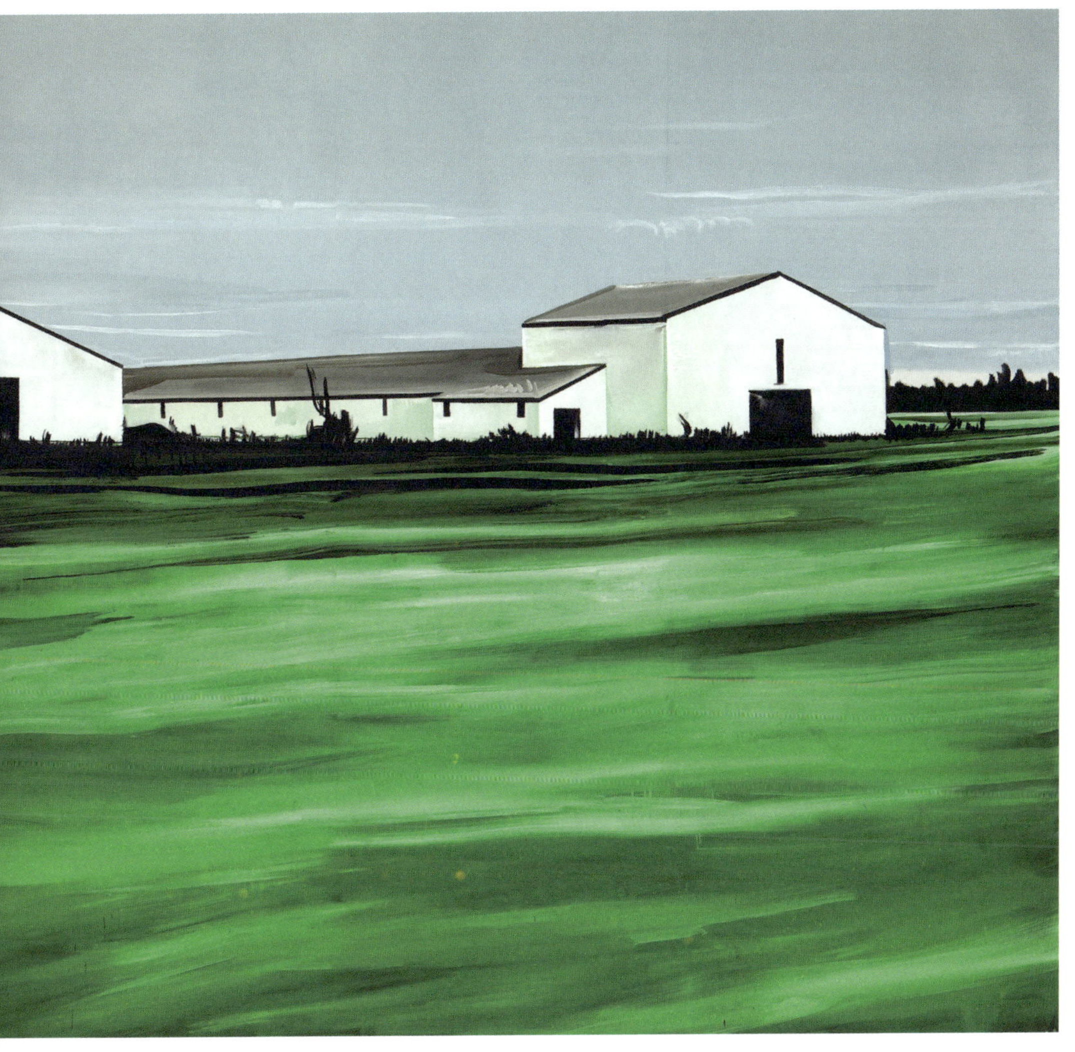

It Looks Gloomy Up Close
By Piotr Forecki

Translated from the Polish by Aleksandra Paszkowska

Since the debate around the Jedwabne pogrom - the massacre of Jews in the Polish town of Jedwabne on 10 July 1941 - began in the early 2000s, a wave of Holocaust negationism in Poland has spilt into the centre of public discourse. Rather than somewhere in the periphery, pages of fascist papers or clandestine samizdats, it is right there, in the so-called mainstream. This Polish kind of negationism does not involve claims that the Holocaust never happened, that gas chambers never existed or were used for something else. Such a radical variant has never taken root locally, invalidated by the official martyrological vision of the Second World War, whose memory serves as the basis for national identity. The Holocaust denialism that is currently practised in Poland, which consists of rejecting various forms of Polish people's complicity, can best be described by Michael Shafir's term 'deflective negationism'. According to Shafir, a strong presence of deflective negationism is especially felt in countries whose citizens aided Nazi Germans in killing Jews - and attempts are now being made to undermine that fact. In Poland, evidence testifying to the scale of complicity has only been mounting. With it, negationism advances, dictated by a desire to return to a time before Jan Tomasz Gross - to an innocent and idyllic Poland whose boundaries have been violated by the writer's 2000 book *Sąsiedzi. Historia zagłady żydowskiego miasteczka* (*Neighbors: The Destruction of the Jewish Community in Jedwabne, Poland*, 2001); to the homeland of

Żegota, Jan Karski, Irena Sendlerowa, the Ulma family and perhaps poor Christians looking at the ghetto.[1]

Gross's discussion of Jedwabne was followed by a backlash. This term 'defensive negationism' aptly describes the defensive yet confrontational reactions to the problem. The so-called 'new memory policy' tied to no specific party is the defining feature of this defensive campaign, in progress for more than fifteen years addressing Poles and an international public. Although the policy has been applied regardless of party in power, it intensified under the Law and Justice Party when the right-wing populist party regained the presidency and parliamentary majority in 2015.

Law and Justice (*Prawo i Sprawiedliwość*) had laid the politics of memory as the foundation of its agenda. It set domestic and foreign tasks for its historical policy, and, most importantly, institutionalised history making by establishing or supporting institutes, museums and redoubts to defend Poland's good name. Moreover, Law and Justice has persistently tried to subordinate existing institutions that shape the memory of the Holocaust by filling public offices with faithful practitioners of the new memory policy, case in point: the nominations of former Law and Justice Prime Minister Beata Szydło as board member of the Auschwitz-Birkenau State Museum Council and non-scholar Monika Krawczyk as director of the Jewish Historical Institute, Warsaw. The POLIN Museum of the History of Polish Jews, Warsaw has also been subject to political personnel changes. More than a decade earlier, party activists teamed up with intellectuals from the conservative think tank Ośrodek Myśli Politycznej (Center for Political Thought) in Kraków to coin the vocabulary for deflective negationism, which has circulated in the public arena ever since. Key terms from their post-Jedwabne

1 Żegota was the code name for the Council to Aid Jews with the Government Delegation for Poland. Jan Karski was an official of the Polish underground government under Nazi occupation who famously reported on the extermination of Jewish people to Western authorities from 1940–43. Polish social worker Irena Sendler, who has been recognised as Righteous Among the Nations, is said to have saved 2,500 Jewish children with her network of collaborators. Villagers Józef Ulma and Wiktoria Ulma are considered martyrs by the Polish Catholic Church as they were executed by Nazi Germans for hiding Jews in their home. 'A Poor Christian Looks at the Ghetto' is the ironic title of a 1943 poem by Nobel Prize winner Czesław Miłosz.

handbook include: 'getting Poland off its knees', 'the pedagogy of shame', 'affirmative patriotism', 'the patriotism of tomorrow' and 'an end to self-flagellation'.

Examples of deflective negationism abound in statements by major Polish politicians, journalists, commentators and clergy. Consider these public appearances by successive ministers of education. When political journalist Monika Olejnik on her popular talk show *Kropka nad i* in July 2016 asked Minister Anna Zalewska who committed the Jedwabne atrocity, the official was evasive and apparently unwilling to quote the investigation's official findings: 'Jedwabne is a historical fact that has attracted many misunderstandings, many very biased opinions.' To Olejnik's correction that Polish people burnt their Jewish neighbours alive in a locked barn, Zalewska replied that this was merely the journalist's opinion 'repeated after Mr Gross'. She also stated that 'an in-depth analysis of Mr Gross's books' by other historians had shown how 'biased, full of lies and confusion' their content was. Zalewska's successor, Minister Dariusz Piontkowski, advocated for the exhumation of the pogrom victims in order to 'resolve everything once and for all'.[2] In October 2019, the current Minister of Education Przemysław Czarnek called an art installation by Dorota Nieznalska with the names of towns where Poles had murdered Jews 'an anti-Polish scandal'.[3] 'Anti-Polish slander'[4] was what Czarnek said of the monumental publication *Dalej jest noc. Losy Żydów w wybranych powiatach okupowanej Polski* (2018; *Night without End: The Fate of Jews in German-Occupied Poland*, 2022), the product of long and arduous research by a team of experts edited by Barbara Engelking and Jan Grabowski.

2 Anna Zalewska in an interview with Monika Olejnik, *Kropka nad i*, TVN24, 13 July 2016, https://tvn24.pl/programy/kto-odpowiada-za-pogrom-kielecki-rozne-byly-zawilosci-historyczne-ra660807-3187927.

3 Sebastian Białach, 'Wojewoda lubelski chce usunięcia instalacji artystycznej. "To antypolski skandal"' (The Lublin Voivode Wants Artistic Installation Removed: 'This is an anti-Polish scandal'), Onet.pl, 19 October 2019, https://wiadomosci.onet.pl/lublin/lublin-przemyslaw-czarnek-chce-usuniecia-instalacji-doroty-nieznalskiej/4zh29ek.

4 Przemysław Czarnek in an interview with Dorota Kania, *Rozmowy poranka*, Polskie Radio 24, 23 March 2021, https://www.polskieradio.pl/130/5553/Artykul/2702449,Minister-edukacji-12-kwietnia-mozliwy-powrot-uczniow-do-szkol.

Questions about attitudes towards Jedwabne as well as Gross's *Neighbors* and the author himself have become a test of 'patriotism' - or more accurately: of readiness for performing negationism as a public service. For example, this was the case during the 2015 presidential campaign. At a debate on the public television channel TVP1, the incumbent President Bronisław Komorowski was put on the spot by Law and Justice candidate Andrzej Duda to explain why Komorowski had written in his 2011 letter on the seventieth anniversary of the Jedwabne pogrom that 'a nation of victims had to acknowledge the inconvenient truth that it had also been the perpetrator'.[5] Duda asked:

> Mr President, tell me what your policy for protecting Poland's good name looks like if you have used phrases in your speeches that destroy actual historical memory, belying what is so extraordinarily important to us so that we are not falsely accused by others that we participated in the Holocaust. You know very well, sir, that the Polish nation did not take part in the Holocaust.[6]

In the summer of 2016 - shortly before the seventy-fifth anniversary of the Jedwabne massacre - candidates for the new Board of Experts of the Institute of National Remembrance (INR), routinely selected by the Senate of the Republic of Poland, were subjected to a peculiar test of readiness for defending Poland's good name against accusations of the Polish people's complicity in the Holocaust. The test question on their attitude to Gross's scholarship was posed by Law and Justice Senator and historian Jan Żaryn. The Jedwabne problem was evoked once again when the Board of Experts was selecting candidates for the position of the INR's chairman. One candidate was Marek Chrzanowski, a history teacher and school director in the town of Puławy. He declared that he

5 The Chancellery of the President of the Republic of Poland, 'Uroczystości w 70. rocznicę mordu w Jedwabnem' (Celebrations on the 70th Anniversary of the Murder in Jedwabne), Bronisław Komorowski Archive, official website of the President of the Republic of Poland, 10 July 2011, https://www.prezydent.pl/kancelaria/archiwum/archiwum-bronislawa-komorowskiego/aktualnosci/wydarzenia/uroczystosci-w-70-rocznice-mordu-w-jedwabnem,14322.

6 'Polityka historyczna w debacie. Duda zagrał Jedwabnem. Prezydent zrewanżował się pytaniem o SKOK i dał miniwykład' (Historical Politics in the Debate. Duda Played Jedwabne. ...), TVP, 18 May 2015, https://www.tvp.info/20106395/jedwabne-w-debacie-prezydenckiej-tvp.

considered a reassessment of the crime and the exhumation of victims an important task for the INR. 'As a history teacher, I don't know what I'm supposed to tell the children – what happened there,' the candidate claimed. He added that Gross's book contained 'allegations that attack Poland's good name', while the INR's 2002 publication *Wokół Jedwabnego* (Around Jedwabne) was 'a failure'; therefore, according to Chrzanowski, one should 'reach the truth because the affair is damaging to Poland's image'.[7]

At that time, the INR's Board of Experts recommended Dr Jarosław Szarek as chairman. At a hearing in the Parliament's Komisja Sprawiedliwości i Praw Człowieka (Justice and Human Rights Commission) on 19 July 2016, Szarek explicitly admitted to having a fixed opinion on Gross and Jedwabne. To the simple question 'What happened on 10 July 1941 in Jedwabne and who was the perpetrator of the crime that took place that day?', asked by MP Michał Szczerba from Civic Platform (Platforma Obywatelska), Szarek replied: 'The perpetrators were Germans who forcibly exploited a group of Poles in the [Nazi] machine of terror. The full responsibility rests with German totalitarianism.'[8]

The rhetoric is continued by Karol Nawrocki, the former Director of the Gdańsk Museum of the Second World War in Gdańsk and INR chairman since July 2021. In an interview for Radio Gdańsk in May 2021, he revealed what he had to say about Jedwabne. He deemed the perpetrators of that crime to have been traitors of the Polish state as they had committed the act against the official position of the local government. According to Nawrocki, they had thus been expelled from the Polish national community. Nawrocki did not stop there. 'Fabulists, haters and academic charlatans'[9] – he said of researchers from the Polish Center for

7 'Kandydat na prezesa IPN pytany o Jedwabne. "Nie wiem, co się tam wydarzyło"' (Candidate for the President of the Institute of National Remembrance When Asked About Jedwabne: 'I don't know what happened there'), *Gazeta.pl*, 18 July 2016, https://wiadomosci.gazeta.pl/wiadomosci/7,114883,20416764,kandydat-na-prezesa-ipn-pytany-o-jedwabne-nie-wiem-co-sie.html.

8 Komisja Sprawiedliwości i Praw Człowieka /nr 31/, Zapis przebiegu posiedzenia komisji (Commission Hearing Minutes), Sejm.gov.pl, 19 July 2016, https://www.sejm.gov.pl/Sejm8.nsf/biuletyn.xsp?skrnr=SPC-31.

9 Norbert Nowotnik, 'Doktor Karol Nawrocki o roli IPN, zbrodni w Jedwabnem

Holocaust Research at the Institute of Philosophy and Sociology of the Polish Academy of Sciences in Warsaw, adding that the INR would not welcome them for debate if he became chairman. Apparently, attitudes towards the centre and its publications - alongside quizzes on Jedwabne - had become another qualification test to hold public office in Poland.

In recent years, similar statements have only been growing in number. Together, they constitute a curious Polish lexicon of deflective Holocaust negationism - which will perhaps someday be recorded in writing or at least be used as an expanding body of evidence in a trial against 'the assassins of memory',[10] as Yosef Hayim Yerushalmi called Holocaust deniers. For the moment, Holocaust researchers have been taken to court instead. An organisation called Reduta Dobrego Imienia (Good Name Redoubt) or the Polish League Against Defamation, which is closely tied to the ruling Law and Justice Party, sought to discredit and publicly stigmatise scholars Barbara Engelking and Jan Grabowski. The Redoubt was not the first to do so. After the 2018 publication of *Night without End*, the Polish Center for Holocaust Research (the book's editors Engelking and Grabowski work at the centre) came under attack by the authorities with support from the INR, the Pilecki Institute, Radio Maryja and other right-wing media outlets. The role of the media was also evident in February 2019 when recent findings on Polish people's complicity in the Holocaust were presented at a conference in Paris. TVP's evening news broadcast *Wiadomości* showed photographs of Gross, Grabowski, Engelking and Jacek Leociak stylised to resemble arrest warrants and captioned 'a festival of anti-Polish lies'. The faces of the centre's researchers have frequently appeared on magazine covers and circulate online as the embodiment of the anti-Polish element that fouls its own nest. Also on TVP's *Wiadomości*, right-wing journalist and Law and Justice backer Bronisław Wildstein simply called these scholars 'Poland's enemies'.

i kontrowersjach ws. "Burego"' (Doctor Karol Nawrocki on the Role of the Institute of National Remembrance, the Jedwabne Crime and the Controversy Over 'Bury'), *Polska Agencja Prasowa*, 19 May 2015, https://www.pap.pl/aktualnosci/news%2C874882%2Cdoktor-karol-nawrocki-o-roli-ipn-zbrodni-w-jedwabnem-i-kontrowersjach-ws.

10 Yosef Hayim Yerushalmi, *Zakhor: Jewish History and Jewish Memory*, Seattle: University of Washington Press, 1996, p. 116.

At the same time, if someone from a distance calls by its proper name what can be seen up close and what has long been known, a wave of outrage surges. This happened after then-FBI Director James B. Comey's speech at the United States Holocaust Memorial Museum Annual Dinner in Washington DC on 15 April 2015. Comey pointed out that not only Germans, but also the 'good people' of Poland, Hungary and many other countries 'helped murder millions' of Jews. An astonishing avalanche of criticism against the American official rolled out in the Polish media, combined with demands for corrections and an apology. Though astonishing, it was not surprising: despite Comey's not having said anything shocking or untruthful, the reaction was easy to predict knowing the Poles' hypersensitivity to the subject matter - which, crucially, is relatively widespread rather than limited to the ruling party and its supporters.

This was highlighted by the Polish readers' reactions to Masha Gessen's opinion piece on the court case against Grabowski and Engelking, published in *The New Yorker* on 26 March 2021. The reactions were inflamed by the article's unfortunate lead: 'Scholars face defamation suits, and potential criminal charges, in the Polish government's effort to exonerate the nation of any role in the murders of three million Jews during the Nazi occupation.' Gessen's explanations of what they had in mind or what the English syntax and the logical order of that sentence means in the broader context of their text were futile. The public closed its ears to assurances that the piece did not preposterously assign responsibility to Poles for the deaths of three million Jews. The Polish media seethed with indignation, the Polish embassy in Washington 'undertook measures' and the Vice Minister of Foreign Affairs Szymon Szynkowski vel Sęk talked of a firm reaction by the diplomatic service. The Polish Center for Holocaust Research issued its own statement, while director Piotr Cywiński responded on behalf of the Auschwitz-Birkenau State Museum. Gessen was also sent hateful, threatening e-mails. In their statement, published in *Gazeta Wyborcza*, Gessen said that the situation gave them 'barely a taste of the intellectual climate in which Polish historians of the Holocaust now live'.[11]

11 Masha Gessen, 'Gessen: "it is shocking that so many people have chosen to ignore the rules of logic in reacting to my piece"', statement sent to *Gazeta Wyborcza*, 30 March 2021, https://wyborcza.pl/7,173236,26935568,gessen-it-is-shocking-that-so-many-people-have-chosen-to-ignore.html?disableRedirects=true.

The media frenzy exposed the effects of the politics of memory and deflective Holocaust negationism pursued in Poland for the last fifteen years. Was it not for a historical policy, which, perforce, feeds national narcissism, the one sentence from Gessen's opinion piece might have never attracted the attention of *New Yorker* readers across the pond. However, as a result of Polish moral outrage, a scandal erupted and our native patriots were once again able to take a roll-call among their ranks. Piotr Cywiński did not meet with equally universal disapproval when he had accused Gessen of negationism (*sic!*) and incompetence in a specially issued statement. Cywiński wrote that he had found 'so many lies and misrepresentations' in the opinion piece that it was hard to believe in 'such a coincidence'. Most of all, the Director of the Auschwitz-Birkenau State Museum apparently must have ignored all recent scholarly findings, including ones regarding the third phase of the Holocaust, if he used the word 'incidents' (*przypadki*) when referring to the denunciation and murder of Jews by Poles during the Second World War.

Unlike Gessen's opinion piece, Cywiński's statement did not come under close linguistic scrutiny. After a brief consultation of the Polish dictionary, one will immediately realise that *przypadki* are unforeseeable events, coincidences, isolated incidents, unpleasant and unusual. The word cannot apply to Polish people's complicity in the Holocaust because - rather than being 'incidental' - that complicity was characterised by repeated patterns of behaviour and large-scale tendencies. Using the word 'incident' to talk about a vast body of scholarship on Poles aiding Germans in murdering Jews diminishes the crimes committed. It is an instance of deflective negationism that Cywiński supported through the power of his authority as Auschwitz-Birkenau Museum Director.

The word 'incidents' has its place in a more complex vocabulary of the Polish elites who are trying to erase the problem of Polish people's complicity in the Holocaust or at least distance themselves from it. In recent years, as a result of discursive actions, the blame for murdering Jews has been shifted to Polish peasants - who are usually portrayed as primitive and demoralised people acting on their lowest impulses. The rural working class has been depicted as the 'ignorant masses', ready to rob and barbarically murder Jews out of wartime poverty; a hungry, poor, greedy and contemptible mob whose crimes arise from 'peasant mentality' and circumstance. Such interpretations have been penned by historians, sociologists and commentators as early as the Jedwabne debate; since then, their number has only grown.

The theme of the common people's wrongdoings against Jews or 'folk antisemitism' has also entered Polish cinema. It has been explored in different ways using different conventions by, for instance, Anka Sasnal and Wilhelm Sasnal (*Z daleka widok jest piękny* (*It Looks Pretty from a Distance*), 2011), Władysław Pasikowski (*Pokłosie* (*Aftermath*), 2012), Przemysław Wojcieszek (*Sekret*, 2012), Marcin Wrona (*Demon*, 2015), Piotr Chrzan (*Klezmer*, 2015), Paweł Pawlikowski (*Ida*, 2013) and Michał Rogalski (*Letnie przesilenie/Unser letzter Sommer* (*Summer Solstice*), 2015). The list of titles testifying to 'the rural turn' in the search for Jewish corpses and antisemitism is indeed long. So far, no films have been produced about ghetto benches at universities, young National Democratic racists from the 'good homes' of the intelligentsia or the clergy setting their Catholic audience against Jews. As an exception, Wojciech Smarzowski's *Wesele* (2021) was the first feature in the history of Polish cinema to draw attention to the Catholic Church's role in inciting hatred that leads to physical violence - but one swallow does not a summer make. The problem of the Poles' complicity in the Holocaust has not only had a peasant's face - or rather, an ugly and primitive mug - on the big screen, but it has also been mapped onto the Polish countryside, the backwoods, far away from the whitewashed manors of the nobility, from universities and the newsrooms of respected periodicals - from the gentle and good people. This is where it is endemically localised and locked away, surrounded by a thick wall of class distinction and distance if not outright contempt. One can hardly find a word other than contempt to equate poverty with immorality - to consider destitution tantamount to criminal tendency.

'The country is Jedwabne, the city is Żegota'[12] - these words by novelist Sylwia Chutnik capture this strain of classism in the context of the Polish reckoning with the past. Her ironic phrase emphasises that Jedwabne is not perceived as a symbol of the entire Polish nation's complicity in the Holocaust, but that of the peasants, who

12 Sylwia Chutnik, *Dzidzia* (Baby), Warsaw: Świat Książki, 2009.

are demonised, exoticised and unequivocally held accountable for murdering Jews. This is a practical ruse for shifting responsibility that guarantees the Polish elites a safe place in the name of maintaining a good self-image and an unblemished identity. However, the ongoing process of externalising the 'banal evil' - distancing it from educated and cultured people - does not eliminate the question of origin. Where did these Jedwabne peasants and all the other people murdering Jews in rural areas during the third phase of the Holocaust come from?

This class body had been shaped by their clergy, their teachers, their landowners and their local administrators. Rural Poland had been chosen by radical, nationalist students as a target of indoctrination: they spread antisemitism there in the 1930s. It was no coincidence that a wide stream of antisemitic popular press was flowing to villages and small towns from publishing centres including the Franciscan monastery in Niepokalanów. In other words, that class body would not have existed had it not been for its earlier socialisation for which the landowner and the parson were equally responsible. It is also not without reason that almost forty per cent of Poles today agree that scholars who reveal shameful episodes from Polish history should be punished. The deflective negationism spewed by representatives of the Polish elites continues to impact social consciousness and mould opinions. Just like it did decades ago.

Untitled (The Eye Swallows the Landscape. The Landscape Gouges the Eye), 2017

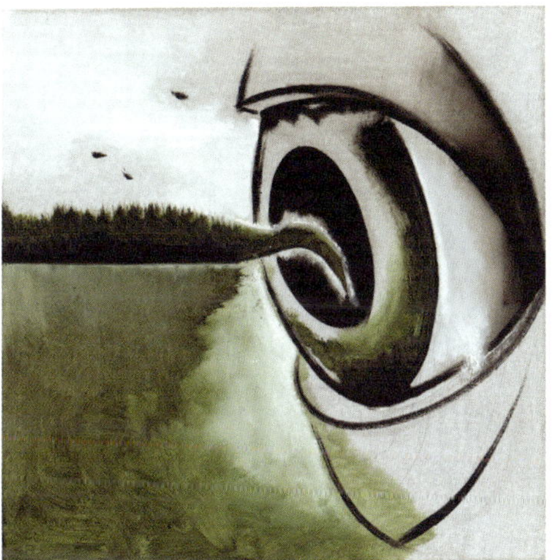

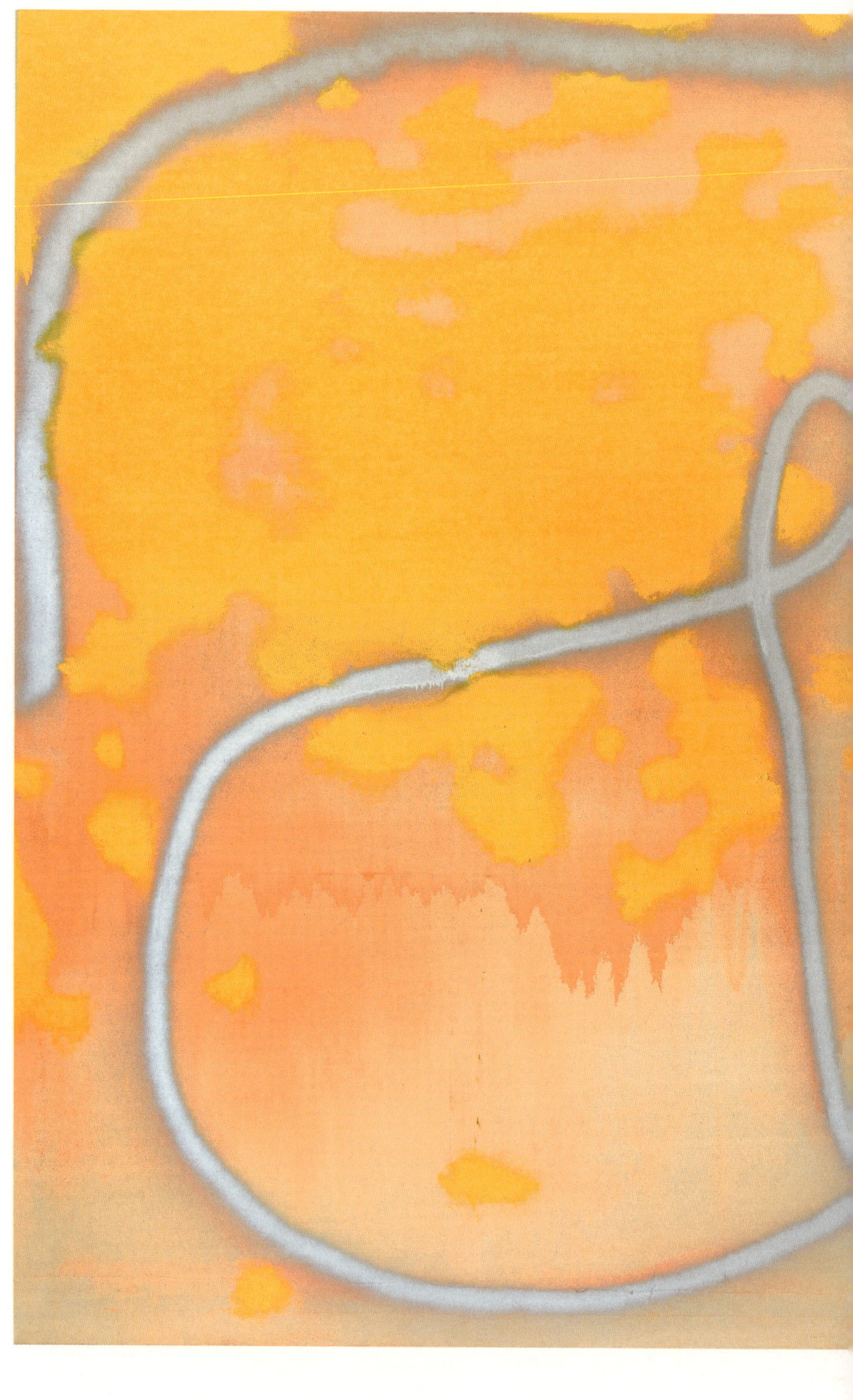

Untitled (Afterimage), 2019

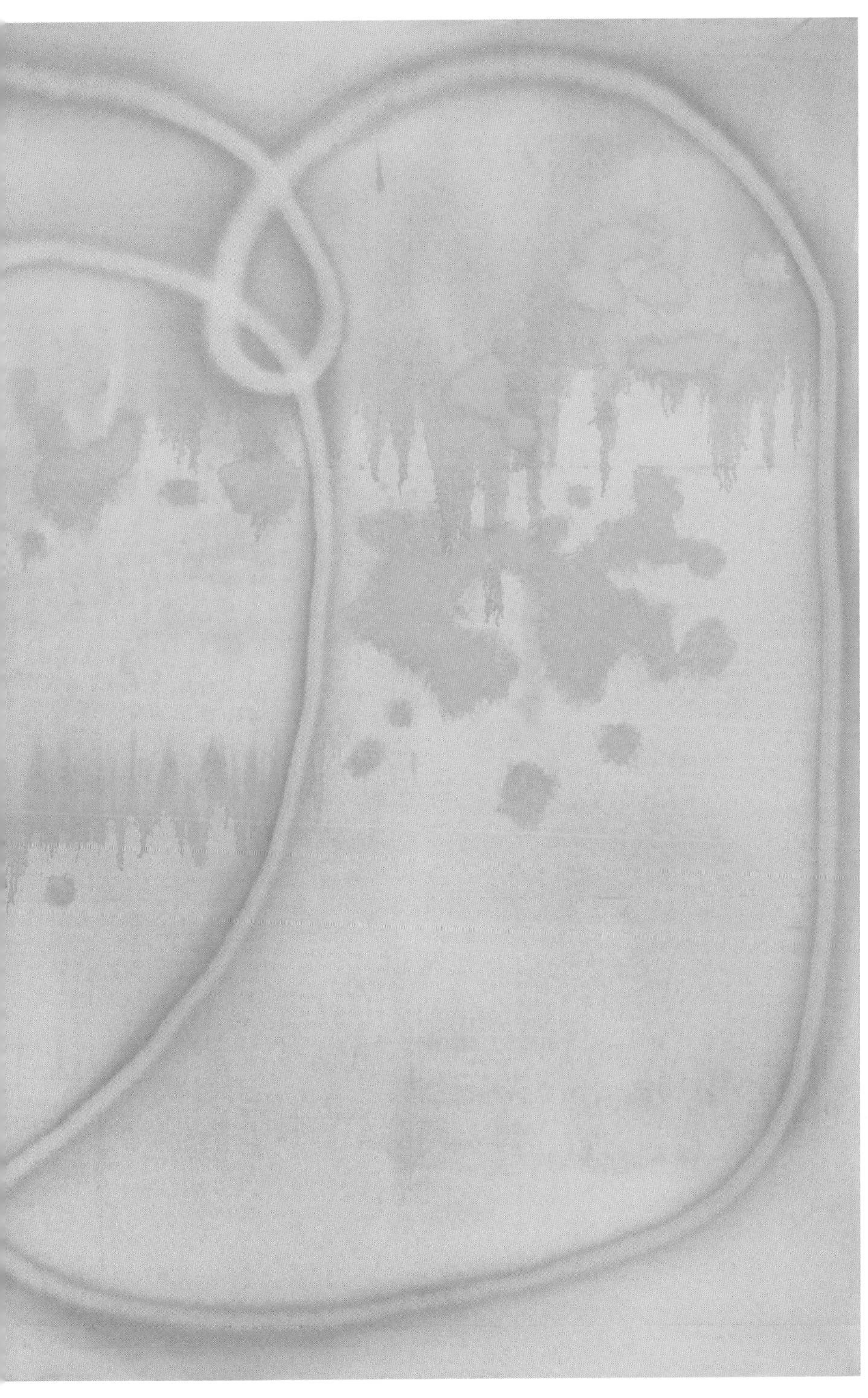

A Summons to See: *It Looks Pretty from a Distance*

By Luiza Nader

Translated from the Polish by Eliza Rose

The Sun - The Heart of the Day (1948) belongs among Władysław Strzemiński's most ecstatic afterimage paintings, despite being deemed a failure by its artist. This text centres on Anka Sasnal and Wilhelm Sasnal's film *It Looks Pretty from a Distance* (*Z daleka widok jest piękny*, 2011). The optical consciousness (one of Strzemiński's key terms) embodied in *The Sun*, the concept of the afterimage and the Freudian notion of screen memory as revised by Michael Rothberg have been guideposts informing my path into select works from Wilhelm Sasnal's oeuvre. In what follows, I reflect on the multilayered and multidirectional scenes of screen memory (*Deckerinnerung*) engendered by Sasnal. Among these scenes, guilt and shame loom large.

Theory of Seeing Revisited on Its Terms

Władysław Strzemiński's *Theory of Seeing* is a moebius strip of several concepts overlaid: knowing and seeing, cognition and the sense of sight, cultural memory, historical transmission and (physiological) afterimages. Strzemiński writes:

> Let us come to know the world not only by seeing it but by thinking and detecting what each optical sensation communicates: which piece of worldly knowledge is imparted by the eye.

> In a word, let us analyse optical sensations by extrapolating from them and restaging them to test their effects. Our field of vision is not determined by some 'innate' or 'normal' capability. Rather, it is a working process that emerges out of a reciprocal relationship between cognition and biological sight (as interdependent terms). Yes, this is how optical consciousness is achieved, and it is this process that limits the scope of worldly phenomena accessible by means of the eye.[1]

With these words, Strzemiński summons his reader to an exercise of optical consciousness that cannot be reduced to the basic act of seeing or being aware, for it comes laden with dynamics of cultural memory and personal memory acts, just as it is anchored in the physiology of seeing and neurological activity of the body. Strzemiński's call to awareness is an ethical imperative in which several ingredients blend: quotidian experience, an emboldened way of witnessing the world, the artist's empirical toolkit and neurological sight activated by the trembling body (for Strzemiński, seeing is a feedback loop between eye, body and brain). Also inherent in this exercise is the work of taking in and contemplating a whole complex of historical, social, cultural and political processes in order to articulate, here and now, the artist's response *to* and responsibility *for* the present and past. Optical consciousness is thus visual awareness in its most tensile form, for it straddles biology and history, the individual and social body, autobiographical memory and the cultural politics of memory. What is more, optical consciousness - realised in its full theoretical and visual potential in a series of eight afterimage paintings made by Strzemiński in 1948–49 - carries associations with light, the outside world, limit-experience and finally, visual testimony.[2] This last aspect necessarily occurs at the level of individual experience and

1 Władysław Strzemiński, *Teoria widzenia* (Theory of Seeing), 3rd ed., Kraków: Wydawnictwo Literackie, 1972, p. 14. All translations from *Teoria widzenia* (hereafter *Theory of Seeing*) are by Eliza Rose.

2 In the Polish language, the words collected here (light, world, experience, consciousness, testimony) share etymological and philosophical roots. On this topic, see Luiza Nader, *Afekt Strzemińskiego. Teoria widzenia, rysunki wojenne, Pamięci przyjaciół - Żydów* (Strzemiński's Affect: Theory of Seeing - the Wartime Drawings - In Memory of Friends - Jews), Warsaw: Akademia Sztuk Pięknych w Warszawie - Muzeum Sztuki w Łodzi - Wydawnictwo Instytut Badań Literackich PAN, 2018, pp. 111-12.

answers to real and pressing circumstances (in a materialist, existential or anthropological sense). Yet the record of personal accountability contained in visual testimony remains inseparable from the fluttering movement of the observer's eye, body and mind. Optical consciousness understood by these terms is a summons: it enjoins us to take up the labour of seeing and to bear witness. It calls on us to answer to extant reality as it unfolds and to take responsibility for the future and past.[3]

Afterimages

While Wilhelm Sasnal has made direct reference to Strzemiński on only the rare occasion, it is for good reason that the term afterimage (associated with *Theory of Seeing*) is an operative concept in his critical reception.[4] Iwona Kurz has compellingly observed that:

> the images generated by the Sasnals are in fact afterimages - representations persisting long after their object vanishes from the visual field. Theirs is a dual nature: they simultaneously confirm and refute the possibility of directly tracing reality, for the mark resulting from this procedure is but an outline or sketch - a dialectical status vividly expressed in [Zbigniew] Libera's 'Positives' (2002-2003). In the Sasnals' case, however, it is instead 'negatives' that emerge.[5]

Karol Sienkiewicz treats this same concept in technical terms, as one of many devices available to painterly practice but also as an idiomatic mode of reception: 'What distinguishes Sasnal from other

3 On reading *Theory of Seeing* as visual testimony, see L. Nader, *Afekt Strzemińskiego*.
4 See, for instance: Jakub Banasiak, 'Sto utraconych kawałków' (One Hundred Missing Pieces), in *Sasnal. Przewodnik Krytyki Politycznej* (Sasnal: A Guide to Polish Criticism), Warsaw: Wydawnictwo Krytyki Politycznej, 2007, p. 29; Iwona Kurz, 'Ani z bliska ani z daleka. Klisze i powidoki' (Not from Afar; Not at Close Range: Afterimages and Clichés), *Dwutygodnik*, February 2012, https://www.dwutygodnik.com/artykul/3205-ani-z-bliska-ani-z-daleka-klisze-i-powidoki.html; Karol Sienkiewicz, 'Sasnal wchodzi do kina' (Sasnal Goes to the Cinema), *Dwutygodnik*, February 2012, https://www.dwutygodnik.com/artykul/3185-sasnal-wchodzi-do-kina.html.
5 I. Kurz, 'Ani z bliska ani z daleka'.

artist-filmmakers is that he has always remained a painter. His work exhibits a unique sensitivity to images, afterimages and colors (!) registered in long shots.'[6]

Wilhelm Sasnal made two (never released) posters for Andrzej Wajda's film *Afterimage* (*Powidoki*) (2016). The film dramatises the post-war episode of Strzemiński's life, which contextually ties it to *Theory of Seeing*, his afterimage paintings and his series *In Memory of Friends - Jews* (*Pamięci przyjaciół - Żydów*).[7] Sasnal's first poster alludes to an illustration from *Theory of Seeing* by way of a synthetic graphic line depicting a single wide-open eye somewhat like the Eye of Providence (Strzemiński tended to be single-minded yet authoritative in his theoretical tone). The eye looms up from behind a cloud-like shape (perhaps a drifting afterimage?). The second poster is an array of simple abstract forms that diminish in size towards the poster's base. Our 'visual brain' will be tempted to translate these shapes into birds in flight. At the bottom of the poster, just above the film's title, rise curving lines denoting an iris and pupil (and perhaps conjuring the wheel of history). Converging on this shape (or peeling away from it) are black forms (or signs, or birds) in a state of dispersion, snatching away bits and pieces of the iris. Sasnal's posters convey the ambivalence of a transient reality submitted to observation while actively altering its observer in turn. In 2019, an enigmatic afterimage painting by Sasnal (*Untitled*, 2019) appeared in the exhibition *The Sign of Inequality* at Warsaw's Foksal Gallery Foundation, where it was displayed alongside interpretations of canonical works: realist depictions of physical toil by Gustave Courbet, Jean-François Millet and Carlo Pittara. As astutely noted by Stach Szabłowski, Sasnal

> expands on this rural triptych with two contributions. The first is an intimate landscape seen from behind some kind of scaffolding: [we see] decaying vegetation, a dark wall of trees girding

6 K. Sienkiewicz, 'Sasnal wchodzi do kina'. Translation by E. Rose.

7 Here, following Strzemiński, I deliberately use the title *In Memory of Friends - Jews* (*Pamięci przyjaciół - Żydów*) in lieu of the standard art historical title *To My Friends, the Jews* (*Moim przyjaciołom - Żydom*). On this subject, see L. Nader, *Afekt Strzemińskiego*.

> the horizon and a washed-out sky. There are no peasant-serfs or comparable identifying staffage, but surely, we're in Poland. The second painting is powerful and, at first glance, abstract: a meandering, stunningly white line descends on afterimage-sunspots of harsh yellow hue. If this painting responds to Courbet, does it not also summon Strzemiński? The exhibition text informs us that the artist was inspired to make the painting while sitting [in] a dentist's chair, staring open-eyed into the surgical lamp overhead.[8]

The Sign of Inequality commented on the social, political and practical obligations attending artistic practice. The show combined images of social class with the active articulation of a history of the disenfranchised (the peasantry), while drawing on aesthetic modes of realism. Strzemiński can be treated as an avatar for one such realism: a realism born in a moment of optical consciousness, at the exact interface between body and world. The afterimages of Strzemiński and Sasnal are united by flashes of sunlight and pain: blinding light, the sensation of a dentist's drill penetrating the tooth, and in the grips of this feeling – the registration of flickering afterimages.

Paweł Mościcki, describing Strzemiński's work, follows Leszek Brogowski in stating that 'afterimages are a primal form of memory'. For Mościcki, the afterimage (a visual remnant lingering fleetingly under the eyelid) is tied to the Freudian logic of *Nachträglichkeit* (often translated as 'deferred action' or 'afterwardness') and thus constitutes 'an intermediate form between perception and memory'.[9] Mościcki goes on: 'Inscribed in the aesthetics of afterimages [...] is a peculiar temporality, aptly conveyed by Jerzy Ficowski's poetic formula: "being on time too late". Above all, the time of afterimages is a time of imagination, of viewing with eyes shut.'[10]

8 Stach Szabłowski, *Chłopi, realizm i ateizm* (Peasants, Realism and Atheism), *Dwutygodnik*, October 2019, https://www.dwutygodnik.com/artykul/8519-chlopi-realizm-i-ateizm.html. Translation by E. Rose.

9 Paweł Mościcki, 'Being on Time too Late. On Władysław Strzemiński's Encounters with History', in *Afterimages of Life. Władysław Strzemiński and Rights for Art*, ed. Paulina Kurc-Maj and Jarosław Lubiak, Łódź: Muzeum Sztuki w Łodzi, 2012, p. 338. Translation by Marcin Wawrzyńczak.

10 *Ibid.*

In Sasnal's work, the afterimage is radically evolved. It emerges through his paintings and films as a conceptual constellation in motion: a physiological act in the literal sense (as it was for Strzemiński), as an image generated by retinal lag. It is also the automatic memory of visual input accrued through everyday experience: of mediascapes and images codified in culture, and of the mind's internal screening mechanism activated as a line of psychological defence. These images registered under the eyelids are saturated and fed each day through exposure to culture, media, family scenarios and arbitrary images glimpsed by chance. From this onslaught of content, certain categories come to the fore. First, there are places, spaces, environments and settings populated by beings human and otherwise: plants, animals, things, landscapes and the aggregate soundscape and iconosphere of the moment at hand. A second category consists of painterly afterimages associated with a cultural lineage of social consciousness and collective memory, such as the Polish canon with all its stock staffage of romantic nationalist myths. The afterimage thus understood is carried onward and expanded upon in Sasnal's art, where it continues to exist as a transient, fluid form in which contrasting memory imprints pool together. Here accumulate layers of personal and collective memory (as Maurice Halbwachs might put it) or memories universal and shared (in Avishai Margalit's terms). In its biographical and physiological scope, the afterimage corresponds to (and, in a cultural sense, answers to) the Freudian notion of *Deckerinnerung*, which refers to the image of a cover or screen that both conceals and exposes repressed memories.[11]

Complicit Art History

In his book *Wielki retusz. Jak zapomnieliśmy, że Polacy zabijali Żydów* (The Great Makeover: How We Forgot That Poles Killed Jews), Tomasz Żukowski reconstructs how concern for self-image and fear of an impending breach of the Polish imaginary have led to a tendency to idealise images of Poles, in particular by pushing knowledge of their complicity in the Holocaust to the margins of social discourse.

11 I draw this language from Michael Rothberg, *Multidirectional Memory: Remembering the Holocaust in the Age of Decolonization*, Stanford: Stanford University Press, 2009, p. 13.

Żukowski's object of study is cultural representation: films and texts that use misinformation and stereotypes to 'embellish' Polish identity. Yet the blemishes painted over in this process are liable to return. When they do, they expose certain cultural constructs to be rooted in phantasm and myth.[12] Wilhelm Sasnal shares Żukowski's interest in this process of cosmetic embellishment perpetrated in culture and art. His analysis, however, unfolds in the visual field, through mediums like painting, posters and comics and - in collaboration with Anka Sasnal - film.

Sasnal's art is often formatted in iterations (serial versions distinguished by targeted modifications) and operates in the cultural register of phantasmal images (often but not always particular to Poland). These include stereotypes that aid the rewriting of history and memory by helping to whitewash the collective self-image. Sasnal's art features blurry, partially effaced images that simultaneously amplify and neutralise the grotesque until an uncanny effect is achieved. Examples include heroic stock images of Polish horseback riders who hail back to classical paintings like Piotr Michałowski's *Maksymilian Oborski on Horseback* (*Maksymilian Oborski na koniu*, c. 1840–48 found in Sasnal's untitled painting from 2010); antisemitic, racist or xenophobic images freely circulating in culture (e.g. *Untitled*, 2007; *Jews, After Degas*, 2014; *After Degas*, 2014 and *Murzynek Bambo*, 2014);[13] media clichés such as partisans (*Fire*, 2008) and Catholic believers (*Częstochowa*, 2010) and finally, national landscapes (e.g. *Kraków-Warszawa (Cracow Warsaw)*, 2006; *Stork*, 2014 and *Highlander*, 2016). Sasnal reproduces and tampers with a particular visual canon that, in this process, becomes a screen memory mediated by art history. The resulting memory cannot be erased; it can only be reconstructed and scrutinised to determine what it conceals and why.

I have so far discussed only a subset of the memory-afterimages imposed on sight by art history and culture and engaged in Sasnal's art. The full range includes fully developed images alongside visual

12 See Tomasz Żukowski, *Wielki retusz. Jak zapomnieliśmy, że Polacy zabijali Żydów* (The Great Makeover: How We Forgot That Poles Killed Jews), Warsaw: Wielka Litera, 2018.

13 *Murzynek* is a diminutive of the Polish N-word 'Murzyn'. For more on the term see pp. 17 and 139, n. 41 in this book.

remnants (blinks of the eye) circulating in Polish culture yet downplayed or outright ignored. Some remnants, here 'on the outskirts of Auschwitz',[14] need to be visually underscored. Others, conversely, are so conspicuous that they elude the eye, their meaning buried under accretions of other 'screen meanings'. It is this kind of content that stimulates afterimages (covers, screens) on the level of culture, art history and history writ large, thus reversing the cosmetic embellishment described above. An example of this procedure can be found in the film *Shoah* (dir. Claude Lanzmann, 1985). Despite its status as a staple on humanities syllabi, Lanzmann's film has been largely excluded from the discursive field in Poland on the Holocaust. In a series of paintings, Sasnal extracts and recreates the interpreter figure from the film, accenting her subjective 'bystander' position, linguistic acrobatics, efforts to explain and emotional wavering (*Shoah: Translator*, 2003). From Lanzmann he also adopts the no less vital figure of the nonhuman witness in the form of the landscape itself (*Shoah (Forest)*, 2003) and - for the film *It Looks Pretty from a Distance* - Polish villagers (to whom I will soon return).

A cultural text of comparable status to Lanzmann's film is Art Spiegelman's multi-part graphic novel *Maus* (volume 1, 1986; volume 2, 1991 and the complete edition, 2011). The Polish edition was published to bitter controversy in 2001 (volumes 1-2) and 2016 (complete edition). Its initial release met with public protests and allegations that Spiegelman and his translator Piotr Bikont were guilty of 'anti-Polish sentiment'.[15] The Polish edition's release coincided in time with other seminal publications seeding similarly aggressive uproar: most notably, Jan Tomasz Gross's book *Sąsiedzi. Historia zagłady żydowskiego miasteczka* (2000; *Neighbors: The Destruction of the Jewish Community in Jedwabne, Poland*, 2001), which quickly fell prey to heated media debates due to its discussion of the cooperation of Poles in crimes perpetrated against Jews. Sasnal made five works alluding to *Maus* in 2001. The works both reproduce and abstract his source text. In each case, Sasnal underscores, duplicates or rhetorically amplifies the visual effects of a particular component from the novel, such as beds in a camp

14 I borrow this term from Katarzyna Bojarska.
15 See Katarzyna Bojarska, 'Wilhelm Sasnal's transitional images', special issue, 'The History of Art in Poland and the Holocaust', *Miejsce*, no. 6, 2020, p. 17, https://www.doi.org/10.48285/8kaewzjo3p.

barrack, the entrance to a gas chamber, or a Pole portrayed (after the novel) as a pig.[16] Drawing from the source novel in this way, he contrived potent visual figures that operate in a manner analogous to rhetorical figures in language.[17] He creates metonyms (especially pars-pro-toto synecdoche and the singular standing in for the plural) for conformism, the fear and horror of the death camps, and the complicity of Polish bystanders.

In a literal sense, Sasnal also centres *Maus* in the 'primal scene' of fear, betrayal, abasement and depredation. Such was the case with a mural covering one wall of Galeria Bielska BWA in Bielsko-Biała during the painting competition *Bielska Jesień* (curated by Adam Szymczyk in 2001). For the mural, Sasnal reproduced page 157 of *Maus* (Polish edition, 2001; see pp. 6-7 in this book) but erased the drawings, leaving only speech bubbles. The excerpted page recounts the experiences of Spiegelman's parents (Władek and Andzia) during the Holocaust, covering events that took place in the city surrounding the gallery.[18] Here, in Bielsko-Biała, Spiegelman's parents were blackmailed by Polish informants (known in Polish as *szmalcowniks*).[19] The mural was originally conceived for a wall of the local Museum of Technology and Textile Industry - a former factory that once belonged to the Spiegelman family (and appears in this capacity in *Maus*). When Sasnal sought permission to use this venue, his request was refused.[20] The mural found its eventual home on a wall inside Galeria BWA, which stands on the site of a demolished synagogue. In Sasnal, Spiegelman finds an ally who

16 In *Maus*, Art Spiegelman portrays Jewish characters as mice, Germans as cats, Poles as pigs, French as frogs, Americans as dogs and so on. This device may, for instance, evoke the fairy tales of the Brothers Grimm, where humanlike characters often appear in animal form.

17 Adam Szymczyk has also observed Wilhelm Sasnal's use of rhetorical figures. See 'Adam Szymczyk/Ulrich Loock', in *Images in Painting: Eberhard Havekost, Johannes Kahrs, Magnus Plessen, Wilhelm Sasnal*, exh. cat., Porto: Fundação Serralves, 2006, p. 18.

18 In 1951, the cities Bielsko and Biała were incorporated into one city bearing both names (Bielsko-Biała). See https://sztetl.org.pl/pl/miejscowosci/b/407-bielsko-biala/96-historia-miejscowosci/69637-historia-miejscowosci. See also pp.133-34, n. 23 in this book.

19 For more on *szmalcowniks*, see p. 133, n. 22 in this book.

20 K. Sienkiewicz, 'Maus - Wilhelm Sasnal', Culture.pl, https://culture.pl/en/work/maus-wilhelm-sasnal. For a close analysis of Sasnal's *Maus* cycle, see K. Bojarska, 'Wilhelm Sasnal's transitional images'.

situates the reception of *Maus* in the material afterlife of the events it describes.[21] Here, the work comes into contact with descendants of those who related to the Holocaust as observers, onlookers, watchers,[22] beneficiaries, facilitators[23] and informed participant-observers.[24] The mural also maps sites of betrayal, such as properties requisitioned from Jews while the Holocaust was still ongoing and where former bystanders continue to draw profit from what is known as the 'excluded economy'.[25]

This last practice is documented in the film *The Beater* (*Naganiacz*, dir. Ewa Petelska and Czesław Petelski, 1963). As recently noted by Żukowski, the film's brutal accuracy has been overlooked in cultural discourse, for it depicts the historical practice known as *Judenjagd* (so-called 'Jew-hunts' in which Poles participated), which forms the subject of a recent book by Jan Grabowski.[26] The protagonist of *Beater* also makes a cameo in Sasnal's work (*Untitled (from the movie 'The Beater')*, 2010). These many borrowings and allusions all transmit and reinforce a consistent message regarding the multiple diverse ways in which Poles participated in the Holocaust - as bystanders and as direct facilitators of death.

21 For a broad discussion of Polish bystanders of the Holocaust and their language of dissimulation, see, for instance, *Świadek: jak się staje? Czym jest?* (Witness: How Does It Happen? What Is It?), ed. Agnieszka Dauksza, Warsaw: Wydawnictwo IBL PAN, 2019.

22 I borrow these terms differentiating the bystander's position into its constituent aspects from Roma Sendyka, 'Od obserwatorów do gapiów. Kategoria bystanders i analiza wizualna' (From Observers to Gawkers: The 'Bystander' Category and Visual Analysis), *Teksty drugie*, no. 3, 2018, pp. 117-30.

23 Jan Tomasz Gross, 'Sprawcy, ofiary i inni' (Perpetrators, Victims and Others), *Zagłada Żydów. Studia i materiały*, vol. 10, Warsaw: Stowarzyszenie Centrum Badań nad Zagładą Żydów & IFiS PAN, 2014, p. 888.

24 'Informed participant-observer' is Elżbieta Janicka's term. See E. Janicka, 'Pamięć przyswojona. Koncepcja polskiego doświadczenia zagłady Żydów jako traumy zbiorowej w świetle rewizji kategorii świadka' (Assimilated Memory: The Polish Experience of the Genocide of Jews as a Collective Trauma in Light of the Revised Category of the Witness), *Studia Litteraria Historica*, no. 3/4, 2014/2015, pp. 148-226.

25 Kazimierz Wyka, 'Gospodarka wyłączona' (Excluded Economy) (1945), in *Życie na niby* (Make-Believe Life), Kraków: Universitas, 2010.

26 T. Żukowski, *Wielki retusz*, p. 44. See also Jan Grabowski, *Hunt for the Jews: Betrayal and Murder in German-Occupied Poland*, Bloomington: Indiana University Press, 2013.

'The "daytime" history of the Poles, filled with toxic martyrological clichés will not yield until the "nocturnal" history of the Poles is revealed,' writes Joanna Tokarska-Bakir. To this, Elżbieta Janicka adds: 'what hinders critical analysis and the working through of the past on a social scale is not ignorance of the "nocturnal" history of the Poles, but a "system of mental and moral organization of this knowledge".'[27] In Sasnal's art, this knowledge-ordering system is deconstructed and disarmed. His work renders visible certain substrates in which we are steeped: the iconosphere of daily life, the image canon of art history, and (cultural) history as both discipline and inheritance. All of the above are sites of reception as well as institutions in which we participate, be it as viewers or determining agents. By making visible these institutions, Sasnal reveals them to be complicit, non-neutral and non-autonomous. At the same time, as Janicka, Wojciech Wilczyk, Artur Żmijewski and others have done, he contributes to the visual labour of reading and decoding 'Polish culture [that] unconsciously or semi-consciously hints at knowledge it nonetheless declines to overtly discuss'.[28] Sasnal summons an overlooked and underappreciated aspect of this complex, multidirectional, complicit visual memory and knowledge - of afterimages in the term's broadest meaning, as veil, cover and screen.

Screen Memory

Moving on from the afterimage as a primal memory form and as the conceptual constellation outlined above and transmitted in Sasnal's art, I will now trace how these concepts enter into the film *It Looks Pretty from a Distance*. First, some attention is due to a specific form of memory corresponding, as I see it, to the afterimage: that form is *Deckerinnerung* (screen memory). Memory, Michael Rothberg tells us, is always a form of work, labour, action or intervention engaged in the moment at hand. To repeat Richard Terdiman's minimalist but incisive

27 E. Janicka, 'Instead of Negationism: The Symbolic Topography of the Former Warsaw Ghetto Vis-à-Vis Holocaust Narratives', in *Holocaust: Studies and Materials*, Warsaw: Stowarzyszenie Centrum Badań nad Zagładą Żydów & IFiS PAN, vol. 10, 2017, p. 256. Translation by Jerzy Giebułtowski. Joanna Tokarska-Bakir's comment is cited in this article, p. 256.

28 T. Żukowski, *Wielki retusz*, p. 44. Translation by E. Rose.

definition: 'memory is the past made present.'[29] These words take literal form in Sasnal's painterly practice. Each iteration, repetition, erasure, defacement, re-enactment, duplication or amplification of a (visual or textual) narrative from or referencing the past is both a labour of and intervention in habitual ways of representing that past. In his book *Multidirectional Memory*, Rothberg offers a productive revision of the Freudian notion of screen memory (*Deckerinnerung*):

> As Freud clarifies in 'On Childhood Memories and Screen Memories,' a chapter in *The Psychopathology of Everyday Life*, the content of the screen memory has a variety of '*temporal* relation[s]' with 'the subject it has screened out.' He distinguishes between 'retrospective,' 'anticipatory,' and 'simultaneous' screen memories in order to clarify that the content of a screen memory can be formed by projections from repressed memories that happened after, before, or at the same time as the remembered events. Noting the temporal complexity that Freud finds in childhood memories (and pointing out that the memories at stake in 'Screen Memories' are probably Freud's own), Hugh Haughton writes that 'the notion of the "screen" or "cover" becomes increasingly many-layered and multidirectional.' The English translation of *Deckerinnerungen* (literally, 'cover memories') as 'screen memories' is thus apt, if not literal, since such memories do encapsulate two notions of the 'screen': they serve both as a barrier between consciousness and the unconscious, and as a site of projection for unconscious fantasies, fears, and desires, which can then be decoded. *Consequently, screen memory is, in my terminology, multidirectional not only because it stands at the center of a potentially complex set of temporal relations, but also - and perhaps more importantly - because it both hides and reveals that which has been suppressed.*[30]

Following Freud, Rothberg contends that *Deckerinnerung* is neither pathology nor fantasy: it occupies the space of more painful memories while revealing memory's latent force (the persisting relation between that which is remembered and suppressed). The mechanism thus

29 M. Rothberg, *Multidirectional Memory*, pp. 3-4.
30 *Ibid.*, pp. 13-14. Emphasis mine.

illustrates how 'a kind of forgetting accompanies acts of remembrance, but this kind of forgetting is subject to recall'.[31] In Rothberg's conception, *Deckerinnerung* seems tied to the mnemic experience described by Zofia Rosińska as a continuous process of 'psychomachia' (a battle of the psyche) applied to memory's readily apparent contents through memorisation, recall, recognition, forgetting, coding, decoding, narrating, interpreting, constructing and so on.[32]

I wish to draw a parallel between the expansive understanding of afterimages proposed here - encompassing physiological and visual cultural 'sediments' - and the concept of screen memory. In its principal definition, an afterimage is also a cover or screen: a physiological memory of colour and form that transmits an act of seeing. To see in this manner is to see 'with eyes closed', even if what precedes it is the risky venture of gazing into blinding light. Here and now, to consider the afterimage and its physical effects, I open my eyes, close them, and repeat. In this procedure, seeing and not seeing begin to overlap and a paradox emerges: eyes open, I am blind (a sensation registered as a flash of light). Conversely, eyes closed, I see (the afterimage and its analysis). The afterimage's first effect is to make visible the screen of the body: it sensitises the embodied subject to their porous interface with the world and to the way in which external reality inevitably 'seeps in', infiltrating physiological acts of perception. Secondly, to produce an afterimage, one has no choice but to close one's eyes. This act installs a very real cover or screen on which the afterimage's colourful forms are 'projected'. By the same measure, afterimages obstruct our ability to see with eyes open. Thirdly, the afterimage is the product of open-eyed contact with a bright source of light. Metaphorically, this seems a kind of limit-experience whose remnants are subsequently retained under the eyelids. Strzemiński tried to describe these visual 'relicts' in optical and physiological terms. These drifting residues, sediments, remainders and constructs of cultural memory that persistently structure the Polish imaginary from the source text that Sasnal then translates into bodily memory.

31 *Ibid.*, p. 13.

32 Zofia Rosińska, 'Doświadczenie mnemiczne czyli fenomen pamięci według Zygmunta Freuda' (Mnemic Experience, or: Memory According to Sigmund Freud), *Dialogi. Zeszyty Instytutu Psychoanalizy i Psychoterapii*, no. 1-2, 2002, pp. 66-72.

It Looks Pretty from a Distance

An additional meaning of *Deckerinnerung* is operative in Sasnal's art: its associative force in unlocking access to a repressed experience or event. This force, as Rothberg insists, is mulidirectional and many-layered: it tends to refer to looping units of place and time (the present notwithstanding).

Such a beautiful sunny day... Night without end... Among the poisoned knives... Keys and cash... - these and other phrases from eyewitness statements of Jewish victims and non-Jewish bystanders (phrases also used as book titles for scholarship on Poles' multifaceted complicity in the Holocaust) form the rhizomatic matrix of images, textual associations, personal memories and cultural tropes in which the film *It Looks Pretty from a Distance* is steeped. Rather direct points of reference for the film are several books by Jan Tomasz Gross: *Neighbors* and also (2006; *Strach. Antysemityzm w Polsce tuż po wojnie. Historia moralnej zapaści*, 2008) *Fear: Anti-Semitism in Poland after Auschwitz* and finally, *Złote żniwa* (2011; *Golden Harvest: Events at the Periphery of the Holocaust* (co-authored with Irena Grudzińska Gross).[33] The film

33 My aim here is not to suggest a literal or chronological correlation. Rather, I wish to point out how Anka and Wilhelm Sasnal identify certain motifs in the visual sphere that have deep resonance in humanities scholarship on the genocide of Jews by seminal scholars like Barbara Engelking, Jan Tomasz Gross, Jan Grabowski, Agnieszka Haska, Dariusz Libionka, Jacek Leociak and Alina Skibińska. See Barbara Engelking, *Such a Beautiful Sunny Day... - Jews Seeking Refuge in the Polish Countryside, 1942-1945*, Jerusalem: Yad Vashem, 2016; *Klucze i kasa. O mieniu żydowskim w Polsce pod okupacją niemiecką i we wczesnych latach powojennych 1939 - 1945* (Keys and Cash: On Jewish Property in Poland Under Nazi Occupation and in the Early Wartime Years, 1939-1945), ed. Jan Grabowski and Dariusz Libionka, Warsaw: Stowarzyszenie Centrum Badań nad Zagładą Żydów, 2014; *Night without End: The Fate of Jews in German-Occupied Poland*, ed. Barbara Engelking and Jan Grabowski, Bloomington: Indiana University Press, 2022 (Polish edition published in 2018). Other major publications on the Holocaust that may contribute to the associations summoned in this film include: J. T. Gross, *Neighbors: The Destruction of the Jewish Community in Jedwabne, Poland*, Princeton, NJ: Princeton University Press, 2001; *Prowincja noc. Życie i zagłada Żydów w dystrykcie warszawskim* (Province of the Night: The Life and Destruction of Polish Jewish in the Warsaw District), ed. B. Engelking, Jacek Leociak and D. Libionka, Warsaw: Wydawnictwo IFiS PAN, 2007 [2006]; J. T. Gross, *Fear: Anti-Semitism in Poland after Auschwitz - an Essay in Historical Interpretation*, New York: Random House, 2007; *Zarys krajobrazu.*

(together with its title) rests, visually and verbally, on word clouds made of received figures of speech. Its viewers face a peculiar task: the imperative to unearth knowledge by sharpening the way in which they see.

In making this film, Anka and Wilhelm Sasnal were less concerned with *what* (*what* is this film about?) than with *how: how* to articulate the contemporary social condition through the specific medium of film.[34] *It Looks Pretty* takes place in a generic impoverished Polish village. The filmmakers' intent is not to criticise this particular village, for Poland has no shortage of such settings. After all, rural villages are places of origin for the bulk of Polish society (largely descended from peasantry). For this very reason, the village exists as a site of shame for the urban middle class eager to deny their peasant background. Terms like 'village', 'rural', 'bumpkin' or phrases like 'hay coming out of their shoes' colloquially double as epithets synonymous with embarrassment, obscurity, simplicity, vulgarity, dimness, or a lack of culture and pedigree. The film's viewers contend with a village that is less an actual place than a figure of latent anxieties and fears that stingingly reminds them of their own denied origins. As Andrzej Leder writes, the middle class 'knows nothing of its origins and wrestles with the bad conscience attending the repressed memory of violence associated with those origins'. This operation of denial results in a potent urge to, as Leder puts it, 'avoid defining one's identity and to instead either bask in hazy dreams of a pseudo-noble past of multihectare estates, uprisings and cemeteries, or "flee" toward hyperglobal templates, as made spectacularly clear in the bourgeois class's passionate penchant for sushi.'[35]

The village setting of *It Looks Pretty* suffers from economic decline. Its inhabitants live at poverty's brink. Little has changed here since the

Wieś polska wobec zagłady Żydów 1942–1945 (Outline of a Landscape: The Polish Village and the Genocide of Jews, 1942–1945), ed. Barbara Engelking and Jan Grabowski, Warsaw: Stowarzyszenie Centrum Badań nad Zagładą Żydów, 2011; J. Grabowski, *Hunt for the Jews*; J. T. Gross and I. Grudzińska Gross, *Golden Harvest: Events at the Periphery of the Holocaust*, Oxford: Oxford University Press, 2012.

34 Statement by Wilhelm Sasnal in an interview with Max Cegielski, Culture.pl, 10 February 2012, https://culture.pl/pl/wideo wilhelm-sasnal-w-studio-kultura-cz2-wideo.

35 Andrzej Leder, *Prześniona rewolucja. Ćwiczenie z logiki historycznej* (Sleepwalking the Revolution: An Exercise in Historical Logic), Warsaw: Wydawnictwo Krytyki Politycznej, 2014, p. 7.

Second World War; perhaps more things have broken or fallen apart. With the exception of one minor character (the brother of the protagonist called the Girl), the village inhabitants are selfish, envious, irreverent and greedy. Together they sow a violence whose psychological, symbolic and physical effects begin in the body of the self and from there, bleed into relations with family, neighbours, people 'on the other side of the river', and even material things, animals and the landscape. A deficit of empathy is the governing principle of this world. Relationships are forged and community is fostered solely for material gain.

Paweł, who sells scrap metal to make a living, moves his psychologically and physically ailing mother into an institution. The camera surveys his half-ruined home, keenly registering its filthy, shoddy interior and façade as the Girl moves in. For the first time, she almost feels 'at home'. Then Paweł disappears, leaving the Girl vulnerable to public humiliation. At her father's command, she goes home to her family. Paweł's household is gradually picked clean by his neighbours. The Girl's father takes his rabbits. One neighbour cruelly shortens the chain of Paweł's dog and kicks over its water bowl, leaving the animal to die of thirst. Looting ensues. At first, only trivial objects are claimed: preserve jars, dirty curtains, a shabby sheepskin coat – things easily filched under cover of night. Bulkier objects soon follow. In a final gesture, the entire village ransacks the home and burns what remains of Paweł's belongings. The Girl does not abstain from the raiding of Paweł's precarious estate, which had never consisted of more than low-grade, broken-down things. The next day, the Girl poisons several dogs in the village including her own family pet. But Paweł returns. Neighbours observe him from inside their houses. The Girl, unafraid, joins him in his car. During an aggressive drive, she kills him with a knife. The film ends with a shot of the Girl exiting the car and traversing the country road, walking towards (perhaps coming for?) the viewers.

The film grants equal weight to its narrative and visual content, treating the viewer to landscapes, views, isolated images, the blinking of an eye and an immersive soundscape. One particular view of Paweł's house and land recurs several times. The small, dull-grey house (surely once white) has a leaking roof and collapsed fence but no garden. In its vicinity lie dismantled car parts and debris of some former structure amidst scattered rubble and dust. The house will be cleaned by the abandoned Girl, but this won't change much. Paweł's domestic space broadcasts a picture of anomie, poverty and decline. As if swept out from its interior, this impression of disintegration permeates the surrounding land, undercutting an otherwise serene backdrop of forest and fields. As household objects submit to decay (a maggot-ridden bed dragged outdoors), this process merges with the sights and sounds of scorching summer: bird songs, the buzzing of bees, vibrating colours, rippling wheat fields. The landscape's searing, blinding, incapacitating beauty lords over the narrative. The sole elements disturbing the scene are people: dirty, corpulent, angry and poor, they are consumed by a lust to possess, lay claim and destroy. Their interactions with the natural world are tinged with aggression (the film's opening scene depicts people laying animal traps). Their social relations are similarly empty of tenderness: the film's dialogue mainly consists of monosyllabic, incomplete sentences amidst a soundtrack of cursing, snorting, spitting, sniffling and clearing of throats. This same aggression taints their treatment of objects (as when Paweł and his friends crudely saw a car down into parts). All is in a state of decay. With no empathy to cement them, social bonds are fragile and fleeting. These people live outside of culture and hold nature in contempt.

Wilhelm Sasnal has said that this is, first and foremost, a film about avarice.[36] To this I would add that it is also a film about the lust of possession, relentless looting, circulation of stolen goods, objectification of women and a culture steeped in intergenerationally transmitted violence that is psychological, symbolic and physical. The whole film operates on an anti-psychological register: viewers are granted no access to the protagonists' thoughts, feelings or motives. And yet everything seems uncannily familiar, as if we've seen it all before, or heard it, or dreamt it. The pillaging of Paweł's house seems to invoke Erna Rosenstein's painting *Looters* (*Szabrownicy*, 1946). A boy painting a gate blue seems to echo paintings by Andrzej Wróblewski. Strips of lush forest and scenes of arresting beauty conjure, via similar camerawork, Lanzmann's *Shoah* together with myriad nineteenth-century Polish landscape paintings well-known to viewers from museums.

36 Statement by W. Sasnal in an interview with M. Cegielski.

The villagers seem cast straight out of Lanzmann's film. The scrawny dog on a short chain is an afterimage associated with widespread animal cruelty (not limited to rural Poland). Rubble, decay, the entropy of spaces and things - this is the Polish reality that can be found anywhere, even in the centre of our capital city. This film tells a parable in hyperbole that is nonetheless anchored in real visual afterimages ceaselessly supplied by our cultural and educational institutions, mediascapes and everyday life. Despite our inability to identify with the protagonists, we are not impervious to the shame projected on-screen: shame for the filth in which these people live, for their amoral behaviour, for their anger and the scars it leaves, and for witnessing how they revel in the suffering of another. Shame is an unusually contagious affect. To shame another, it suffices to simply draw on one's own store of shame. Conversely, to behold shamelessness in another is often to take that shame upon oneself.

Shame

It was Adam Szymczyk who first noted the affect of shame in Wilhelm Sasnal's work. In his interview with Ulrich Loock, we read:

> Loock: How would you describe the logic of his choices?
> Szymczyk: I think they are driven by the need for touching shame. He is putting himself in the position of someone who takes the blame... although it may not be his.
> Loock: Himself?
> Szymczyk: Yes, as somebody whose aim is to represent subjects that are shameful, which he is not doing in a shameless way. He is rather modest in approaching the subject matter. So there is a lot of hesitation, but nonetheless he always surpasses this, and he's trying to reach things that are somehow... I'm not saying that they are impossible to represent, but the fact is that in Polish art, the Polish-Jewish relationships before, during and after the Second World War have never been addressed directly.[37]

37 'Adam Szymczyk/Ulrich Loock', in *Images in Painting*, pp. 13-14.

Shame comes up again in Katarzyna Bojarska's article 'Wilhelm Sasnal's Transitional Images',[38] where the author parses Szymczyk's suggestion about Sasnal's 'need for touching shame'. Sasnal does not broadcast a message of shame, nor does he seek to shame his own community. Rather, '[h]is paintings seem to be coming to life through an encounter with shame which is neither staged nor reproduced for others.' His painterly practice culls from images operative in the public sphere and thus fashions for each person their own distinct moment of shame.[39] Drawing from Silvan Tomkins and Eve Kosofsky Sedgwick, Bojarska suggests that we understand this practice in dual terms, for it marks the artist's separateness from *and* receptivity to his community. Expanding on this line of thought, I will now propose an alternative way of looking at shame.

Silvan Tomkins, the pioneering affect theorist cited by Bojarska, has delineated seven basic affect pairs (experienced at low and high intensity) that correspond to specific facial responses: interest/excitement, enjoyment/joy, distress/anguish, fear/terror, shame/humiliation, contempt/disgust and anger/rage. For Tomkins, it is not drives but affects that form the baseline of human behaviour and motives. From among these affects, he singles out shame as a decisive factor in subject formation. In his view, children develop the affect of shame around the eighth month of life, when they are not yet capable of grasping prohibition. Shame is thus subjectivity's defining force, for it is through shame that the child develops a sense of self.[40] Eve Kosofsky Sedgwick takes this notion further by stressing the bodily aspect of affects and the subject difference and relationality they precipitate. For Sedgwick, the performative, fleeting nature of shame does not preclude its power to alter the subject (to monitor subjectivity). Sedgwick thus assigns shame a cardinal role in identity formation and queer politics.[41] Building on this, Ruth Leys adds that shame draws on all an individual's flaws filtered

38 K. Bojarska, 'Wilhelm Sasnal's Transitional Images', pp. 180–84.

39 *Ibid.*, p. 181.

40 Silvan Tomkins, 'What are affects?', in *Shame and its sisters. A Silvan Tomkins reader*, ed. Adam Frank and Eve Kosofsky Sedgwick, Durham, NC: Duke University Press, 1995. The affect pairs are listed on page 74.

41 E. K. Sedgwick, 'Shame, Theatricality and Queer Performativity: Henry James's *The Art of Novel', Touching Feeling: Affect, Pedagogy, Performativity*, Durham, NC: Duke University Press, 2003, pp. 35–66.

through the gaze of the other. While guilt is concerned with deeds (real or imagined, present or past) and their attending accountability, shame is tied to issues of subjectivity - of who the subject is becoming.[42] The feeling, transmission, exposition and sharing of shame are therefore strategies for restoring subjecthood on the microscale of individual experience and the macroscale of the collective. Reflecting on guilt leads to the delegation of responsibility. Shame, conversely, opens fissures in the idealised image of the self. In *It Looks Pretty from a Distance*, shame (one layer of screen memory) is exhibited and projected. Shame, however, is not screen memory itself but merely one of its layers, and the surface layer at that. On its underside lies guilt.

Mother Matrix

It may be worth turning to the figure of Paweł's Mother, whose role is crucial despite her disappearance after the film's opening scenes. What this mother really suffers from is old age: she is defenceless and superfluous. She no longer produces anything. She gets underfoot and runs away from home. Though she never cries out and hardly speaks, she is dangerous - out of control. Against her will, she is moved into an institution. Whether it is a hospital or elderly facility, the film leaves unstated, though she has clearly lost the right to return home. Indeed, it is the mother who loses everything in this film: her family, her home. It is her deprivation that launches the chain of violent expropriative acts constraining the narrative. It is the memory of her that must be pillaged and erased. Yet she, like Paweł, returns: the Girl dreams her. She appears in a window, and a drawn-out cry escapes her mouth, eventually phasing into a droning noise that rattles in the ears. It is perhaps in this very scene that we receive a key for interpreting the film. This old woman moaning in a ruined home - a Mother emitting an obscure, repetitive, long and probing sound that rings with the suffering of a child not yet initiated into language. The Mother suffers from dementia, forgets words and is incapable of verbal communication, yet it is she who embodies the memory of some unsettling, guilt-laden person or thing we care not

42 Ruth Leys, *From Guilt to Shame*, Princeton, NJ: Princeton University Press, 2007, pp. 129-32.

to recall. Denied pangs of conscience attend her. Might this mother serve as an allegory for the internal matrix of sick mental structures undergirding the 'nocturnal history of the Polish conscience'?[43] If so, what is the sickness's root cause? Could it be, for instance, the story recounted in the film of those mothers who 'during the war' drowned their children before taking their own lives (those who, as one villager gruffly notes, were 'not really Polish after all')? If so, does this event - the drowned mother in whom the structure of experience originates - return as the denied pang of conscience that escapes from home and wanders recklessly and that society rushes to dispose of, thereby initiating the film's spiral of violence, plunder and crime? Is this the guilt of doing nothing, of giving the 'evil eye', of falling short in empathy and finally, of direct involvement in chasing down, turning in and murdering Jews? Put otherwise, is this the guilt of Polish bystanders' co-responsibility for the Holocaust and for the psychic, cultural, social and political inheritance left to their descendants?

The Post-*Shoah* Landscape

It Looks Pretty from a Distance and the art discussed above take up the challenge of dismantling the episteme built into the Polish imaginary: its history, art history, art, literature and film. Viewers of these works are confronted with images-as-screen memories: the stock landscapes of romantic Polish painting and poetry and Polish icon painting of the nineteenth and twentieth centuries by artists like Józef Chełmoński, Jan Stanisławski, Wojciech Gerson or Julian Fałat (images still echoed in amateur photography blogs, calendars and souvenirs). Yet as I have mentioned, screen memory unveils its object as it simultaneously marks that which obscures the hidden content. What, then, can we take away from the landscapes summoned by the Sasnals? Close-ups of forests and glades inevitably conjure scenes from Lanzmann's *Shoah* - even particular scenes featuring a Holocaust survivor named Szymon Srebrnik. Could Paweł's home be that 'small white house' from the song sung by the teenage Srebrnik, confined in manacles and watched by Polish onlookers? Having seen *Shoah*, the mere act of taking in the

43 Phrase by Joanna Tokarska-Bakir, see E. Janicka, 'Instead of Negationism', p. 256.

Polish landscape seems to conjure Srebrnik's words: 'Yes, this is the place.' With this association in mind, the laying of animal traps in the film's first scene may covertly allude to the practice of *Judenjagd* - the hunting, turning in and murdering of Jews by Poles during the Holocaust's third phase. Andrzej Leder writes:

> To find our place, we first have a fraught genealogy to reckon with. We must acknowledge that nearly all of us are children of that misfortune perpetrated by others' hands, that cruel revolution, that total undoing and reworking of the Polish social fabric. This means, yet again, taking responsibility for what happened long ago. It means owning up to how our fathers or grandfathers took, intruded, turned a blind eye and even killed, sold information and betrayed. But they also faced difficult decisions and dilemmas. It was thoughts of the future that guided their paths. They built a new world ground-up. Today we should consider the moral but also future-facing function of actions like taking responsibility for Jedwabne. The moral function has to do with bringing justice to the other; the future-oriented function is a matter of taking responsibility for oneself.[44]

Critics have often remarked on how challenging it is to identify with the characters populating *It Looks Pretty from a Distance*. After all, no one is really so one-dimensional, so worthy of contempt. But identification is only one of many possible ways to relate to filmic reality, and a naïve one at that. This particular film, as I argue above, is a hyperbole, and its 'heroes', situations and images are visual allegories for mental structures coercively altered in the 1940s and persisting to this day. To describe the formative period for such mental structures (1939-56), Leder coined the phrase 'slept-through revolution'. Yet Wilhelm and Anka Sasnal's film is more concerned with 'touching shame' with the eye, body and mind. Perhaps it is also guilt they're concerned with: that guilt accrued in the 'nocturnal history of the Polish conscience'. Their film issues an invitation to see and describe one's own multifaceted and memory-engrained shame, to take stock of guilt while taking on responsibility and concern for both future and past. It is a summons to build

44 A. Leder, *Prześniona rewolucja*, p. 199. Translation by E. Rose.

a subjectivity founded on shame that is fragile and vulnerable to injury but overcomes these discomforts to open itself to the other.

A Summons to See

One positive figure recurring in Wilhelm Sasnal's work and present in the film discussed here is a boy carrying notes of hope, concern for the future and past, and mental and emotional emancipation. In *It Looks Pretty*, he takes the form of the Girl's brother. It is he who feeds, walks and eventually buries the family dog. His manner of speech is clear. He is the sole person on-screen to engage in repair work on the farm: he paints a gate blue. This visual pairing of the boy and the colour blue directs us towards another art idiom: direct realism and the painting, aesthetics and ethics of Andrzej Wróblewski. 'We want to paint art that will help us distinguish good from bad,' said Wróblewski during a visit by workers to the Exhibition of Modern Art in Kraków in 1948.

> We make paintings as repugnant as a dead body's stench. We paint even those in whom you sense the nearness of death. Through our paintings, you will peer into the interior of man, and there you will see a weakness you have to resist. In some cases, you will grasp the overpowering temptation to seek oblivion in narcotics, vodka or debauchery. We hide nothing. We believe in you. We believe that you are good and will make the right choice.[45]

As with Strzemiński and Sasnal, Wróblewski's theory of realism was largely extratextual and communicated mainly through paintings and art. For some years now, Sasnal has added his voice to the ongoing debates among artists and curators over how to make politically engaged and emancipatory art. His art seems to answer Wróblewski's demand that artistic practice help its viewer 'distinguish good from bad'. Strzemiński would surely have something to add here - perhaps

45 Andrzej Wróblewski [One of several informational texts prepared for workers' tours of the Exhibition of Modern Art], *I Wystawa Sztuki Nowoczesnej. Pięćdziesiąt lat później* (1st Exhibition of Modern Art: Fifty Years Later), ed. Józef Chrobak and Marek Świca, Kraków: Starmach Gallery, 1998, p. 111. Translation by E. Rose.

a reminder that the aesthetic gaze should also take stock of and reproduce physiological barriers, cultural layers of concealment, and the reflexes and movements of the body standing before a painting and assailed by its 'dead body stench'. The optical consciousness attained in such moments of recognition and blindness spreads over the whole surface of the human body quaking with rhythmic vibrations.[46] It entails the competence to see, recognise, gain new knowledge and testify: the effort of absorbing the world through the highest authority of sovereign thought yet always mediated by the real corporeal eye.

Revisiting Strzemiński's ideas today, I have this to add: to look is not necessarily to know, to see is not to understand, and to understand is not to remember. That historical reckoning and care for the past are intrinsic to memory cannot be taken for granted.[47] Today, *Theory of Seeing* reads as an engaged and prescient theory and practice of testimony, and given its prescience, the optical consciousness it describes is now due for revisions both copious and deep.

We find one such radical revision of this practice of seeing and its attendant theory of knowledge in the art of Wilhelm Sasnal. A small, untitled work from 2017 can be treated as a generative footnote to *Theory of Seeing*: a vast, wide-open eye devours the landscape - the very same scene that is pretty only 'from a distance' (though here, in its greenish-brown hue, its appearance is melancholy). This all-seeing, all-knowing - all-knowing, all-seeing - eye perpetrates the havoc wreaked on the literal level of the image and the symbolic level of the synthetic landscape. Wilhelm Sasnal's art and his film collaborations with Anka Sasnal demand a radical 'optical consciousness' from their viewer but also provide a space in which that consciousness can be cultivated. This state of awareness is born out of recognising, making visible and also disarming the force of afterimages, covers and screens transmitted culturally and interpersonally, encoded in the retina, in the 'mind's

46 W. Strzemiński, *Teoria widzenia*, p. 16.

47 See B. Engelking, Zofia Waślicka-Żmijewska and Artur Żmijewski, *Przestańmy mówić o pamięci, zacznijmy mówić o trosce* (Let's Stop Talking About Memory and Start Talking About Care), *Krytyka Polityczna*, 26 April 2019, https://krytykapolityczna.pl/kultura/historia/waslicka-zmijewski-barbara-engelking-zaglada-wywiad/.

membranes'[48] and in the automatic reflexes of body and speech. Through assiduous excavation of subjective and social ways of seeing, false historical and cultural constructs and the mediascapes, soundscapes and iconospheres of everyday life, this work facilitates a post-Shoah reckoning with conditions still undergirding Polish society. It summons us to see existing knowledge about the deeds of Poles complicit in the Holocaust and to see how the act of seeing itself rests on received clichés, internalised violence, antisemitism, xenophobia and fear of an impending breach of the Polish imaginary (a breach that has in fact already occurred). The work imparts sensations of shame and guilt all too sorely needed in a contemporary Polish sociopolitical landscape suffering from an acute deficit of these affects.

48 I borrow the term 'mind's membranes' (*błony umysłu*) from philosopher and feminist Jolanta Brach-Czajna, *Błony umysłu*, Warsaw: Sic!, 2003.

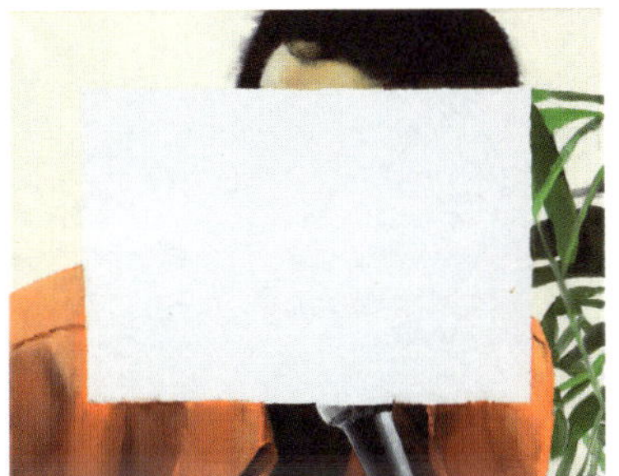

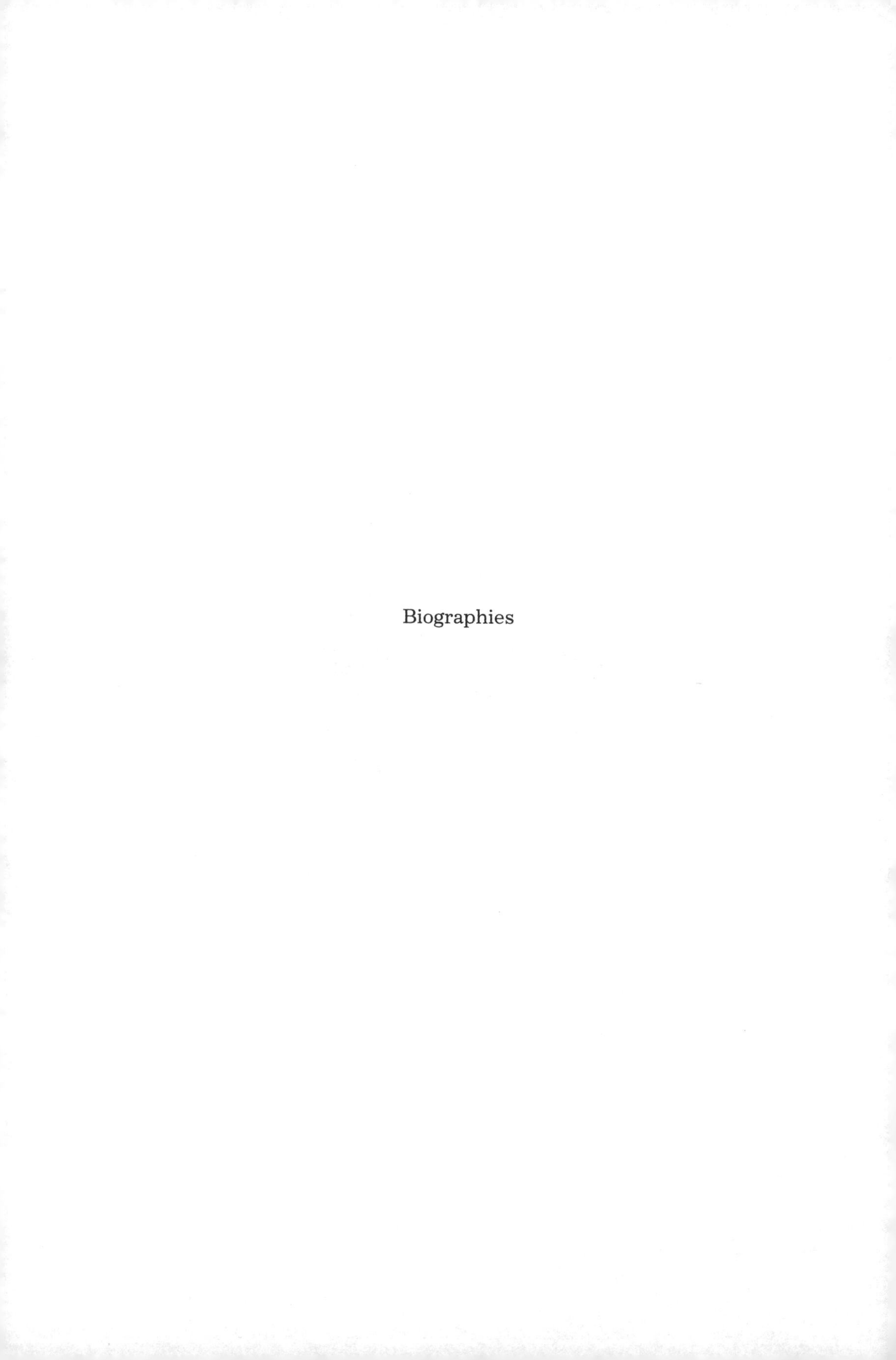

Biographies

Noit Banai

is an art historian and critic who specialises in modern and contemporary art in a global context, with a focus on conditions of migrations, exile, diaspora, border-regimes and statelessness. Before joining Hong Kong Baptist University as Associate Professor, Art and Theory, she was Professor of Contemporary Art in the Department of Art History at the University of Vienna and Lecturer of Modern and Contemporary Art at School of the Museum of Fine Arts at Tufts University, Boston. She is the author of *Being a Border* (2021) and *Yves Klein* (2014), and articles in journals such as *Third Text*, *Stedelijk Studies*, *Public Culture*, *Performing Arts Journal* and *Texte zur Kunst*. She served as assistant editor for the journal *RES: Anthropology and Aesthetics* and is a regular contributor to *Artforum*.

W. E. B. Du Bois

(b. 1868, Great Barrington, MA – d.1963, Accra, Ghana) – was an American writer, sociologist, critic, intellectualist, and political and social activist. A leading activist against discrimination and racial segregation in the United States and critic of colonialism, he was the first black American to be awarded a PhD degree from Harvard University, Cambridge, MA. An active participant in the pan-African movement, at the end of his life, he focused on creating a new encyclopaedia of the African diaspora, financed by the government of Ghana where he became a citizen.

Piotr Forecki

is a political scientist and Professor in the Political Culture Department of the Faculty of Political Science and Journalism at Adam Mickiewicz University, Poznań. He studies the Polish memory of the Holocaust, antisemitism and representations of the Holocaust in popular culture. He is the author of monographs *Od 'Shoah' do 'Strachu'. Spory o polsko-żydowską przeszłość i pamięć w debatach publicznych* (From 'Shoah' to 'Fear': Disputes about the Polish and Jewish Past and Memory in Public Debate, 2010), *Reconstructing Memory: The Holocaust in Polish Public Debates* (2013) and *Po Jedwabnem. Anatomia pamięci funkcjonalnej* (After Jedwabne: The Anatomy of Functional Memory, 2018).

Jan Tomasz Gross

(b. 1947, Warsaw) is Emeritus Professor of History at Princeton University, NJ and author of books including *Złote żniwa* (2011; *Golden Harvest: Events at the Periphery of the Holocaust*, 2012, together with Irena Grudzińska-Gross), *Fear: Anti-Semitism in Poland after Auschwitz - an Essay in Historical Interpretation* (2006; *Strach. Antysemityzm w Polsce tuż po wojnie. Historia moralnej zapaści*, 2008) and *Sąsiedzi. Historia zagłady żydowskiego miasteczka* (2000; *Neighbors: The Destruction of the Jewish Community in Jedwabne, Poland*, 2001).

Milena Jesenská

(b. 1896, Prague - d. 1944, Ravensbrück, Germany) was a Czech journalist, writer and translator and member of Prague literary and intellectual circles. Her many articles were published in the 1920s and 1930s in leading Czech newspapers, as well as in literary and political magazines. She analysed Nazi Germany's politics in Europe as it happened then: the rise of the National Socialist German Workers' Party, the *Anschluss* (the annexation of Austria into Nazi Germany) and the persecution of European Jews. Her communist views evolved, and in the mid-1930s she also opposed Stalin's totalitarian regime. During the German occupation of Czechoslovakia, Jesenská joined the resistance movement, helping Jews and political dissidents leave the country. In 1940, she was imprisoned in Ravensbrück concentration camp, where she died in 1944.

Adolf Muschg

(b. 1934, Zurich) is a Swiss writer and professor of literature. A public intellectual, he has regularly commented on key political issues and events in the press and media for many years. Considered one of most important German-speaking authors living today, he is laureate of numerous literary awards, including the Georg-Büchner-Preis (1994) and the Swiss Grand-Prix for Literature (2015). He is a member of the Academy of Arts in Berlin.

Luiza Nader

(b. 1976) is a Professor at the Academy of Fine Arts in Warsaw. Her work focuses on the twentieth century and contemporary art and in particular testimonies and visual records of and in reaction to the Holocaust. She is inspired by theories of memory, affect, concepts of 'material shift' and affirmative humanities and ethics. Nader is the author of *Afekt Strzemińskiego. 'Teoria widzenia', rysunki wojenne, 'Pamięci przyjaciół - Żydów'* (Strzemiński's Affect: 'The Theory of Vision', War Drawings, 'In Memory of Friends - Jews', 2018) and *Konceptualizm w PRL* (Conceptualism in the Polish People's Republic, 2009).

Bonaventure Soh Bejeng Ndikung

(b. 1977, Yaoundé, Cameroon) is a curator, author and biotechnologist. He is founder and artistic director of SAVVY Contemporary, Berlin and is the artistic director of Sonsbeek 20→24, Arnhem, the Netherlands and Professor in the Spatial Strategies MA programme at the Weissensee Academy of Art in Berlin. He was curator at large from 2014 to 2017 for documenta 14, Athens and Kassel, guest curator of Dak'Art Biennial 2018 and artistic director of Rencontres de Bamako (2019-22), Mali. From 2023 he is director at Haus der Kulturen der Welt, Berlin.

Michael Rothberg

(b. New Haven, CT) is Chair of the Department of Comparative Literature, Professor of English and Comparative Literature, and the 1939 Society Samuel Goetz Chair in Holocaust Studies at the University of California, Los Angeles (UCLA). He is co-organiser of the Working Group in Memory Studies at UCLA and an affiliate of the Alan D. Leve Center for Jewish Studies, and teaches on contemporary literatures, critical theory, cultural memory, Holocaust studies, human rights and postcolonial studies. Rothberg is the author of *The Implicated Subject: Beyond Victims and Perpetrators* (2019), *Multidirectional Memory: Remembering the Holocaust in the Age of Decolonization* (2009) and *Traumatic Realism: The Demands of Holocaust Representation* (2000). He has also co-edited *The Holocaust: Theoretical Readings* (2003, with Neil Levi) and special issues for the journals *Studies in American Jewish Literature, Yale French Studies, Interventions, Occasion* and *Criticism*. His work is published in journals such as *American Literary History, Contemporary Literature, Critical Inquiry, Cultural Critique, History and Memory, Memory Studies, New German Critique* and *PMLA*. He writes regularly for public-facing venues such as *Inside Higher Ed, Los Angeles Review of Books* and *The Nation*, as well as German-language publications *Die Zeit, Berliner Zeitung* and *Geschichte der Gegenwart*.

Dariusz Stola

is a historian at the Institute for Political Studies, Polish Academy of Sciences, Warsaw. He has published ten books and over one hundred articles on the history of Polish-Jewish relations, the communist regime in Poland and international migrations in the twentieth century, including *Nadzieja i Zagłada* (Hope and the Holocaust, 1995), *Kampania antysyjonistyczna w Polsce 1967-1968* (The Anti-Zionist Campaign in Poland, 1967-1968, 2000), *Kraj bez wyjścia? Migracje z Polski 1949-1989* (A Country with No Exit? Migrations from Poland, 1949-1989, 2010), *Patterns of Migration in Central Europe* (2001, co-edited with C. Wallace) and *PZPR jako machina władzy* (Polish United Workers Party as a Ruling Machine, 2012, co-edited with K. Persak). His books have received several awards and he was awarded the Knight's Cross of the Order of Polonia Restituta and the Medal of the University of Warsaw. He serves at the Polish Academy of Sciences' Committee on History and Committee on Migration

Research, and advisory boards at Polish and international institutions and journals. From 2014 to 2019 has was the director of the POLIN Museum of the History of Polish Jews, Warsaw.

Adam Szymczyk

(b. 1970, Piotrków Trybunalski, Poland) is a curator and author based in Zurich. He was artistic director of documenta 14 in Athens and Kassel between 2013 and 2017 and served as director and chief curator of Kunsthalle Basel between 2002 and 2014. At present, he is curator at large at the Stedelijk Museum Amsterdam. In 2022, he co-founded Verein by Association in Zurich, with the aim to initiate and realise exhibitions, publications and other public projects in the realm of contemporary culture.

Joanna Tokarska-Bakir

(b. 1958) is a cultural anthropologist and religious studies scholar at the Institute of Slavic Studies at the Polish Academy of Sciences. She is author of books including *Légendes du sang. Une anthropologie du préjugé antisémite en Europe* (2015; *Legendy o krwi. Antropologia przesądu* [Legends of Blood: Anthropology of Vorurteile], 2008); *Okrzyki pogromowe. Szkice z antropologii historycznej Polski lat 1939–1946* (2012; *Pogrom Cries*, 2017), *Społeczny portret pogromu kieleckiego* (The Social Portrait of the Kielce Pogrom, 2 volumes, 2017) and *Bracia miesiące. Studia z antropologii historycznej Polski 1939–1945* (*Jewish Fugitives in the Polish Countryside, 1939–1945*, 2021). She received her PhD from the University of Warsaw and is a scholarship holder of, among others, A.W. Mellon; A. von Humboldt; Marie Curie Fellowship at Institute for Advanced Study, Princeton, CT and Imre Kertész Kolleg, Jena.

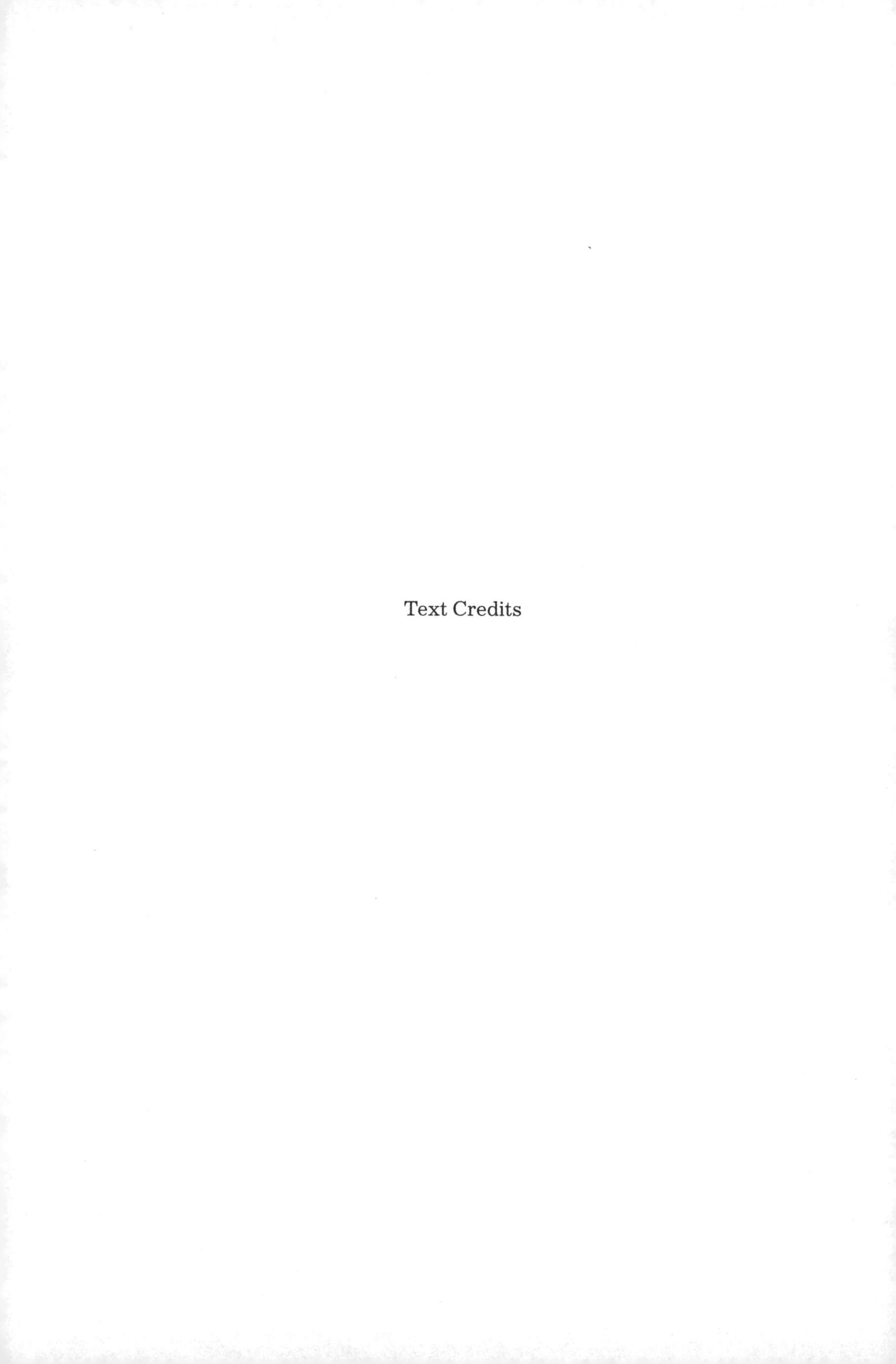

Text Credits

pp. 10–15

'Invitation to Read, Call to See' © Adam Szymczyk, translated by Eliza Rose.

pp. 18–27

'Judge Lynch in Europe' © Milena Jesenská, first published in *The Journalism of Milena Jesenská: A Critical Voice in Interwar Central Europe*, edited and translated by Kathleen Hayes, New York and Oxford: Berghahn Books, 2003. The original Czech text 'Soudce Lynch v Evropě' was published in *Přítomnost*, 30 March 1938.

pp. 30–47

'A Monologue for Claude Lanzmann' © Joanna Tokarska-Bakir, translated by Jerzy Juruś.

pp. 52–58

'The Negro and the Warsaw Ghetto' © W. E. B. Du Bois and 2019 The University of Chicago, first published in *Jewish Life* (now *Jewish Currents*), vol. 6, no. 7, pp. 14–15, New York: Orthodox Jewish Congregations of America, 1952.

pp. 62–71

'Distancing from Participation: If Auschwitz Were in Switzerland – On Not Acknowledging Historical Guilt and the Long Slumber of the Self-Righteous' © Adolf Muschg, translated by Andrew Boreham with Colin Shepherd, and edited for this book, first published as 'Wenn Auschwitz in der Schweiz liegt', *Die Zeit*, no. 7, 7 February 1997 and revised for A. Muschg, *Wenn Auschwitz in der Schweiz liegt: Fünf Reden eines Schweizers an seine und keine Nation*, Frankfurt am Main: Suhrkamp, 1997.

pp. 74–80

'The Spectres of Comparison: On the Mbembe Affair' © Michael Rothberg, first published as 'The Specters of Comparison: On the Mbembe Affair', *Zeitgeister: International*

Perspectives from Culture and Society, Goethe-Institut, May 2020, https://www.goethe.de/prj/zei/en/pos/21864662.html.

pp. 84–89

'Run Baby Run. Run Like the Wind. Memory Is the Most Unusual Thing' © Bonaventure Soh Bejeng Ndikung, first published as 'Curator Bonaventure Soh Bejeng Ndikung on Why Germany's Struggle Against Imperialism Is Far From Over', *frieze*, 20 October 2020.

pp. 92–101

'We Cannot Escape Our Own History' © Jan Tomasz Gross, first published as 'Eastern Europe's Crisis of Shame', *Project Syndicate*, 13 September 2015 , https://www.project-syndicate.org/commentary/eastern-europe-refugee-crisis-xenophobia-by-jan-gross-2015-09. Expanded in 2021 for this publication.

pp. 104–21

'Reactions, Discussions and Disputes: Polish Controversies Over the Shoah' © Dariusz Stola, translated by Zofia Sochańska © POLIN Museum of the History of Polish Jews, Warsaw.

pp. 124–54

'Formlessness Versus Formalisation: Towards a Post-National Culture of Remembrance' © Noit Banai.

pp. 158–68

'It Looks Gloomy Up Close' © Piotr Forecki, translated by Aleksandra Paszkowska.

pp. 172–97

'A Summons to See: *It Looks Pretty from a Distance*' © Luiza Nader, translated by Eliza Rose.

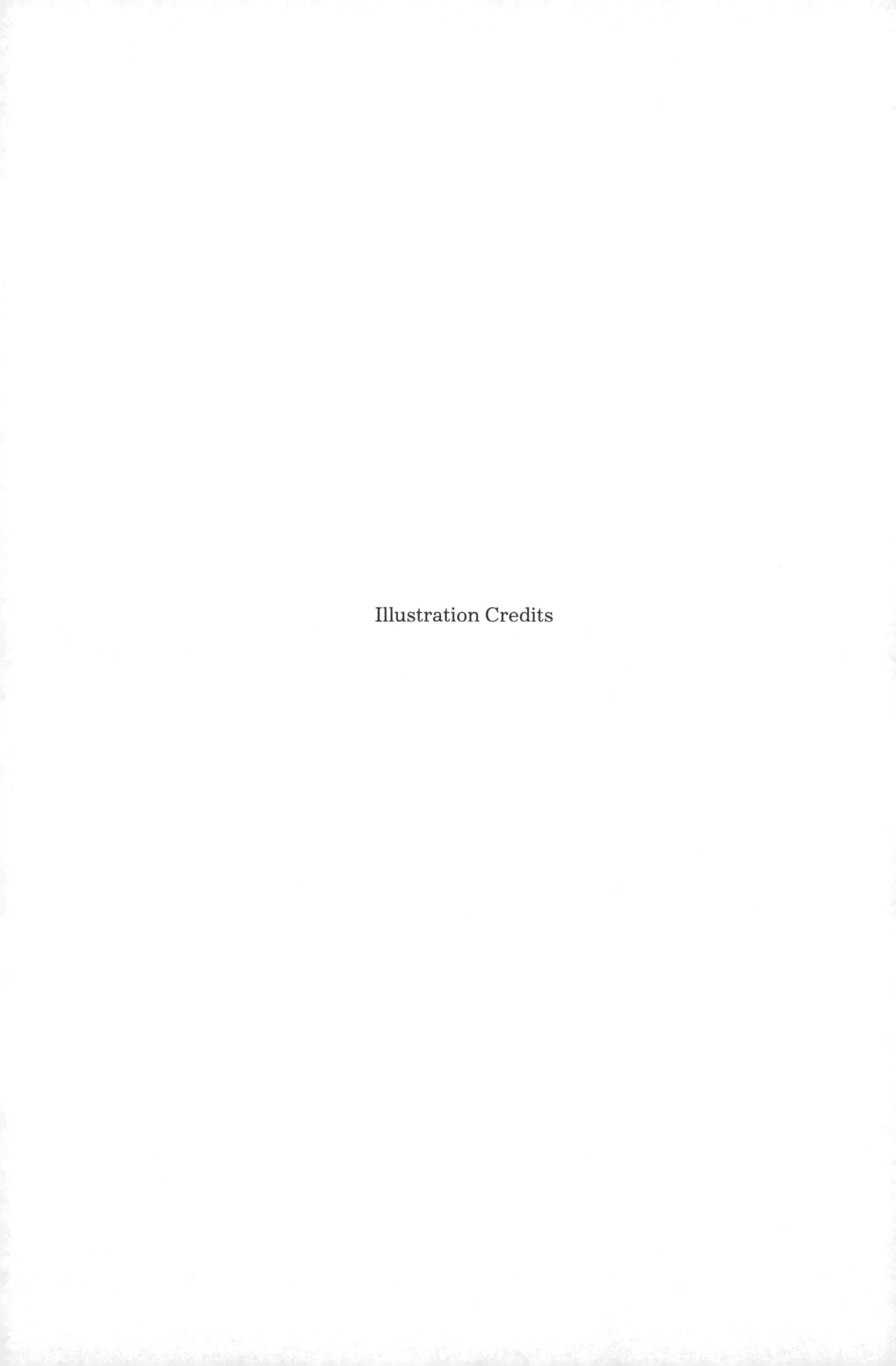

Illustration Credits

Cover:
Wilhelm Sasnal: Such a Landscape, 2021-22
Exhibition view, POLIN Museum of the History of Polish Jews, Warsaw
Exhibition architecture: Johanna Meyer-Grohbrügge
Courtesy of Foksal Gallery Foundation, Warsaw
Photo: Marek Gardulski

Cover, front:
Untitled (Afterimage), 2019
Oil and spray paint on canvas, 220 x 300 cm
Courtesy of the artist and Foksal Gallery Foundation, Warsaw

Cover, back:
Stork, 2014
Oil on canvas, 90 x 120 cm
Courtesy of Fondation Beyeler, Riehen/Basel

p. 7
Maus, 2001
Mural, 450 x 300 cm
Galeria Bielska BWA, Bielsko-Biała, Poland
Courtesy of the artist
Photo: Grażyna Cybulska

p. 8
Untitled, 2007
Oil on canvas, 40 x 40 cm
Collection of Peter Handschin, Switzerland
Courtesy of the artist
Photo: Gina Folly

p. 9
Untitled (Hitler), 2010
Oil and wooden board on canvas, 40 x 35 cm
Kontakt Collection, Vienna
Courtesy of the artist
Photo: Marek Gardulski

p. 16
Untitled, 2017
Oil, spray paint and rope on canvas, 180 x 150 cm
Courtesy of the artist and Foksal Gallery Foundation, Warsaw
Photo: Marek Gardulski

p. 17
Murzynek Bambo, 2014
Oil and spray paint on canvas, 220 x 160 x 2.5 cm
Courtesy of the artist and Sadie Coles HQ, London
Photo: Marek Gardulski

p. 28
Shoah (Translator), 2003
Oil on canvas, 40 x 30 cm
Boros Foundation, Berlin
Courtesy of the artist

p. 29
Shoah (Forest), 2003
Oil on canvas, 45 x 45 cm
Private Collection
Courtesy of the artist and Hauser & Wirth, Zurich

pp. 50–51
Maus 3, 2001
Oil on canvas, 90 x 190 cm
Private Collection of Dr Isabella von Moreau-Johnen
Courtesy of the artist

p. 60
First of January (Side), 2021
Oil on canvas, 70 x 100 cm
Courtesy of the artist and Foksal Gallery Foundation, Warsaw
Photo: Marek Gardulski

p. 61
First of January (Back), 2021
Oil on canvas, 70 x 100 cm
Courtesy of the artist and Foksal Gallery Foundation, Warsaw
Photo: Marek Gardulski

pp. 72–73
Skeleton of Water, 2008
Oil on canvas, 160 x 200 cm
Private Collection
Courtesy of the artist and Anton Kern Gallery, New York
Photo: Marek Gardulski

p. 82
Maus 4, 2001
Oil on canvas, 115 x 130 cm
POLIN Museum of the History of Polish Jews, Warsaw
Courtesy of the artist
Photo: Marek Gardulski

p. 83
Untitled (Majdanek), 2016
Oil on canvas, 160 x 220 cm
Courtesy of the artist and Foksal Gallery Foundation, Warsaw
Photo: Marek Gardulski

p. 90
Population, 2000
Oil on canvas, 50 x 50 cm
Courtesy of the artist and Foksal Gallery Foundation, Warsaw
Photo: Marek Gardulski

p. 91
Untitled (Fear), 2008
Oil on canvas, 40 x 40 cm
Private Collection
Courtesy of the artist
Photo: Marek Gardulski

p. 102
Untitled (Borowski), 2002
Oil on canvas, 150 x 150 cm
Private Collection
Courtesy of the artist
Photo: Stefan Altenburger Photography

p. 103
Untitled (Borowski), 2002
Oil on canvas, 100 x 100 cm
Courtesy of the artist and Foksal Gallery Foundation, Warsaw
Photo: Marek Gardulski

p. 122
Shoah (Forest-Ner River), 2003
Oil on canvas, 40 x 50 cm
Courtesy of the artist and Foksal Gallery Foundation, Warsaw
Photo: Marek Gardulski

p. 123
Untitled, 2003
oil on canvas, 45 x 50 cm
Collection of Christine Binswanger, Switzerland
Courtesy of the artist
Photo: Marek Gardulski

p. 155
Kraków-Warszawa (Cracow-Warsaw), 2006
Oil on canvas, 55 x 70 cm
Zachęta - National Gallery of Art, Warsaw
Courtesy of the artist
Photo: Jerzy Jacek Gładykowski

pp. 156–57
Pigsty, 2011
Oil on canvas, 200 x 440 cm
Courtesy of the artist and Foksal Gallery Foundation, Warsaw
Photo: Marek Gardulski

p. 169
Untitled (The Eye Swallows the Landscape. The Landscape Gouges the Eye), 2017
Oil on canvas, 40 x 40 cm
Jakub Szkudlarek Collection
Courtesy of the artist
Photo: Marek Gardulski

pp. 170–71
Untitled (Afterimage), 2019
Oil and spray paint on canvas, 220 x 300 cm
Courtesy of the artist and Foksal Gallery Foundation, Warsaw
Photo: Marek Gardulski

p. 199
Gonzalez, 2002
Oil on canvas, 24 x 30 cm
Courtesy of the artist and Foksal Gallery Foundation, Warsaw
Photo: Marek Gardulski

pp. 222–23
Untitled (Road), 2011
Oil on canvas, 200 x 220 cm
Collection of Christine Binswanger, Switzerland
Courtesy of the artist
Photo: Marek Gardulski

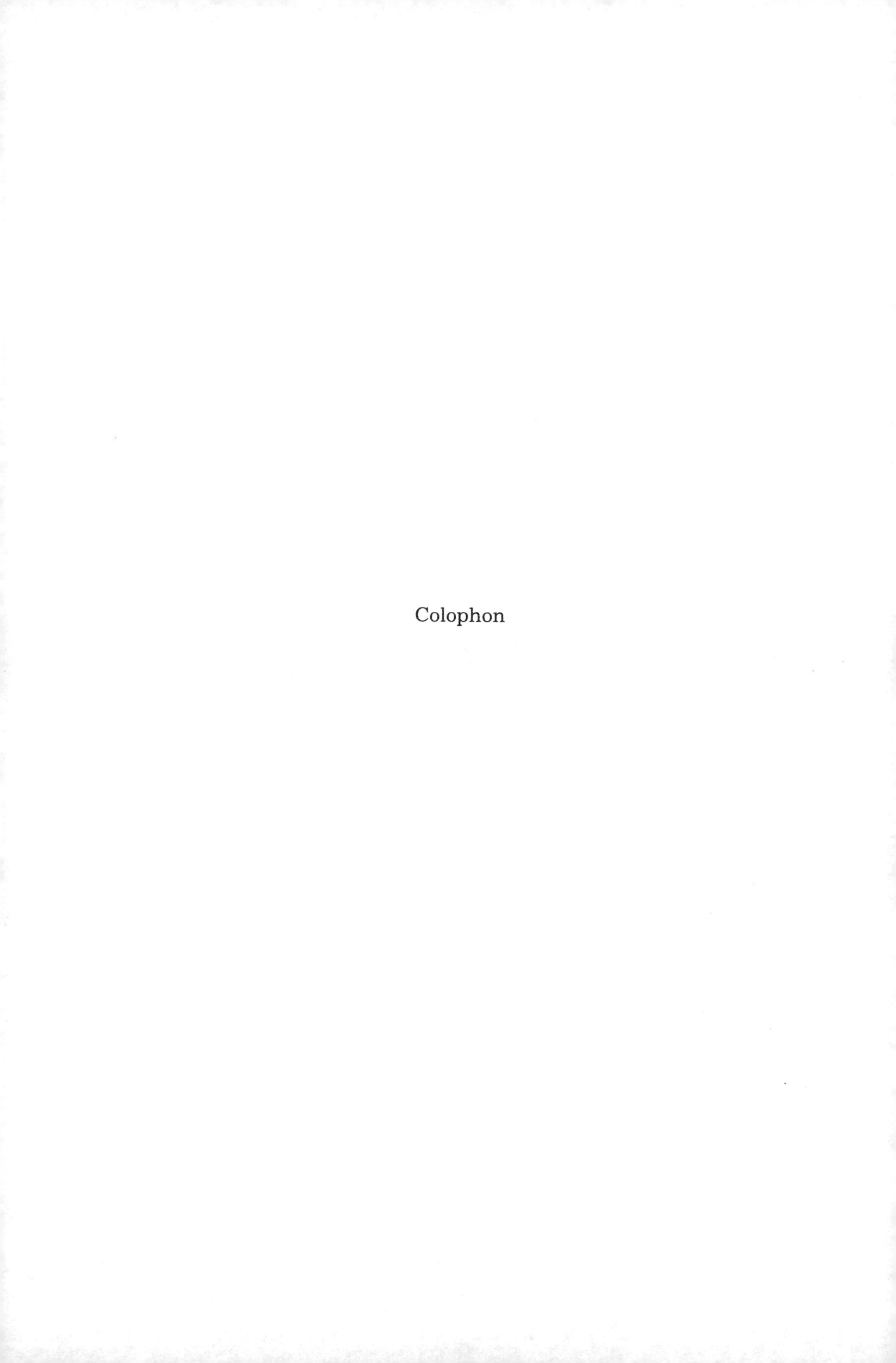

Colophon

Wilhelm Sasnal:
Untitled (Reader)
is published following
the exhibition
Wilhelm Sasnal:
Taki pejzaż
(Such a Landscape)
at POLIN Museum
of the History of Polish
Jews in Warsaw,
curated by
Adam Szymczyk
(17 June 2021–
10 January 2022).

Editor:
Adam Szymczyk

Managing editor:
Janine Armin

Copy-editors:
and proofreading (EN):
Janine Armin
and
Eva Wilson

Proofreader (PL):
Patryk Walaszkowski

Editorial co-ordination:
Miriam Sadowska

Designer:
Agata Biskup

Printer:
Drukarnia Skleniarz, Kraków

Paper:
Munken Pure

Fonts:
Borgis Pro

Publisher:
Verlag der Buchhandlung
Walther und Franz König
Ehrenstraße 4
50672 Köln
www.buchhandlung-walther-koenig.de

The editor and the artist wish to thank the following individuals who in many ways contributed to the book and its preceding exhibition: Ewa Chomicka, Marta Dziewulska, Joanna Fikus, Scott & Jill Forbes, Ewa Jasiecka, Aneta Jasionek, Erika Krzyczkowska-Roman, Michał Kulisiewicz, Julian Kutyła, Tamara Łozińska, Marta Markowska, Johanna Meyer-Grohbrügge, Sylwia Narewska, Agata Polak, Anna Pokłosiewicz, Zofia Sochańska, Marta Stawińska, Zygmunt Stępiński, Katarzyna Tomczak-Wysocka, Patryk Walaszkowski and Jakub Woźniak; and also the institutions, collections and galleries that made the exhibition and this book possible: Anton Kern Gallery (New York), Boros Foundation (Berlin), Collection of Christine Binswanger (Switzerland), Collection of J&M Donnelly, Collection of Mario Testino (London), Collection of Peter Handschin (Switzerland), The District Museum in Tarnów, Foksal Gallery Foundation (Warsaw), Fondation Beyeler (Riehen/Basel), Fundacja Signum (Poznań), Hauser & Wirth (Zurich), ISelf Collection (London), Jankilevitsch Foundation, Krytyka Polityczna (Warsaw), Museum of Modern Art in Warsaw, The National Museum of Art in Warsaw, POLIN Museum of the History of Polish Jews (Warsaw), Raster Gallery (Warsaw), Sadie Coles HQ (London) and Zachęta - National Gallery of Art (Warsaw).

Wilhelm Sasnal would like to extend special thanks to Anka Sasnal, Paweł Gardynik, Andrzej Przywara and Joanna Diem.

A Polish version of this book
will be published in 2022
by Krytyka Polityczna, Warsaw.

Distribution:
Buchhandlung Walther König
Ehrenstraße 4
D - 50672 Köln
www.buchhandlung-walther-koenig.de
Tel: +49 221 20596-53
verlag@buchhandlung-walther-koenig.de

ISBN: 978-3-7533-0237-9

Printed and bound in Poland

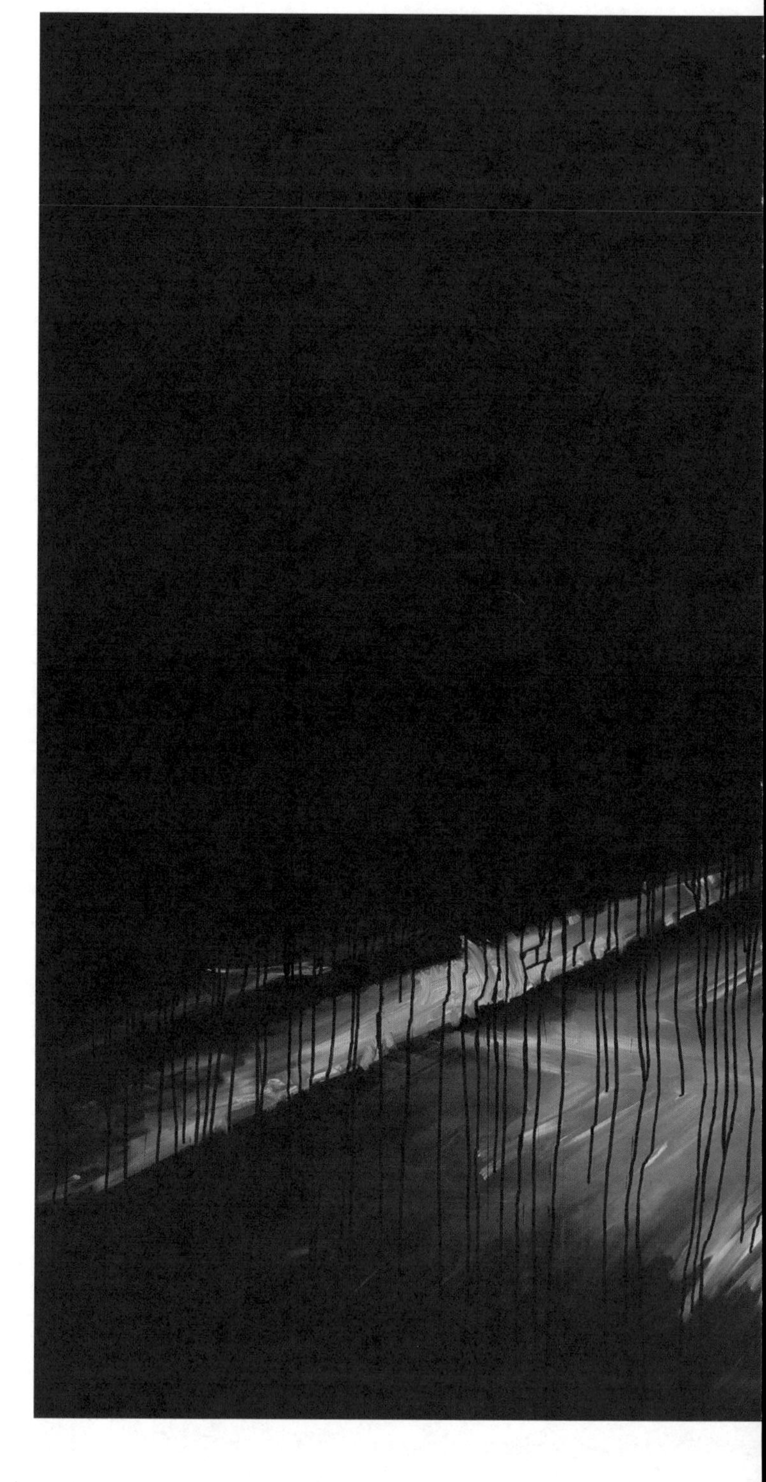